Also by Robert Parry

Fooling America
Trick or Treason
The October Surprise X-Files

Lost History

Lost History:

Contras, Cocaine, the Press & 'Project Truth'

Robert Parry

The Media Consortium
Arlington, Virginia

To my children
-- Samuel, Nathaniel, Elizabeth and Jeffrey --
and to their generation.

Grateful acknowledgement is made to Samuel and Nathaniel Parry for their assistance in preparation of this book and the cover design. Thanks is also given to Diane Duston for her help throughout this project

Library of Congress Catalog Card Number: 99-93363

Parry, Robert, 1949-

Lost History: Contras, Cocaine, The Press & 'Project Truth' / Robert Parry.

Includes index.

ISBN 1-893517-00-4

Printed in the United States of America

9 8 7 6 5 4 3 2

CONTENTS

Introduction: A Search for Lost History   3

PART ONE: THE 1980s -- THE MISSING LINK

Chapter 1:   'Project Truth'   31

Chapter 2:   'Perception Management'   56

Chapter 3:   Containment   79

Chapter 4:   A Breakthrough, of Sorts   109

Chapter 5:   'Good for the Country'   127

Chapter 6:   Tale of Two Scandals   145

Chapter 7:   Cuban Connection   159

Chapter 8:   Contra-Coke   178

Chapter 9:   Crumbling Cover-up   193

Chapter 10:   Justice Denied   207

Chapter 11:   CIA Confession   224

PART TWO: BEFORE, AFTER & DURING

Chapter 12:   How Others See It   248

Chapter 13:   Lying First   265

Chapter 14:   The CIA Analysts   272

Chapter 15:   Sins of the Father   279

Index: 293

"...it has never yet been discovered,
how to make man *unknow* his
knowledge, or *unthink* his thoughts."

Thomas Paine, *Rights of Man,* 1791

Introduction
A Search for Lost History

There is a cynical old saying that the victors write the history. For those of us brought up on Westerns that made the Indians the aggressors and the U.S. cavalry the peacekeepers, we know there's something to that.

But it is one of the ironies of the long Cold War that it is the American people -- the supposed victors -- who are seeing their own history sanitized and miswritten. Even as the archives of ex-communist nations are opened, even as truth commissions wring the painful reality out of ex-rightist regimes, the American people are the ones most thoroughly kept in the dark about the unsavory secrets of the past half century.

Without doubt, the conventional history is more comforting, less troubling, the American government making the right decisions or at least ones justified by the exigencies of a long struggle against a ruthless enemy. To encounter the secret history is disturbing, unnerving. It comes with a sense of vertigo, the uneasy discovery that what one assumed to be true might not be. The secret history is a challenge. It is the unpleasant reality that exists beneath the surface of our time.

It also is a history in danger of being lost, possibly forever. With a national news media absorbed by tabloid journalism and disinterested in serious research, many U.S. operatives who prosecuted the Cold War are aging and passing away without their experiences being recorded. Other times, the glut of trivial information obscures the pieces of valuable evidence that do enter the public domain. At least in the near term, our understanding of this recent era -- and our nation's role in it -- is way off the mark.

It is as if the final price for winning the Cold War is our national confinement to a permanent childhood, where reassuring fantasies and endless diversions shield us from the hard truth of our own recent history.

One can argue that perhaps history has always been this way, a chancy business with the truth sometimes seeping out in unexpected ways, sometimes not. Rarely is the full picture ever known and never are the chroniclers free of political bias. There is certainly merit in that view. Many historical events are understood only hazily, anecdotally, sometimes through popular fiction or from slanted textbooks.

It's certainly true that many unsavory chapters of American history have been "lost" before, or are known but not generally accepted in the national consciousness. Only recently have historians begun devoting significant time and effort excavating and compiling the record of African-American slavery. For centuries, too, mainstream historians glossed over the genocide against America's Native population. One also can argue that American history -- like the histories of all countries -- tends to skim over the unpleasant chapters and dwell on the positive.

But the "lost history" of this era is a different breed. It cannot be rationalized by the needs of a struggling young nation. It cannot be explained as some event from a long-ago time, or by the remoteness of a conflict, or by poor communications, or by the boosterism of some over-eager patriots. This "lost history" has a component of coercion to it, a calculated abuse of information in the cause of raw power. In this era, there were cover-ups of horrendous crimes often behind flimsy excuses of ideology and geopolitics. In Raymond Bonner's perceptive phrase, this was a time of "weakness and deceit."

Among the worst examples of this "lost history" were the crimes committed in Latin America where countless civilians were slaughtered by U.S.-backed military forces. In Guatemala, the genocidal death toll reached an estimated 200,000, including the annihilation of hundreds of Mayan Indian villages. In El Salvador, the numbers of dead reached 70,000, the vast majority unarmed men, women and children. Tens of thousands more died in Nicaragua where the United States defied international law and supported the Nicaraguan contras trained by the exemplars of "dirty wars," the Argentine intelligence services.

Sometimes, the contras and other U.S. allies doubled as international drug traffickers exploiting their cozy relationships with the American government to smuggle cocaine into the United States, a crime that exacted another kind of destruction on the American population. These crimes were then concealed, obfuscated or excused. No U.S. official was punished for these acts carried out under the justification of fighting the Cold War, even though many of the crimes had only the most tangential connection to any real power struggle between East and West.

But what made this new breed of "lost history" even more troubling was that the crimes were not unknown. Indeed, many were reported by human rights investigators and courageous journalists. The crimes simply disappeared into some historical nether world. They were known, but not known. They were ignored, studiously, willfully, criminally at times -- by the press as well as by the government. They became "lost history," with Americans often believing in "facts" that were the opposite of what was real -- for instance, thinking that the contra-cocaine charges were disproved when, in truth, the CIA had confessed to the core allegations.

How did this happen? How did the vaunted Watergate press corps of the 1970s -- which exposed abuses such as the Pentagon Papers' deceptions on Vietnam and the CIA's spying on American citizens -- turn into the tabloidish Monica Lewinsky news media of the 1990s? How did the national press lose its way? What happened during the 1980s, the "missing link" between the two eras?

By cluing the American people into the hidden world of Washington's "national security" crimes, the Watergate-era press corps had made life a bit too difficult for those who saw themselves as protectors of U.S. interests around the world. In effect, these individuals were faced with a new twin challenge: how to wage successful counterinsurgency warfare against Third World forces threatening U.S.-backed governments while simultaneously curtailing dissent in the United States, opposition that could limit the military options as the Vietnam War protests did.

Military concern about public opinion was a less serious problem in the early days of American history. In the 19th Century and the early 20th Century, the wars were waged in relative secret, in distant territories, mostly out of public view. That was no longer possible in the media-saturated modern age of the late 20th Century. So, this need to control images became the new imperative in post-Vietnam counterinsurgency doctrine.

In that sense, the goal was to create more political space for the military so it could carry out the often messy business of counterinsurgency, without the carnage showing up on the evening news or in the morning newspapers. The logical answer became: limit the news media's coverage of the violence overseas while pressuring journalists in Washington to frame the issues in ways more supportive of U.S. policy. In this endeavor, the editorial offices in Washington and New York were viewed as the crucial switching points for limiting or shutting off the flow of troubling information to the American people.

But for this strategy to work, new techniques were needed to convince much of the press corps and influential elements of the citizenry that the apparent facts before them were not the real facts, that those who seemed to be telling the truth were not. In the early 1980s, Reagan administration officials sometimes called their ambitious program "perception management." Another name for the operation was "Project Truth." At least in a public relations sense, they believed, counterinsurgency warfare could be sold to the American people.

As historian Peter Dale Scott has noted, America sees itself as a land of decency and democratic values, but that image can contrast sharply with the reality of brush wars whether on the old American frontier or in today's Third World nations. "There is a dark -- seldom acknowledged -- thread that runs through U.S. military doctrine," Scott wrote in 1998. "Dating back to the founding of the Republic, this military tradition explicitly defended the selective use of terror, whether in suppressing Indian resistance on the frontiers in the 19th Century or in quelling rebellion against U.S. interests abroad in the 20th Century."[1]

Though counterinsurgency warfare is as old as time, some historians trace its modern tenets to the Civil War success of Gen. William Tecumseh Sherman and his famous March to the Sea in 1864. Sherman's army cut a swath of destruction through the Confederacy with the goal of breaking the South's will to fight. By targeting civilian homes and food stocks, not just the opposing army on the battlefield, Sherman revived the ancient practice of total war.

The U.S. Army refined its counterinsurgency skills with the repression of the western Indians in the latter half of the 19th Century. That strategy applied selective terror against rebellious Indians while isolating others in restricted zones -- reservations -- where some government social programs were provided. Gen. Philip H. Sheridan, who led the Indian wars, succeeded Sherman as the U.S. Army's commanding general in 1883 and etched these strategies deeper into military doctrine.[2]

From the start of the 20th Century, the mix of terror and beneficence would become a hallmark of U.S. counterinsurgency as that doctrine traveled with the U.S. military through interventions in Latin America, the Caribbean and Asia. This doctrine was followed when a U.S. expeditionary force put down a nationalist uprising in the Philippines in 1900.

Under the command of Gen. J. Franklin Bell, U.S. troops summarily executed captured Filipinos in contested areas. But there were quirky twists to intimidate the broader population. To coerce assistance from wealthy Filipinos in bringing the rebellion to an end, some rich landowners were forced to burn down their own homes. In pacified areas, U.S. forces built schools and provided other social amenities.[3]

Half a century later, the Cold War gave a new impetus to refinement of these counterinsurgency strategies. The problem

---

[1] Scott wrote about these developments in the context of upheavals in Indonesia. For details, see *iF Magazine*, July-Aug. 1998.
[2] See Ward Churchill, *A Little Matter of Genocide.*
[3] See Stuart Creighton Miller's *"Benevolent Assimilation."*

grew after World War II when subjugated people around the world demanded independence from the weakened colonial powers of Europe. Washington, however, viewed many of these uprisings as communist-led or communist-inspired and, therefore, threats to U.S. interests. In all corners of the world, the United States stepped forward to counter the perceived communist expansion by bolstering colonial regimes or propping up pro-U.S. governments.

Fittingly, the newly formed CIA got its first test of Cold War counterinsurgency back in the Philippines where the so-called Huk rebellion threatened a U.S.-backed government. CIA advisers to the pro-U.S. Filipino forces applied the tried-and-true counterinsurgency doctrines with some more new wrinkles.

The CIA's Maj. Gen. Edward G. Lansdale experimented with the modern concept of psychological warfare, or "psy-war," a new spin to the old game of breaking the will of a target population. Lansdale analyzed the supposed psychological weaknesses of the Filipinos and then developed "themes" to induce their acquiescence to U.S. desires.

Lansdale's psy-war tactics relied heavily on propaganda and disinformation, but also used selective terror of a demonstrative nature. An Army psy-war pamphlet, drawing on Lansdale's experiences in the Philippines, recommended "exemplary criminal violence -- the murder and mutilation of captives and the display of their bodies," according to Michael McClintock's *Instruments of Statecraft*.

Lansdale himself described an example of his psy-war tactics in his memoirs, *In the Midst of Wars*. Lansdale noted that the Huks were considered superstitious and fearful of a vampire-like creature called an *asuang*. So, one of his psy-war teams played on that fear to spook the enemy. Lansdale wrote:

> The psy-war squad set up an ambush along a trail used by the Huks. When a Huk patrol came along the trail, the ambushers silently snatched the last man on the patrol, their move unseen in the dark night. They punctured his neck with two holes, vampire-fashion, held the body up by the heels, drained it of blood, and put the corpse back on the trail. When the Huks

returned to look for the missing man and found their bloodless comrade, every member of the patrol believed the *asuang* had got him.

Militarily more significant, however, was the refinement of "free-fire zones" as a tactic. After cordoning off sections of disputed territory, the Philippine army judged anyone caught in the "free-fire zone" an enemy who should be killed. With American assistance and the application of far-greater firepower than was possible in earlier times, the Philippine government defeated the Huk rebellion.

After that success, U.S. military advisers sought to apply the new lessons to other rebellious populations. Personifying this modern American warrior, Lansdale set up shop in Vietnam, devising more propaganda and disinformation, "themes" to exploit Vietnamese cultural weaknesses. The Vietnamese, too, were judged superstitious, so the psy-war teams prepared bogus astrology reports predicting doom for Ho Chi Minh's communist-led forces.

There were also the bloodier tactics. Before long, South Vietnamese troops backed by American advisers were burning down villages and herding civilians into "strategic hamlets." Outside the hamlets, "free-fire zones" were declared for hunting Viet Cong. More selectively, CIA-run "Phoenix" units extracted information from captives and used it to wage ambush attacks that decimated the Viet Cong's political infrastructure. The Phoenix program was widely regarded as an assassination campaign, though CIA officials disputed that allegation.

The expanding experience in counterinsurgency warfare had another consequence. The U.S. intelligence community decided to compile the hard-learned lessons into a more formal doctrine.

In 1965, a top-secret program was started at the U.S. Army Intelligence Center at Fort Holabird, Md. Given the spooky name "Project X," the program pulled together the field lessons from U.S. counterinsurgency operations around the world. Project X then boiled down what had been learned and put that material into training manuals. Translated into many languages, the booklets were to "provide intelligence training to friendly foreign countries," according to a Pentagon history of Project X.

Called "a guide for the conduct of clandestine operations," Project X material "was first used by the U.S. Intelligence School on Okinawa to train Vietnamese and, presumably, other foreign nationals," the history stated. Linda Matthews of the Pentagon's Counterintelligence Division recalled that in 1967-68, some of the Project X training material was prepared by officers connected to the Phoenix program.

"She suggested the possibility that some offending material from the Phoenix program may have found its way into the Project X materials at that time," the Pentagon report said.

In the 1970s, the U.S. Army Intelligence Center moved to Fort Huachuca in Arizona and began exporting Project X to U.S. military assistance groups working with "friendly foreign countries." By the mid-1970s, the Project X lessons were going to armies all over the world. In a 1992 review of these U.S. training programs, the Pentagon acknowledged that Project X was the source for some of the "objectionable" lessons taught at the School of the Americas. There, Latin American officers were trained in blackmail, kidnapping, murder and spying on non-violent political opponents, the Pentagon admitted.

In the final days of the Bush administration, senior Pentagon officials ordered the collection of all Project X documents. After the records were centralized, they were destroyed, ostensibly to prevent accidental use of the material in the future. But the destruction also prevented the U.S. public from ever knowing the details of the operation. The brief Project X history, which was written in 1991, and some of the more innocuous Project X records survived and were released in 1997.

But the consequences of the Project X training were not as easily managed. Around the world, the U.S.-refined techniques of counterinsurgency warfare were copied in ruthless struggles against communists and perceived communist sympathizers. The death toll was staggering in countries from Indonesia to Korea, from Iran to South Africa.

The American hand was especially heavy in Latin America. From Chile and Argentina to El Salvador and Guatemala, graduates from the School of the Americas and other U.S. intelligence-training centers blended their U.S. advice with more traditional brutality. In country after country, U.S.-backed security forces waged "dirty wars" that kidnapped, tortured and executed political dissidents judged threats to the state.

Vietnam had another effect on the secretive world of counterinsurgency. As the first televised war, Vietnam let average Americans see what the U.S. military had kept mostly under wraps since the days of the Indian wars. In Vietnam, camera crews were present as U.S. soldiers set fire to the ancestral homes of crying old women. Scenes appeared on the nightly news of brutalized Viet Cong suspects, including one captured VC officer being shot in the head. Americans witnessed civilians, including children, burned with napalm. TV showed Agent Orange sprayed as a defoliant on vast tracts of "free-fire zones."

The Vietnam image problem was compounded by the disclosure of the Pentagon Papers in 1971. The internal Pentagon history exposed the deceptions that the U.S. government had employed to justify the war. Opposition to the Vietnam conflict sent millions of Americans into the streets and finally led Congress to end U.S. participation in the Vietnam conflict in 1974.

By the mid-1970s, other national security secrets were spilling out in Congress and in the national news media. The Church and Pike committees pulled back the veil around the CIA, exposing scandals such as spying on Americans, Mafia-connected assassination plots and drug experiments on unsuspecting subjects. Some investigative reporters were digging into evidence that the CIA had collaborated with drug traffickers. In the post-Watergate commitment to government openness, the Freedom of Information Act gave even ordinary citizens a chance to pry loose government records. National security scandals were appearing regularly in the major newspapers and on TV.

By 1976, however, with George H.W. Bush as CIA director, the national security agencies were striking back. They warned that government openness had gone too far and was threatening the nation's safety. Under pressure from hardliners in the late 1970s, President Carter implemented new secrecy rules. Then, in the 1980s, President Reagan moved even more aggressively against those in government and in the media who made unauthorized disclosures. Tougher security regulations were imposed to keep information from the public and to punish leakers.

Beyond defensive steps, Reagan implemented a pro-active "public diplomacy" strategy to push the administration's foreign policy arguments on the American people and on the opinion leaders of Washington. Based at the National Security Council and overseen by CIA director William J. Casey, "public diplomacy" had as its overriding goal the Orwellian concept of "perception management." The initial operation was called "Project Truth."

The core idea was to enable the government to manipulate how the American people perceived U.S.-supported counterinsurgency operations around the world. To minimize critical information, this tough "public diplomacy" apparatus challenged independent-minded journalists, congressmen and citizens groups. Meanwhile, military "psy-war" experts were assigned to develop "themes" for generating public support for foreign conflicts, to analyze what excited or frightened the American people. Gen. Lansdale's strategies had come home.

Soon, it became clear to reporters and other Washington figures that telling the truth about national security secrets could be dangerous to one's earning potential. Fewer and fewer journalists would take those chances at a time when plum assignments in Washington carried lucrative rewards, from a high salary to moonlighting deals on TV pundit shows. Members of Congress knew that to expose wrongdoing by the U.S. government only guaranteed a well-funded challenge in the next election, not to mention accusations of disloyalty as someone who would "blame America first" in U.N. Ambassador Jeane Kirkpatrick's classic formulation delivered at the 1984 Republican National Convention.

The writing was on the wall. As a reporter for *The Associated Press, Newsweek* and the Public Broadcasting System's FRONTLINE program in the 1980s and early 1990s, I witnessed first-hand how Washington powerbrokers perfected these skills for managing unpleasant facts and shaping national perceptions. I also was one of the reporters who tried to resist the pressures.

In doing so, in the mid-1980s, I managed to break many of the stories that we now know as the Iran-contra scandal. Those articles included the first story about Oliver North's secret Nicarguan contra supply network and -- with my AP colleague Brian Barger -- the first story about drug trafficking by contra organizations. But that work simply earned me a place on a list of "enemy" reporters. As the 1980s wore on, my editors showed declining interest in going against the grain. By the 1990s, little by little, the Washington news media had been transformed, back to the more compliant press corps that existed before the 1970s.

As communist governments collapsed in Eastern Europe, the dominant view among the Washington media elite was that the Cold War justified almost any act by anti-communist forces, that the ends truly did justify the means. Capturing this sense of *realpolitik* situational ethics was a column written in 1990 by *Washington Post* senior editorial writer Stephen S. Rosenfeld. Responding to a press disclosure that U.S. diplomats had supplied lists of suspected communists to the Indonesian military in 1965, Rosenfeld acknowledged that the lists might have helped fuel the massacres of an estimated one million people, including vast numbers of unarmed men, women and children.

But Rosenfeld defended "this fearsome slaughter" as an act that "was and still is widely regarded as the grim but earned fate of a conspiratorial revolutionary party that represented the same communist juggernaut that was on the march in Vietnam." In a column entitled "Indonesia 1965: The Year of Living Cynically?" Rosenfeld reasoned that "either the army would get the communists [the PKI] or the communists would get the army, it was thought. Indonesia was a domino, and the PKI's demise kept it standing in the free world. ... Though the means were grievously tainted, we -- the fastidious among us as well as the hard-headed and cynical -- can be said to have enjoyed the fruits in the geopolitical stability of that important part of Asia, in the revolution that never happened."[4]

---

[4] *The Washington Post,* July 13, 1990. In the years that followed, Rosenfeld continued to promote the same Cold War double standard, denouncing human rights crimes by leftists while often ignoring or minimizing atrocities by pro-U.S. forces. On May 18, 1999, Rosenfeld was named the *Post's* editorial page editor.

The "public diplomacy" tactics -- and the government's continued control over millions of pages of secret documents -- put Americans in another peculiar position. Citizens of the world's preeminent democracy often knew more about the actions of old communist adversaries and some of America's authoritarian allies, whose archives had been thrown open, than about the decisions of the U.S. government. The United States, after all, had not suffered the political ruptures that tore the lid off secret files of the communist states and many right-wing governments.

South Africa's Truth and Reconciliation Commission investigated and disclosed human rights crimes committed by both the white supremacist government and the insurgent African National Congress during the bitter conflict over racial apartheid. The old Soviet Union and its satellites experienced similar excavations of their archives, sometimes after angry mobs sacked government offices.

Truth commissions also peeled back the layers of lies in El Salvador, Guatemala, Honduras and elsewhere in Latin America. In Argentina, witnesses described barbaric military practices of torture and mass executions. Sometimes, Argentine army doctors used Caesarian sections or induced labor to "harvest" babies from female political prisoners. The babies then were removed, often for distribution to military families, and the new mothers were sent off to their deaths, sometimes shackled naked with other victims and dumped from planes into the Atlantic Ocean to drown.[5]

At times, Americans got the clearest view of their own government's actions not from voluntary disclosures by the U.S. government but from investigations conducted in foreign countries. The case of Guatemala was perhaps the most striking.

In February 1999, a Guatemalan truth commission reported on the murderous practices of that country's U.S.-backed security forces. Guatemala's nightmarish violence dated back to 1954, when the CIA engineered a coup against the elected government of Jacobo Arbenz. The truth commission report then traced the slaughter through the 1960s and 1970s to the 1980s when Ronald

---

[5] For details, see *iF Magazine*, Nov.-Dec. 1997.

Reagan stepped up overt and covert support despite intelligence reports confirming massacres inflicted on Mayan Indian villages.

After the war ended in the mid-1990s, the truth commission persuaded the Clinton administration to declassify internal U.S. documents for the investigation. The documents revealed that American officials played important supporting roles in the Guatemalan counterinsurgency war for four decades, as security forces butchered some 200,000 people.[6] The documents described in chilling detail, often in cold bureaucratic language, how American advisers and their Cold War obsession spurred on the killings and hid the horrible secrets.[7]

In the mid-1960s, for instance, the Guatemalan security forces were disorganized, suffering from internal divisions, and possibly infiltrated by leftist opponents. So, the U.S. government dispatched U.S. public safety adviser John Longon from his base in Venezuela. Arriving in late 1965, Longon sized up the problem and began reorganizing the Guatemalan security forces into a more efficient -- and ultimately, more lethal -- organization.

In a Jan. 4, 1966, report on his activities, Longon said he recommended both overt and covert components to the military's battle against "terrorism." One of Longon's strategies was to seal off sections of Guatemala City and begin house-to-house searches. "The idea behind this was to force some of the wanted communists out of hiding and into police hands, as well as to convince the Guatemalan public that the authorities were doing something to control the situation," he wrote. Longon also arranged for U.S. advisers to begin giving "day-to-day operational advice" to Guatemalan police.

On the covert side, Longon pressed for "a safe house [to] be immediately set up" for coordination of security intelligence. "A room was immediately prepared in the [Presidential] Palace for this purpose and ... Guatemalans were immediately designated to put this operation into effect." Longon's operation within the

---

[6] Based on a review of about 20 percent of the dead, the Guatemalan truth commission blamed the army for 93 percent of the killings and leftist guerrillas for three percent. Four percent were listed as unresolved.

[7] For the full documents, see the National Security Archive's Web site at www.seas.gwu.edu/nsarchive/

presidential compound was the starting point for the infamous "Archivos" intelligence unit that became the clearinghouse for Guatemala's most notorious political assassinations.

Longon also recommended assignment of special U.S. advisers to assist in the covert operations and the delivery of special intelligence equipment, presumably for spying on Guatemalan citizens. With the American input, the Guatemalan security forces soon became one of the most feared counterinsurgency operations in Latin America. The modern Latin American "death squad" was born.

Just two months after Longon's report, a secret CIA cable noted the clandestine execution of several Guatemalan "communists and terrorists" on the night of March 6, 1966. By the end of the year, the Guatemalan government was bold enough to request U.S. help in establishing special kidnapping squads, according to a cable from the U.S. Southern Command that was forwarded to Washington on Dec. 3, 1966.

By 1967, the Guatemalan counterinsurgency terror had gained a fierce momentum. On Oct. 23, 1967, the State Department's Bureau of Intelligence and Research noted the "accumulating evidence that the [Guatemalan] counter-insurgency machine is out of control." The report noted that Guatemalan "counter-terror" units were carrying out abductions, bombings, torture and summary executions "of real and alleged communists."

The mounting death toll in Guatemala disturbed some of the American officials assigned to the country. One official, the embassy's deputy chief of mission Viron Vaky, expressed his concerns in a remarkably candid report that he submitted on March 29, 1968, after returning to Washington.

Vaky framed his arguments in pragmatic, rather than moral, terms. But his personal anguish broke through. He wrote:

> The official squads are guilty of atrocities. Interrogations are brutal, torture is used and bodies are mutilated. ... In the minds of many in Latin America, and, tragically, especially in the sensitive, articulate youth, we are believed to have condoned these tactics, if not actually encouraged them.

Therefore our image is being tarnished and the credibility of our claims to want a better and more just world are increasingly placed in doubt. I need hardly add the aspect of domestic U.S. reactions.

This leads to an aspect I personally find the most disturbing of all -- that we have not been honest with ourselves. We have condoned counter-terror; we may even in effect have encouraged or blessed it. We have been so obsessed with the fear of insurgency that we have rationalized away our qualms and uneasiness.

This is not only because we have concluded we cannot do anything about it, for we never really tried. Rather we suspected that maybe it is a good tactic, and that as long as Communists are being killed it is alright. Murder, torture and mutilation are alright if our side is doing it and the victims are Communists. After all hasn't man been a savage from the beginning of time so let us not be too queasy about terror. I have literally heard these arguments from our people.

Have our values been so twisted by our adversary concept of politics in the hemisphere? Is it conceivable that we are so obsessed with insurgency that we are prepared to rationalize murder as an acceptable counter-insurgency weapon? Is it possible that a nation which so revers the principle of due process of law has so easily acquiesced in this sort of terror tactic?

Though kept secret from the American public for three decades, the Vaky memo obliterated any claim that Washington simply didn't know the reality in Guatemala. Still, with Vaky's memo squirreled away in State Department files, the killing went on. The repression was noted almost routinely in reports from the field.

On Jan. 12, 1971, the Defense Intelligence Agency reported that Guatemalan forces had "quietly eliminated" hundreds of "terrorists and bandits" in the countryside. On Feb. 4, 1974, a State Department cable reported resumption of "death squad" activities.

On Dec. 17, 1974, a DIA biography of one U.S.-trained Guatemalan officer gave an insight into how U.S. counterinsurgency doctrine had imbued the Guatemalan strategies. According to the biography, Lt. Col. Elias Osmundo Ramirez Cervantes, chief of security section for Guatemala's president, had trained at the U.S. Army School of Intelligence at Fort Holabird in Maryland, the center for Project X, the distillation of U.S. lessons learned in conducting counterinsurgency warfare. Back in Guatemala, Lt. Col. Ramirez Cervantes was put in charge of plotting raids on suspected subversives as well as their interrogations.

As brutal as the security forces were in the 1960s and 1970s, the worst was yet to come. In the 1980s, the Guatemalan army escalated its slaughter of leftists and their suspected supporters to unprecedented levels.

Ronald Reagan's election in November 1980 set off celebrations in the well-to-do neighborhoods of Central America. After four years of Jimmy Carter's human rights nagging, the region's anticommunist hardliners were thrilled that they had someone in the White House who understood their problems.

The oligarchs and the generals had good reason for optimism. For years, Reagan had been a staunch defender of right-wing regimes that engaged in bloody counterinsurgency campaigns against leftist enemies. In the late 1970s, when Carter's human rights coordinator, Pat Derian, criticized the Argentine military for its "dirty war" -- tens of thousands of "disappearances," tortures and murders -- then-political commentator Reagan joshed that she should "walk a mile in the moccasins" of the Argentine generals before criticizing them.

Despite his aw shucks style, Reagan found virtually every anticommunist action justified, no matter how brutal. From his eight years in the White House, there is no historical indication that he was troubled by the bloodbath and even genocide that occurred in Central America during his presidency, while he was shipping hundreds of millions of dollars in military aid to the implicated forces.

After his election, Reagan pushed aggressively to overturn an arms embargo imposed on Guatemala by President Carter because of the military's wretched human rights record. Reagan saw bolstering the Guatemalan army as part of a regional response to growing leftist insurgencies. Reagan pitched the conflicts as Moscow's machinations for surrounding and conquering the United States. His administration gave little heed to persistent reports about the Guatemalan army carrying out massacres.

According to these "secret" cables, the CIA was confirming Guatemalan government massacres in 1981-82 even as Reagan was moving to loosen the military aid ban. In April 1981, a secret CIA cable described a massacre at Cocob, near Nebaj in the Ixil Indian territory. On April 17, 1981, government troops attacked the area believed to support leftist guerrillas, the cable said.

A CIA source reported that "the social population appeared to fully support the guerrillas" and "the soldiers were forced to fire at anything that moved." The CIA cable added that "the Guatemalan authorities admitted that 'many civilians' were killed in Cocob, many of whom undoubtedly were non-combatants."

Despite that CIA account and other similar reports, Reagan permitted Guatemala's army to buy $3.2 million in military trucks and jeeps in June 1981. To permit the sale, Reagan removed the vehicles from a list of military equipment that was covered by the human rights embargo. The bureaucratic maneuver averted an open clash with Congress about the actions of Guatemala's security forces, while helping to improve the Guatemalan army's mobility.

Apparently confident of Reagan's sympathy, the Guatemalan government continued its political repression without apology, even defiantly. According to a State Department cable on Oct. 5, 1981, Guatemalan leaders met with Reagan's roving ambassador, retired Gen. Vernon Walters, and left no doubt about their plans.

Guatemala's military leader, Gen. Fernando Romeo Lucas Garcia, "made clear that his government will continue as before -- that the repression will continue. He reiterated his belief that the repression is working and that the guerrilla threat will be successfully routed." Human rights groups saw the same picture.

The Inter-American Human Rights Commission released a report on Oct. 15, 1981, blaming the Guatemalan government for "thousands of illegal executions."[8]

But the Reagan administration was set on whitewashing the ugly scene. A State Department "white paper," released in December 1981, blamed the regional violence on leftist "extremist groups" and their "terrorist methods" prompted and supported by Cuba's Fidel Castro.

Yet, even as these rationalizations were presented to the American people, U.S. agencies in the Central America continued to pick up clear evidence of government-sponsored massacres. One CIA report in February 1982 described an army sweep through the so-called Ixil Triangle in central El Quiche province.

"The commanding officers of the units involved have been instructed to destroy all towns and villages which are cooperating with the Guerrilla Army of the Poor [known as the EGP] and eliminate all sources of resistance," the report stated. "Since the operation began, several villages have been burned to the ground, and a large number of guerrillas and collaborators have been killed."

The CIA report explained the army's modus operandi: "When an army patrol meets resistance and takes fire from a town or village, it is assumed that the entire town is hostile and it is subsequently destroyed." When the army encountered an empty village, it was "assumed to have been supporting the EGP, and it is destroyed. There are hundreds, possibly thousands of refugees in the hills with no homes to return to. ...

"The army high command is highly pleased with the initial results of the sweep operation, and believes that it will be successful in destroying the major EGP support area and will be able to drive the EGP out of the Ixil Triangle. ... The well documented belief by the army that the entire Ixil Indian population is pro-EGP has created a situation in which the army can be expected to give no quarter to combatants and non-combatants alike."

---

[8] *The Washington Post,* Oct. 16, 1981.

In March 1982, Gen. Efrain Rios Montt seized power in a military coup. An avowed fundamentalist Christian, he immediately impressed Washington. Reagan hailed Rios Montt as "a man of great personal integrity." By July 1982, however, Rios Montt had begun a new scorched-earth campaign called his "rifles and beans" policy. The slogan meant that pacified Indians would get "beans," while others could expect to be the target of army "rifles."

In October, Rios Montt secretly gave carte blanche to the feared "Archivos" intelligence unit to expand "death squad" operations in the cities. The U.S. embassy was soon hearing more accounts of the army conducting Indian massacres in the countryside, though the Reagan appointees did not investigate too aggressively.

On Oct, 21, 1982, one cable described how three embassy officers tried to check out some of these reports but ran into bad weather and canceled the inspection. The cable put the best possible spin on the situation. Though unable to check out the massacre reports, the embassy officials did "reach the conclusion that the army is completely up front about allowing us to check alleged massacre sites and to speak with whomever we wish."

The next day, the U.S. embassy went further in defending the Guatemalan military. The embassy sent a cable to Washington portraying major human rights groups as communist dupes. The analysis claimed "that a concerted disinformation campaign is being waged in the U.S. against the Guatemalan government by groups supporting the communist insurgency in Guatemala." The cable asserted that "conscientious human rights and church organizations," including Amnesty International, had been taken in and "may not fully appreciate that they are being utilized. ... The campaign's object is simple: to deny the Guatemalan army the weapons and equipment needed from the U.S. to defeat the guerrillas. ...

"If those promoting such disinformation can convince the Congress, through the usual opinion-makers -- the media, church and human rights groups -- that the present GOG [government of Guatemala] is guilty of gross human rights violations they know that the Congress will refuse Guatemala the military assistance it needs. Those backing the communist insurgency are betting on an application, or rather misapplication, of human rights policy so as to damage the GOG and assist themselves."

Reagan personally picked up this theme of a falsely accused Guatemalan military. During a swing through Latin America, Reagan discounted the mounting reports of hundreds of Mayan villages being eradicated. On Dec. 4, 1982, after meeting with Rios Montt, Reagan hailed the general as "totally dedicated to democracy." Reagan declared that Rios Montt's government had been "getting a bum rap."

Internally, however, the U.S. government knew that the Guatemalan military indeed was engaged in a scorched-earth campaign against the Mayans. Still, with the documents kept secret, President Reagan moved forward with his plan to ship more military aid to Guatemala.

On Jan. 7, 1983, Reagan lifted the aid ban and authorized the sale of $6 million in military hardware. Approval covered spare parts for UH-1H helicopters and A-37 aircraft used in counterinsurgency operations. Radios, batteries and battery charges were also in the package. State Department spokesman John Hughes explained that political violence in the cities had "declined dramatically" and that rural conditions had improved too.

In February 1983, however, a secret CIA cable noted the opposite: a rise in "suspect right-wing violence" with kidnappings of students and teachers. Bodies of victims were appearing in ditches and gullies. CIA sources traced these political murders to Rios Montt's order to the "Archivos" in October to "apprehend, hold, interrogate and dispose of suspected guerrillas as they saw fit."

Despite these grisly facts on the ground, the annual State Department human rights survey praised the supposedly improved human rights situation in Guatemala. "The overall conduct of the armed forces had improved by late in the year" 1982, the report stated. A different picture -- far closer to the secret information held by the U.S. government -- was coming from independent human rights investigators.

On March 17, 1983, Americas Watch representatives condemned the Guatemalan army for human rights atrocities against the Indian population. New York attorney Stephen L. Kass said these findings included proof that the government carried out "virtually indiscriminate murder of men, women and children of any farm regarded by the army as possibly supportive of guerrilla insurgents." Rural women suspected of guerrilla sympathies were raped before execution, Kass said. Children were "thrown into burning homes. They are thrown in the air and speared with bayonets. We heard many, many stories of children being picked up by the ankles and swung against poles so their heads are destroyed." [AP, March 17, 1983]

Publicly, however, senior Reagan officials continued to put on a happy face. On June 12, 1983, special envoy Richard B. Stone praised "positive changes" in Rios Montt's government. But Rios Montt's vengeful Christian fundamentalism was hurtling out of control, even by Guatemalan standards. In August 1983, Gen. Oscar Mejia Victores seized power in another coup.

Despite the power shift, Guatemalan security forces continued to act with impunity. When three Guatemalans working for the U.S. Agency for International Development were slain in November 1983, U.S. Ambassador Frederic Chapin suspected that "Archivos" hit squads were sending a message to the United States to back off even the mild pressure for human rights improvements. In late November, in a brief show of displeasure, the administration postponed the sale of $2 million in helicopter spare parts. The next month, however, Reagan sent the spare parts.

Though a staunchly conservative ambassador, Chapin continued to protest. In one cable, Chapin denounced the "horrible human rights realities in Guatemala," adding: "we must come to some resolution in policy terms. Either we can overlook the record and emphasize the strategic concept or we can pursue a higher moral path. We simply cannot flip flop back and forth between the two possible positions."

Of course, lying was always another option. In February 1984, Reagan's State Department submitted a secret report to Congress arguing that the Guatemalan human rights situation was brightening and that more security assistance "could act as a catalyst for further improvements."[9] Later that year, Reagan

---

[9] See *Harper's Magazine,* June 1999.

succeeded in pressuring Congress to approve $300,000 in military training for the Guatemalan army.

By mid-1984, Chapin, embittered over the army's stubborn brutality, was gone, replaced by a far-right political appointee named Alberto Piedra. Piedra was all for increased military assistance to Guatemala. In January 1985, Americas Watch issued a report observing that Reagan's State Department "is apparently more concerned with improving Guatemala's image than in improving its human rights."

Meanwhile, the Guatemalan security forces continued their grim reaping of individuals who were considered "subversive." The logbook of one security unit, which surfaced in early 1999, described the fate of 183 victims from August 1983 to March 1985. The document, presumably one of thousands from the files of Guatemala's security forces, listed the circumstances of captures, interrogations and executions. The victims' photos -- torn from passports and driver's licences -- were glued next to the text.

This one death list started three weeks after Gen. Mejia Victores took power and marked an escalation of the dirty war against urban dissidents. The document also cited other individuals implicated by the kidnap victims during interrogation. Many of those implicated were then themselves captured. Of the 183 people kidnapped, more than 100 were killed, with the death code "300" as the last entry and a date marking when the execution was carried out.

"Given the brutality of the torture applied to the disappeared, it is not surprising that many of them provided information, both real and fabricated, about colleagues, friends, even family members," wrote Kate Doyle, an analyst at the National Security Archive, an independent research group that authenticated the death list. "The log was probably generated by the Archivos."[10]

According to other declassified U.S. records, the Guatemalan government's brutality included torture out of the Middle Ages. A Defense Intelligence Agency cable reported that the Guatemalan military used an air base in Retalhuleu during the mid-1980s as a

---

[10] See *Harper's Magazine*, June 1999.

center for coordinating the counterinsurgency campaign in southwest Guatemala.

At the base, pits were filled with water to hold captured suspects. "Reportedly there were cages over the pits and the water level was such that the individuals held within them were forced to hold on to the bars in order to keep their heads above water and avoid drowning," the DIA report stated. Later, the pits were filled with concrete to eliminate the evidence.

Other pits inside the base perimeter were used as mass graves, according to the DIA report. Another dumping spot for political victims was the Pacific Ocean. Bodies of insurgents tortured to death and of live prisoners marked for "disappearance" were loaded on planes that flew out over the ocean where the soldiers would shove the victims into the water, the disposal technique favored by the Argentine military.

The history of the Retalhuleu death camp was uncovered by accident in the early 1990s, the DIA reported on April 11, 1994. A Guatemalan officer wanted to let soldiers cultivate their own vegetables on a corner of the base. But the officer was taken aside and told to drop the request "because the locations he had wanted to cultivate were burial sites that had been used by the D-2 [military intelligence] during the mid-eighties."

Though the U.S. government knew much of Guatemala's bloody history as it was unfolding, the truth was withheld from the American people until the late 1990s. When Guatemala's Historical Clarification Commission finally secured the U.S. records, it was able to document the breadth of the calamity. In the 1080s alone, the army had committed 626 massacres against Mayan villages, the commission found.

"The massacres that eliminated entire Mayan villages ... are neither perfidious allegations nor figments of the imagination, but an authentic chapter in Guatemala's history," the commission concluded. The army "completely exterminated Mayan communities, destroyed their livestock and crops," the report said. In the north, the report termed the slaughter a "genocide."[11]

---

[11] *The Washington Post,* Feb. 26, 1999.

Besides carrying out murder and "disappearances," the army routinely engaged in torture and rape. "The rape of women, during torture or before being murdered, was a common practice" by the military and paramilitary forces, the report found. The report added that the "government of the United States, through various agencies including the CIA, provided direct and indirect support for some [of these] state operations." The report concluded that the U.S. government also gave money and training to a Guatemalan military that committed "acts of genocide" against the Mayans.

"Believing that the ends justified everything, the military and the state security forces blindly pursued the anticommunist struggle, without respect for any legal principles or the most elemental ethical and religious values, and in this way, completely lost any semblance of human morals," said the commission chairman, Christian Tomuschat, a German jurist. "Within the framework of the counterinsurgency operations carried out between 1981 and 1983, in certain regions of the country agents of the Guatemalan state committed acts of genocide against groups of the Mayan people." But the report did not single out culpable individuals either in Guatemala or the United States. [12]

The major American newspapers did cover the findings, but provided little follow-up. *The New York Times* made the report's release the lead story on Feb. 26, 1999. *The Washington Post* played the story inside on page A19. Both newspapers cited the troubling role of the CIA and other U.S. government agencies in the Guatemalan tragedy.

On March 1, 1999, a *Washington Post* editorial addressed the findings with an odd twist. The only U.S. official singled out for blame was President Carter because he had cut off military aid in response to the slaughters. The editorial argued that the arms embargo removed "what minimal restraint even a feeble American presence supplied." With no apparent irony, the editorial then ended by stating: "We need our own truth commission."

During a visit to Central America, on March 10, 1999, President Clinton apologized for the past U.S. support of right-wing regimes in Guatemala. "For the United States, it is important that I

---

[12] *The New York Times*, Feb. 26, 1999.

state clearly that support for military forces and intelligence units which engaged in violence and widespread repression was wrong, and the United States must not repeat that mistake," Clinton said.

The sketchy apology appeared to be all the Central Americans could expect from El Norte. In the American press, the remarkable disclosures about U.S.-supported genocide were treated as a one-day story receiving little notice on the TV talk shows and soon forgotten.

Even with the Cold War over, the secrets remained, though sometimes they were technically no longer secrets, just forgotten old stories, "lost history." No one important was ever held to account for the mass slaughters, either by war-crimes tribunals or by the news media. Indeed, in the 1990s, ex-President Reagan, one of the American leaders most complicit in these war crimes, had become a national icon.

In books and opinion columns, Reagan was hailed as an inspirational leader and great visionary. More than any recent president, with the possible exception of the assassinated John F. Kennedy, Reagan was bathed in national honors. Washington's National Airport was renamed for him and his name was etched into a new international trade center in Washington. Congressional Republicans even pressed a bill to have his face chiseled into Mount Rushmore, next to Washington, Jefferson, Lincoln and Theodore Roosevelt.

In the celebration over "winning the Cold War," the bloody realities of counterinsurgencies and intelligence abuses were washed from the nation's memory. The tamed national press corps happily moved on to lighter fare and sexier scandals.

The biggest political story of the late 1990s was President Clinton's dalliance with former White House intern Monica Lewinsky, an embarrassment that led to the second impeachment of a U.S. president in history. Only after the Republicans fell short of a two-thirds Senate majority for Clinton's ouster did the year-long scandal finally fade away.

But the Washington press corps still had no interest in revisiting the national security atrocities of the preceding era. The media's working assumption was that the American people just didn't care.

Even earlier, in the pre-Monica days of 1995, tired of
arguments about what constituted "news" in the
modern environment, I started a Web site and
newsletter called *The Consortium*. One of its goals was to help
finance honest reporting about these tough national security
stories from the Cold War.

But, in the nearer term, the publication set out to piece
together what it could about the "lost history." The first series --
and a subsequent monograph -- was entitled *The October Surprise
X-Files*. The series published new documentary evidence about
Republican efforts to disrupt President Carter's desperate attempt
to free 52 American hostages held in Iran before the 1980
presidential election.

In 1997, I launched *iF Magazine*,[13] an investigative publication
that featured the best work generated by *The Consortium*. This
book, *Lost History*, combines information from those publications
with material derived from my first book, *Fooling America*, which
was published in 1992 but has long been out of print.

Lost History starts with the beginning of the Reagan
administration -- a pivotal moment for the nation, for the
Washington press corps and for my career. I had just been placed
on the AP's Special Assignment Team in Washington and thought
the new administration's interest in Central America would be an
important story to follow.

Part One tracks the narrative of the 1980s through the
relentless "perception management" campaigns about Central
America, through the collapse of the Washington press corps'
independence, through the cover-ups of the Iran-contra scandal,
through the dark secret of CIA-protected contra-cocaine trafficking,
and through the press corps' new role as protector of the secrets.

Part Two examines what others discovered about the secret
history of the Cold War and the corresponding decline of
democratic values in the United States. That collection of articles

---

[13] *iF Magazine* was named in recognition of publications by two
iconoclastic journalists of the mid-century, George Seldes's *In
fact* and *I.F. Stone's Weekly*.

comes from the reporting I have done in recent years for *The Consortium* and *iF Magazine*.

Finally, I hope this book will contribute to a citizens effort to build a true historical record of the past half century. Only with a firm commitment to fact, no matter how unpleasant the details, can the United States hope to emerge from the permanent childhood that now entraps us and to build a mature democracy resting on a solid foundation of truth. Only then will the Cold War's victors get to write the history.

Part One
The 1980s –
The Missing Link

Chapter 1
'Project Truth'

T he lies started just weeks after Ronald Reagan's election, when four American churchwomen were raped and murdered by military security forces in rightist-ruled El Salvador.

The evidence was pretty clear. On the night of Dec. 2, 1980, two of the women, Dorothy Kazel and Jean Donovan, drove a white mini-van to the international airport outside San Salvador. There, they picked up Ita Ford and Maura Clarke who had attended a conference in Nicaragua.

Leaving the airport, the van turned onto the long road that heads into the capital city. At a roadblock, a squad of soldiers stopped the van and took the women into custody. After a phone call apparently to a superior officer, the sergeant in charge said the orders were to kill the women. The soldiers raped them first and then executed the women with high-powered rifles. Their bodies were left in the open.

The atrocity was only one of hundreds committed each month by the Salvadoran security forces in a "dirty war" against leftists and suspected leftists, a conflict that was more mass murder than a war, a butchery that would eventually claim some 70,000 lives. The Dec. 2 atrocity stood out only because Americans were the victims and it attracted international attention.

The proper response from U.S. officials would have seemed obvious: to join U.S. Ambassador Robert White in denouncing the brutal rape and murder of four American citizens. But the incoming Reagan foreign policy team didn't see it that clearly. The Reagan team was on the side of the rightist Salvadoran military. So, the rape-murder -- like the other mind-numbing slaughters -- would be treated as a public relations problem, best handled by shifting as much of the blame as possible onto the victims.

Jeane Kirkpatrick, Reagan's choice for United Nations ambassador, found some justification for the crime. The victims, she said, were "not just nuns. The nuns were political activists ... on behalf of the [leftist opposition] Frente." The underlying assumption seemed to be that it was not so bad to rape and murder "political activists" once they were characterized as leftist.

After President Reagan took office, his first Secretary of State Al Haig added some more complexity to the picture. In congressional testimony, Haig suggested that "the nuns may have run through a roadblock or may have accidentally been perceived to have been doing so, and there may have been an exchange of fire." All of a sudden, the new administration was suggesting -- falsely -- that the nuns were packing heat. They weren't just "political activists" now, they may have been armed and dangerous.

This was where I came in. Thirty-one years old, I had been working in *The Associated Press'* Washington bureau more than three years when the Reagan administration took office. Like most AP staffers who get promoted to the national staff in Washington, I started on the night editing desk. After one year on the desk, I went to Capitol Hill, where I covered the budget and economic issues. While on those assignments, I developed some investigative pieces in my spare time, mostly about garden-variety scandals in the Carter administration, such as the misuse of government funds at the General Services Administration.

Eager to specialize in investigative reporting rather than simply cover the surface stories, I asked to be put on the AP's smallish Special Assignment Team. After the 1980 elections, when AP management shifted the staff into new jobs, my name landed as one of four correspondents on the Special Assignment Team. I was the only one designated specifically as an investigative reporter.

My assignment, however, came with no special subject area attached. So, I looked around for what might be a hot topic, one worth investing the time to achieve the necessary expertise. The key to a productive beat, I thought, was choosing a topic that was likely to produce a great deal of action and news. Given the new administration's obvious interest in a hardline national security strategy, the developing Central American story looked like a promising place to start.

As I was learning the ropes of the Central American issues, I attended a Washington news conference held by members of the churchwomen's families. They were describing what they had learned about the murders. They also complained about what they saw as government foot-dragging.

During the questions and answers, a small group of right-wing "journalists" began haranguing the families and accusing them of misrepresenting the facts. "They weren't raped," one of the men yelled at the shocked family members. It seemed Washington was entering a new era in which the capital's traditional political comity was giving way to an ideological fury. In Washington, there was an echo of Central America's extremism.

Beyond the high-profile murders in El Salvador, the Reagan team faced other complaints that Salvadoran security forces were murdering thousands of common citizens who were deemed subversive. When House Democrats toured refugee camps in Honduras in early February 1981, they heard story after story of U.S.-supplied forces terrorizing the population.

"Without exception, the refugees told us ... that they fled the violence of the [Salvadoran] army, which was being supported by the United States," said Rep. Gerry Studds, D-Mass. "Whole villages are being burned."

One refugee described government troops cutting open the abdomen of a pregnant woman, tearing out her unborn child and then killing the woman and the child. "In each and every conversation, it was verified that the military aid from the United States was aiding and abetting the killing and torture of innocent people," said Rep. Barbara Mikulski, D-Md.

The best response to these charges that the new Reagan administration could muster came from State Department spokesman Don Mathes. He argued that impostors might be dressing up in army uniforms to commit atrocities. "It's very difficult to identify where the violence is coming from in El Salvador," he said. [AP, Feb. 6, 1981]

President Reagan seized on another argument to fend off the human rights complaints: he asserted that the Salvadoran security forces were the first line of defense protecting the Americas from an assault by Moscow and Havana. "A friendly country in our hemisphere is trying to halt the infiltration into the Americas by terrorists, by outside interference and those who aren't just aiming at El Salvador but, I think, are aiming at the whole of Central and possibly later South America and, I'm sure, eventually North America," Reagan stated at a news conference on March 6, 1981.

Beyond seeing the hand of international communism at work, Reagan insisted that the Salvadoran security forces were the good guys. "We think we are helping the forces that are supporting human rights in El Salvador," Reagan said during the same news conference. He cited figures that purported to show that the leftist guerrillas "boasted" about committing more than half the political killings in 1980.

Given the contrary assessment by all leading human rights groups, one of my early stories about El Salvador examined how President Reagan had reached that conclusion. It turned out that State Department analysts had used a methodology that multiply counted public statements by the guerrillas. Whenever the guerrillas read a report on radio or published a war bulletin listing enemies killed in action, the numbers were added to the total. It didn't matter that the reports might have referred to the same battle or were a cumulative figure for the year. In other words, the State Department simply counted the same guerrilla battlefield claims over and over again to bring the number to above half the total. The State Department could cite no specific guerrilla "boast" about committing more than half the political killings. [AP, March 19, 1981]

Despite the administration's alarmist rhetoric, the American public remained skeptical about the need to go to war in Central America. Early White House mail ran about 10-to-1 against Reagan's decision to ship military aid to El Salvador and send 55 military advisers. Many letters asserted that Central Americans should be allowed to settle their own political differences and some worried about "another Vietnam." [AP, March 28, 1981]

But the administration's spinning was just beginning. Routinely through 1981, the Reagan administration disputed public accounts of Salvadoran army atrocities and pressed for increased military aid. In one case in April, eyewitnesses described soldiers dragging 30 men, women and teen-agers out of their homes near San Salvador and executing them. The administration tried to shift the blame to "extremist forces" and suggested that the deaths had resulted from a gun battle. [AP, April 11, 1981]

Despite the president's best efforts, however, the evidence kept pointing toward the Salvadoran security forces. By May, the FBI had matched the fingerprint of a national guardsman to one found on the van of the murdered churchwomen. The FBI also linked a bullet casing found at the murder scene to a gun registered to another guardsman. [AP, May 26, 1981]

Still, inside the administration, there was an anything-goes mentality about battling the communist menace and especially countering alleged Cuban penetration of Central America. Besides the leftist guerrillas in El Salvador, the administration was taking aim at the leftist Sandinista government in Nicaragua, where the Sandinista guerrilla army overthrew longtime dictator Anastasio Somoza in 1979.

By 1981, the Sandinistas had been in power nearly two years and were steering that country in a socialistic direction. In solidarity with this new leftist regime, hundreds of Cubans had flocked to Nicaragua to assist in a variety of projects, from military advice to medical service, from intelligence training to teaching literacy and building public works projects. As President Reagan pressed Congress to increase military aid to the Salvadoran army, he also came to view Nicaragua as a test for removing a government that had developed close ties to Moscow.

Many in the administration agreed that the tougher the proposal the better. The CIA's Latin American Division chief, Duane "Dewey" Clarridge, recounted in his memoirs, *A Spy for All Seasons*, that he first rallied support for the contra army by promising that the goal was to "start killing Cubans" inside Nicaragua. "My plan, stated so bluntly, undoubtedly sounds harsh," Clarridge acknowledged. But he knew the idea would sell with hardliners, such as Haig and CIA director William J. Casey.

Clarridge said his Cuban-killing plan "was exactly what Casey wanted to hear. A smile broke across his rumpled countenance as he asked me to produce a Presidential Finding to cover and fund this operation. He knew as well as I did that the idea of killing Cubans was part bravado and part pandering to Haig and his supporters."[14] Already, a small force of contras – remnants of Somoza's national guard – was taking shape in Honduras with training from Argentine intelligence forces.

President Reagan formally authorized the CIA to join in the operation in November 1981. The presidential "finding" was not as blunt as Clarridge's language, however. It stated that the reason for supporting the Nicaraguan contra rebels was to interdict arms shipments from Nicaragua to leftist insurgents in El Salvador. Nothing was mentioned about killing Cubans or another unwritten goal of the covert operation: to overthrow the Sandinistas militarily.

The job of whipping the contras into shape – and coordinating with the Argentine trainers -- fell to Clarridge, Casey's hand-picked can-do guy to run the contra war. A character who sometimes seemed like he had stepped out of a grade-B spy novel, Clarridge had a flamboyant reputation, dressed loudly, smoked cigars, enjoyed red wine and took as his second wife a stunning German woman whom he met on an espionage assignment in Turkey.

---

[14] Inside Nicaragua, Cubans associated with Fidel Castro's government apparently were singled out for death without regard for their civilian or diplomatic status. In 1982, for instance, a U.S. Defense Intelligence Agency report stated that Honduran-based contras had engaged in the "assassination of minor [Nicaraguan] government officials and a Cuban adviser." Five years later, a contra unit ambushed American relief worker, Benjamin Linder, while he was working on a water project. According to forensic specialists, Linder was first wounded and then executed at close range. The contras defended their action by claiming they thought Linder was a Cuban. It is unclear exactly how many Cubans were killed in the Nicaraguan conflict.

B y 1981, Nicaragua had become a sanctuary, too, for dissidents escaping military "death squads" that had ravaged the ranks of South American leftists during the 1970s. Clarridge cited the Sandinistas' harboring of these "terrorists" as another justification for the contra war. He noted that by 1981, as retaliation for the Sandinista protection of Argentine leftists, the Argentine intelligence services had started training the contras.

Argentina's contingent of contra trainers was led by Col. Osvaldo Ribeiro, an expert in the practice of "disappearing" political enemies. He reportedly became a master of these secretive murder techniques after the Argentine military seized power in 1976. The army then launched a "dirty war" that kidnapped and murdered an estimated 30,000 Argentinians, often without any official accounting of their fate. By the early 1980s, Central Americans were calling the tactic of "disappearing" suspected leftists the "Argentine method."[15]

Helped by Ribeiro and other Argentines, the initial contra force coalesced as "the 15th of September Legion." Its military leader was a former Somoza National Guard officer, Col. Enrique Bermudez. Not surprisingly, the early lessons from the Argentines included how to commit acts of terror. At the Argentines' behest, the contras attacked a Costa Rican radio station that was broadcasting news critical of the Argentine "dirty war." Three Costa Ricans died in the raid.

Inside Honduras, the Argentines also organized the contras into roving "death squads" that helped the Honduran military "disappear" nearly 200 labor leaders, students and other political activists during the 1980s. [16] But from the very start, there was

---

[15] See New York Times, June 5, 1988

[16] In 1993, the Honduran human rights ombudsman, Leo Valladares, issued a report on the fate of those who were "disappeared" in Honduras during the 1980s. The report, entitled "The Facts Speak for Themselves," identified for blame a dozen of the contras' Argentine advisers, including Ribeiro and the group's money launderer Leonardo Sanchez-Reisse. In the report, Valladeres said "systematic, clandestine and organized" disappearances started in 1979, coinciding with the arrival of Argentine military advisers who began training the contras. As in

another secret about the Argentine-contra connection that needed to be concealed. The Argentines passed on lessons, too, about using drug money to pay for military operations.

According to a financial specialist for Argentine intelligence, Leonardo Sanchez-Reisse, Argentine trainers arranged an early flow of drug money into the contras' coffers. In closed testimony to Sen. John Kerry's contra-drug investigation in 1987, Sanchez-Reisse said Bolivian drug kingpin Roberto Suarez earmarked more than $30 million to support right-wing paramilitary operations in Central and South America, including the contra war.

Sanchez-Reisse, who oversaw the money laundering, said the drug money first helped finance a 1980 military coup in Bolivia that ousted an elected left-of-center government. Argentine intelligence officers assisted in that putsch, which became known as the Cocaine Coup because it gave the drug lords free run of the country.

Sanchez-Reisse described how he and an Argentine neo-fascist "death squad" leader named Raul Guglielminetti oversaw the Miami-based money-laundering front that also sent drug proceeds to the contras. Sanchez-Reisse said the Miami operation was based in two front companies: Argenshow, a promoter of U.S. entertainment acts in Argentina, and the Silver Dollar, a pawn shop that was licensed to sell guns.

Sanchez-Reisse asserted that the real activity of the companies was to transfer Roberto Suarez's $30 million into various political and paramilitary operations approved by the CIA, which maintained close ties to the Argentine intelligence services. The money for the Argentine-backed Bolivian coup came from "drug traffickers [in Bolivia who] were interested to overthrow the government of Bolivia," Sanchez-Reisse testified. The money "was shipped from Bahamas to United States. ... It was money [that] belonged to people connected with drug traffic in Bolivia at that time, specifically Mr. Roberto Suarez in Bolivia."

Argentina's "dirty war," many Honduran victims were kidnapped, taken to clandestine jail cells and subjected to torture before secret execution.

An architect of the Bolivian coup was World War II Nazi fugitive Klaus Barbie, who was working as a Bolivian intelligence officer under the name Klaus Altmann. Barbie drew up plans modeled after the 1976 Argentine coup and contacted the Argentines for help. As the coup took shape, Barbie organized a secret lodge, called Thule, where he lectured his followers underneath swastikas by candlelight.

The Bolivian military coup leader was Col. Luis Arce-Gomez, the cousin of the drug lord, Roberto Suarez. Besides lining up Bolivian troops, the coup makers also recruited international neo-fascist terrorists, such as Italian Stefano della Chiaie who was already working with Argentine death squads. Dr. Alfred Candia, the Bolivian leader of the World Anti-Communist League, coordinated the arrival of these paramilitary operatives.

Given the left-of-center orientation of the Bolivian government, the CIA apparently viewed the coup developments with some favor. But Michael Levine, a star undercover agent for the Drug Enforcement Administration, saw the geopolitics interfering with major narcotics cases. In May 1980, Levine put together a case in Miami that seized 854 pounds of cocaine base and arrested two top Bolivian traffickers from the Roberto Suarez organization.

The bust, however, was quickly sacrificed for what Levine concluded were political reasons. One suspect, Jose Roberto Gasser, "was almost immediately released from custody by the Miami U.S. atttorney's office," Levine wrote in his book, *Deep Cover*. Gasser was the son of Bolivian WACL associate Erwin Gasser, a leading figure in the upcoming coup. The other defendant saw his bail lowered, letting him flee the United States. Levine complained bitterly about the danger this presented to Bolivian officials who had risked their lives to help the DEA.

On June 17, 1980, six of Bolivia's biggest drug traffickers met with the Bolivian military conspirators to hammer out a financial deal for future protection of the cocaine trade. Because of this near-open collaboration, one La Paz businessman dubbed the coming putsch the "Cocaine Coup," a name that stuck.[17]

Less than three weeks later, on July 6 in Buenos Aires, Argentina, undercover DEA agent Levine met with a Bolivian trafficker named Hugo Hurtado-Candia. Over drinks, Hurtado-Candia outlined plans for Bolivia's "new government." He said his niece, Sonia Atala, a major cocaine supplier, would "be in a very strong position."

Later that day, an Argentine secret policeman told Levine that the CIA knew all about the coup. "You North Americans amaze me. Don't you speak to your own people?" the policeman wondered. "Do you think Bolivia's government -- or any government in South America -- can be changed without your government and mine being aware of it?"

When Levine asked why that affected the DEA's investigation of Hurtado-Candia, the Argentine answered, "Because the same people he's naming as drug dealers are the people we are helping to rid Bolivia of leftists. ... Us. The Argentines ... working with your CIA."[18]

On July 17, 1980, the Cocaine Coup began, spearheaded by Barbie and his neo-fascist goon squad that went by the name "Fiances of Death." "The masked thugs were not Bolivians; they spoke Spanish with German, French and Italian accents," Levine wrote. "Their uniforms bore neither national identification nor any markings, although many of them wore Nazi swastika armbands and insignias."

The slaughter was fierce. When the putschists stormed the national labor headquarters, they wounded labor leader Marcelo Quiroga, who had led the effort to indict former military dictator Hugo Banzer on drug and corruption charges. Quiroga "was dragged off to police headquarters to be the object of a game played by some of the torture experts imported from Argentina's dreaded Mechanic School of the Navy," Levine wrote.

"These experts applied their 'science' to Quiroga as a lesson to the Bolivians, who were a little backward in such matters. They

---

[17] See *Cocaine Politics* by Peter Dale Scott and Jonathan Marshall.
[18] See Levine's *Big White Lie*.

kept Quiroga alive and suffering for hours. His castrated, tortured body was found days later in a place called 'The Valley of the Moon' in southern La Paz." Female captives were gang-raped as part of their torture.

To Levine back in Buenos Aires, it was soon clear "that the primary goal of the revolution was the protection and control of Bolivia's cocaine industry. All major drug traffickers in prison were released, after which they joined the neo-Nazis in their rampage. Government buildings were invaded and trafficker files were either carried off or burned. Government employees were tortured and shot, the women tied and repeatedly raped by the paramilitaries and the freed traffickers."

Col. Arce-Gomez, a central-casting image of a bemedaled, pot-bellied Latin dictator, grabbed broad powers as Interior Minister. Gen. Luis Garcia Meza was installed as Bolivia's new president. After the coup, Arce-Gomez went into partnership with big narco-traffickers, including Mafia-connected Cuban-American smugglers based in Miami. According to DEA agent Levine, Arce-Gomez bragged to one trafficker, "We will flood America's borders with cocaine." It was not an idle boast.

"Bolivia soon became the principal supplier of cocaine base to the then fledgling Colombian cartels, making themselves the main suppliers of cocaine to the United States," Levine wrote. "And it could not have been done without the tacit help of DEA and the active, covert help of the CIA."[19]

The Argentine intelligence officers who assisted in Bolivia's Cocaine Coup followed up their victory by moving to Central America to train a ragtag force of former Nicaraguan national guardsmen. Sanchez-Reisse said the Argenshow-Silver Dollar

---

[19] The importance of Bolivian coca to the early development of the Medellin cartel was corroborated by cartel money-launderer Ramon Milian Rodriguez in Senate testimony on April 6, 1988. Milian Rodriguez stated that "Bolivia was much more significant than the other countries." Nevertheless, the shockingly corrupt Bolivian regime collapsed in 1982. Later, Arce-Gomez was convicted in the United States on drug-trafficking charges, while his boss Gen. Garcia Meza was imprisoned in Bolivia for drug trafficking and human-rights crimes. Klaus Barbie was returned to France where he was jailed for World War II crimes against humanity. He died in prison.

money was soon flowing in the contras' direction, too. In the contra operation, Sanchez-Reisse said, his partner, Guglielminetti, befriended John Hull, a CIA-connected farmer who let contras use his ranch in northern Costa Rica.[20]

There were strong Bolivian drug links to Miami's Cuban exile community as well. On Dec. 16, 1980, Cuban-American intelligence operative Ricardo Morales told a Florida prosecutor that he had become an informer in Operation Tick-Talks, a Miami-based investigation that implicated Cuban-American Frank Castro and other Cuban exiles in a conspiracy to import cocaine from the new military rulers of Bolivia.[21]

By 1981, Argentine-trained contra operatives also were opening their own drug-trafficking channels, U.S. intelligence knew. According to a draft CIA field report in June 1981, the 15th of September Legion, also known as ADREN, chose early on "to stoop to criminal activities in order to feed and clothe their cadre." A September 1981 cable to CIA headquarters stated that ADREN had started using drug trafficking. Two ADREN members made the first delivery of drugs to Miami in July 1981, the CIA cable reported.

Other contra-connected drug dealers had their own connections to Bolivian cocaine suppliers. Norwin Meneses, a notorious Nicaraguan drug smuggler, went to work as a fund-raiser for the contras and gained contra help for his drug deals. One of his lieutenants, Oscar Danilo Blandon, said he and Meneses were en

---

[20] Argentine trainers remained active with the contras until 1983, when an elected civilian government replaced the military junta in Buenos Aires. By then, the Argentines had become a drag on the CIA's goal of sanitizing the contras' image. "Having started out as a great asset, they'd become a liability," wrote senior CIA officer Duane Clarridge in his book, *A Spy for All Seasons.* But the CIA officer did not forget the Argentine contribution in undermining the Sandinista government. When the Sandinistas lost the 1990 election and surrendered power, a celebrating Clarridge called contra commander Enrique Bermudez to get the phone number for the chief Argentine trainer, Osvaldo Ribeiro. "Though Ribeiro and I had had our run-ins, I thought I owed him a call, thanking him for getting the ball rolling," Clarridge wrote. "I suppose Ribeiro was momentarily flabbergasted that I had called. However, he recovered and rather emotionally thanked me." For more details about the Argentine operation, see *iF Magazine,* Nov.-Dec. 1998.

route to Bolivia to complete a drug deal in 1982 when they stopped in Honduras for meetings with contra commander Enrique Bermudez. Bermudez told the drug smugglers that when it came to raising money for the contras, "the ends justify the means."

The next leg of the Meneses-Blandon trip, however, was interrupted when Honduran authorities detained Blandon and seized $100,000 in drug money that was intended as a down-payment on the Bolivian cocaine deal. At that dicey moment, the contras intervened, according to Blandon. They described the smugglers as contras and insisted that the $100,000 belonged to the movement. The Hondurans backed off, returned the drug money and let the traffickers go.

With internal knowledge of the contra-drug connection spreading, the CIA brass came up with a solution to legal requirements about reporting criminal actions by its operatives. In early 1982, CIA director Casey lobbied Attorney General William French Smith to exempt the CIA from a legal duty to report on drug crimes by the spy agency's foreign assets. Smith secretly granted the waiver on Feb. 11, 1982.

Given the shortcomings of these Latin American allies, the Reagan administration had its work cut out for it. But the administration always understood that the Central American conflict was a two-front war: battling leftists in the region, but also winning the public-relations struggle in the United States. Often more important than the reality in Central America was how the opinion leaders in Washington and the American people viewed that reality. "Perception management" soon became the watchword for winning the domestic P.R. war.

"The most critical special operations mission we have ... is to persuade the American people that the communists are out to get us," deputy assistant secretary to the Air Force, J. Michael Kelly, later explained to a National Defense University conference. "If we win the war of ideas, we will win everywhere else."

---

[21] See *Cocaine Politics*. Frank Castro would emerge as a major benefactor of contra operations based in Costa Rica.

An early goal in this "war of ideas" was weeding out American reporters who uncovered facts that undercut the desired public relations images in Central America. One of the first targets was correspondent Raymond Bonner who had been reporting on human rights violations in El Salvador for *The New York Times*, arguably the most influential newspaper in the United States.

The Bonner problem grew critical in late January 1982, when he reported in a front-page article that the Atlacatl Battalion, the first U.S.-trained Salvadoran army unit, had massacred about 800 men, women and children in and around the village of El Mozote in Morazan province in northeast El Salvador in December 1981. Though the province was considered a guerrilla stronghold, the town was inhabited by peasants who were generally not politically active. So, the peasants did not flee into the mountains as inhabitants of other villages did. Still, as part of a strategy to terrorize the population, the soldiers rounded up El Mozote's inhabitants and began to interrogate them on Dec. 10, 1981.

The next morning, the grimly efficient soldiers had another task in mind. The soldiers bound the hands of the men. Then, as the women and children watched, the soldiers methodically used machetes to chop off the heads of many male peasants. Others were executed with bursts of automatic rifle fire into their brains. The wailing women were next, with younger ones, including girls as young as 10, first taken to the hills to be gang-raped before being killed. The older women were dragged into a house and shot to death.

That left the screaming children who had been locked in another house. The soldiers entered and began hacking the children with machetes. Soldiers used rifle butts to smash the heads of other children. Another group was herded into the church sacristy and killed with gunfire from U.S.-supplied M-16s. The remaining children were burned alive when the soldiers set the buildings on fire.[22]

Bonner's *Times* story and a similar one by Alma Guillermoprieto of *The Washington Post* appeared on the front

---

[22] For a detailed account, see Mark Danner's "The Massacre at El Mozote," *The New Yorker*, Dec. 6, 1993.

pages of those two newspapers on Jan. 27, 1982. The next day, President Reagan was set to certify that the Salvadoran government was making a "concerted" effort to respect human rights and was "achieving substantial control over all elements of its own armed forces," a prerequisite for continued U.S. arms shipments to El Salvador. Despite the new atrocity reports, Reagan issued the finding.

But the El Mozote massacre was fast becoming a major P.R. problem. The U.S. embassy in El Salvador dispatched two embassy officers, Todd Greentree and John McKay, to the war zone in Morazan province. They interviewed terrified refugees and concluded that "there had been a massacre." But ongoing military activity in the area prevented the embassy officers from reaching the massacre site, so they lacked details.

Greentree and McKay reported their mixed discoveries to senior embassy officials who then massaged the information into a cable for transmission to Washington. The cable minimized evidence of Salvadoran military guilt. One diplomat who worked on the cable said the embassy knew that the White House did not want confirmation of the massacre, so the report was drafted "intentionally devoid of judgment."[23]

Back in Washington, the watered-down cable allowed the administration to go further. Dropping the Greentree-McKay assessment altogether, Reagan officials challenged the newspaper stories with flat denials and ridicule. Assistant secretaries of state Thomas Enders and Elliott Abrams trooped up to Capitol Hill, where they denounced the El Mozote accusations as false or, at least, wildly exaggerated. "There is no evidence to confirm that government forces systematically massacred civilians in the operations zone, or that the number of civilians even remotely approached the 733 or 926 victims cited in the press," Enders testified.

The *coup de grace* to the massacre tale was Enders's revelation that even before the attack "there were probably not more than 300" people living in El Mozote. That final point was a deft sleight

---

[23] For a detailed account of the embassy maneuvering, see Bonner's *Weakness and Deceit.*

of hand since the newspaper stories had reported that the victims had come not only from El Mozote but from surrounding villages. Enders also understated the refugee-swollen population of El Mozote, which international aid workers put at about 1,000 at the time of the massacre.

Still, the Enders-Abrams performance was good enough for President Reagan's press allies. Accuracy in Media, a right-wing press watchdog group, and *The Wall Street Journal's* editorial page led the attack, pummelling Bonner for alleged leftist sympathies and his gullibility in accepting a false story from Marxist guerrillas. A lead *Journal* editorial accused Bonner of being "overly credulous." The harsh attacks on an individual journalist sent chills through the executive suites of many news organizations, not just those of *The New York Times*.

As political pressure built, *The New York Times'* executive editor Abe Rosenthal flew to El Salvador to assess the complaints about Bonner first-hand. Sympathetic to Reagan's foreign policy, Rosenthal soon limited Bonner's role in the *Times'* bureau in Central America. Word spread that Bonner would be removed.

When I was in El Salvador on an AP reporting assignment in fall 1982, two senior U.S. officials boasted to me about the embassy's success in discrediting Bonner and orchestrating his departure. "We finally got rid of that sonuvabitch," a ranking U.S. military officer told me. In early 1983, Rosenthal did recall Bonner from El Salvador and stuck him in an obscure job on the business desk in New York. Not long after that, Bonner resigned from the *Times*. [24]

---

[24] It would take nearly a decade for the truth about El Mozote to finally come out. After the civil war ended in 1992, a United Nations forensic team excavated the site and discovered hundreds of skeletons, including many tiny ones of children. Bonner was subsequently rehired by *The New York Times*. But no one responsible for the massacre or the cover-up -- either in El Salvador or in Washington -- was held accountable. One of the leading dissemblers, Elliott Abrams, landed a job running an organization called the Ethics and Public Policy Center.

At the time of the El Mozote massacre stories in early 1982, the administration's propaganda efforts still were largely reactive. Privately, Reagan advisers bemoaned what they considered a lack of resources to make their case. According to internal administration assessments, the Executive Branch lacked the machinery to carry out a sustained "political action" campaign aimed at the press, the American people and their congressional representatives.

Summarizing this debate, Kate Semerad, an external-relations official at the Agency for International Development, expressed something like envy for the power of totalitarian states to determine what citizens see and hear. "The totalitarian states whose intelligence and propaganda apparatus we face have no internal problem in denying their citizens access to information or even flagrantly lying to them," Semerad wrote in a memo circulated in the early 1980s. "We have neither the apparatus nor the legal mechanism which would allow the success of an effort to emulate that of Moscow, Habana [sic] and Managua."

But the Semerad memo argued that a U.S. propaganda apparatus was both possible and necessary. "We can and must go over the heads of our Marxist opponents directly to the American people," she wrote. "Our targets would be: within the United States, the Congress, specifically the Foreign Affairs Committees and their staffs, ... the general public [and] the media."

The fledgling operation took the initial nickname of "Project Truth." Later, the idea of a domestic propaganda operation merged with a broader plan for a worldwide information strategy. On June 8, 1982, in London, President Reagan outlined a major new proposal which was to "foster the infrastructure of democracy, the system of a free press, unions, political parties, universities." Reagan gave the concept the name "Project Democracy" and its ostensible focus was international.

But internal Reagan administration records revealed that Project Democracy recruited -- and funded -- influential U.S.-based organizations as part of the international effort. Dated June 14, 1982 and entitled "Project Democracy: Proposals for Action," a draft proposal spelled out plans for drawing non-governmental organizations into the process. The suggested "instruments" for the operation included the Atlantic Institute, the Trilateral Commission and Freedom House. The plan also called for harnessing financial resources from a "coalition of wealthy individuals"; U.S. defense contractors; and private foundations, such as the Twentieth Century Fund.

"Hold a White House meeting of top U.S. business and philanthropic figures to elucidate need and stimulate will to give urgently," stated the proposal. The paper recommended reaching out beyond a base of conservative funders to include more moderate and even liberal foundations, such as the Ford Foundation, Rockefeller Foundation, MacArthur Foundation and the Rockefeller Brothers Fund. The administration also earmarked $200 million in federal money for "political action proposals," ranging from expanded broadcasting to the development of new magazines and the sponsoring of international conferences.

A chart, marked Appendix A and also dated June 14, 1982, identified Freedom House and the Atlantic Institute as important "instruments" for research and contacts with universities. The chart also included boxes for "elite groups" that would be drawn into the operation, including the Trilateral Commission, the Bilderberg Group and the Chamber of Commerce. The Trilateral Commission and the Bilderberg Group are secretive organizations that sponsor closed-door policy discussions involving leading international businessmen, bankers, politicians and media moguls.

The Project Democracy proposal enjoyed the discreet support, too, of CIA director Casey, who wrote in an undated letter to then-White House counsel Edwin Meese III. Casey stated that the plan "has significant merit" and offered to make "suggestions" about who might serve on a working group "to refine the proposal." Casey added, however, that "obviously, we here should not get out front in the development of such an organization, nor do we wish to appear to be a sponsor or advocate. Nevertheless, the needs appear real and I believe our national fabric for dealing with many issues and problems would be well served by such an institute."[25]

---

[25] I found the Casey-to-Meese letter in Walter Raymond's records at the Reagan Presidential Library in Simi Valley, Calif., in May 1999. Like several other documents in Raymond's file, the letter had been torn in half as if he were planning to discard it

The central figure in this fast-growing Project Truth/Project Democracy apparatus was Walter Raymond Jr., a 30-year veteran of CIA propaganda operations who was assigned to the National Security Council staff in 1982. An undated note found in his White House files suggested that the appeal to more moderate foundations was part of a conscious strategy. "Foundations looking leftward ... need to get them committed," the handwritten note stated.

President Reagan took the first formal step to create the propaganda bureaucracy on Jan. 14, 1983, by signing National Security Decision Directive 77, entitled "Management of Public Diplomacy Relative to National Security." The secret directive deemed it "necessary to strengthen the organization, planning and coordination of the various aspects of public diplomacy of the United States Government." He defined public diplomacy broadly as "those actions of the U.S. Government designed to generate support for our national security objectives."

To direct these "public diplomacy" campaigns, Reagan ordered the creation of a Special Planning Group [or SPG] within the National Security Council. "The SPG ... shall ensure that a wide-ranging program of effective initiatives is developed and implemented to support national security policy, objectives and decisions."

To manage the operation, both domestic and foreign, Reagan turned to Raymond. The senior CIA propagandist was a slight, soft-spoken New Yorker who reminded some of a character from a John le Carre spy novel, an intelligence officer who "easily fades into the woodwork," according to one acquaintance. Yet, in small working groups, Raymond could be a standout, assertive, creative, pouring forth ideas, always very serious.

Associates said his CIA career stayed close to headquarters because of special care required for a sick child. Still, he rose to senior levels in the CIA's covert action hierarchy. His last agency job title was considered so revealing of the CIA's disinformation capabilities that it remained a highly classified secret.

---

but later changed his mind. An archivist at the library said she pieced a number of Raymond's torn letters back together and put them in plastic casing for their protection.

Raymond's first concern was the administration's lack of an infrastructure to carry out a domestic "public diplomacy" campaign. "We were not configured effectively to deal with the war of ideas," he recalled in later Iran-contra testimony.

In early 1983, less than two weeks after Reagan signed NSDD-77, Raymond volunteered his professional advice for creating what he called this "new art form" in foreign policy. "It is essential that a serious and deep commitment of talent and time be dedicated to this," Raymond said in a Jan. 25, 1983, memo to then-NSC adviser William Clark. "Programs such as Central America, European strategic debate, Yellow Rain[26] and even Afghanistan have foundered by a failure to orchestrate sufficient resources and forces [for] these efforts."

Raymond recommended a "public diplomacy" apparatus that would "provide central focus for insuring greater commitment of resources, greater concentration of effort in support of our foreign policies: call it political action, if you will." Inside the CIA, "political action" was a term of art encompassing a wide range of activities, both overt and covert, to achieve a desired political result. Historically, "political action" has mixed shades of propaganda, from "white" to "gray" to "black." "White" propaganda is essentially straight information funneled through a cut-out. "Gray" is the blending of truth and half-truth. "Black" is the planting of false stories to damage a political enemy.

But federal law was an obstacle to the domestic side of the operation. Under presidential executive orders, the CIA was specifically barred from influencing U.S. politics and policies, a safeguard established to prevent the spy agency from corrupting U.S. democratic institutions and creating a secret shadow government. Federal law also prohibited the Executive Branch from spending money to lobby Congress, except for the traditional practices of giving testimony, making speeches and talking one-on-one with members. Beyond use of the "bully pulpit," the

---

[26] Yellow rain referred to the administration's allegations that the Soviet Union used a yellow chemical-warfare agent in Indochina. Scientists later concluded that the mysterious yellow substance was bee feces, not a chemical-warfare agent.

administration could not legally spend taxpayers' money to disseminate domestic propaganda or to organize grassroots lobbying campaigns to pressure Congress.

Sensitive to the CIA restriction, Raymond formally resigned from the spy agency in April 1983 so "there would be no question whatsoever of any contamination of this," he said in Iran-contra testimony. But Raymond's CIA training still came in handy as he developed an ambitious public diplomacy strategy. Some of his colleagues remarked that he ran domestic public diplomacy much the same way he would have organized a CIA propaganda operation against a target nation.

Soon, Raymond was cracking the whip within the newly formed Central American Public Diplomacy Task Force, an interagency committee that met every Thursday morning. In that job, he coordinated the public diplomacy work of the State Department, the United States Information Agency, the Agency for International Development, the Defense Department, the CIA and the NSC staff. The minutes of those Thursday-morning meetings showed Raymond as the bureaucratic taskmaster, making sure documents were released on time, checking the budgets and ensuring adequate staffing.

Raymond's immediate challenge was turning the American people around on Central America. On May 5, 1983, a classified "public diplomacy strategy paper" observed that: "Our Central American policy is facing an essentially apathetic and in some particulars hostile U.S. public. There is serious opposition in Congress as illustrated by the two-month battle over the president's request to reprogram $60 million security assistance funds for El Salvador and the current congressional mark-up of the '83 supplemental and '84 authorization bills."

The strategy paper saw a serious problem with the press corps, too. "As far as our Central American policy is concerned, the press perceives that: the USG [U.S. government] is placing too much emphasis on a military solution, as well as being allied with inept, right-wing governments or groups," the paper stated.

"The focus on Nicaragua has not been the repression of pluralism by the Sandinistas but on the alleged U.S.-backed 'covert' war against the Sandinistas. Moreover, the opposition to the

Sandinistas is widely perceived as being led by former Somozistas rather than being broadbased and including many who initially supported the Sandinista revolution. Further areas of press concentration have been the USG is exaggerating the communist threat; the USG is supporting 'covert' efforts to overthrow the Sandinistas in Nicaragua; the USG is not supporting a political solution of the Salvadoran 'civil war'; the USG is opposed to negotiation with Nicaragua to solve outstanding issues."

Perhaps, unintentionally, the internal paper underscored how difficult the administration's job was, because many of the public and press perceptions at that time were accurate. Indeed, the administration *was* supporting a covert war in Nicaragua and had little interest in serious negotiations either in Nicaragua or El Salvador. The contra leaders *were* former Somoza national guardsmen. They *were* vowing to overthrow the Sandinistas. The administration *was* hyping the communist threat in Nicaragua. The Sandinistas had left much of the economy in private hands and the new government's major social policies centered on land reform, literacy programs and health care, more in the style of European social democracies than East Bloc communism.

To "correct" these dominant perceptions, the Reagan administration's internal strategy paper urged that Congress and the news media be subjected to a persistent "public diplomacy" campaign. "Our public diplomacy effort," the paper said, "must be directed to: obtaining congressional support for economic and security assistance [in El Salvador and] to foster a climate of editorial and public opinion that will encourage congressional support of administration policy."

As for the press, "a comprehensive and responsive strategy, which would take timely advantage of favorable developments in the region, could at least neutralize the prevailing climate and perhaps, eventually overcome it," the paper suggested. It also urged use of "opinion leaders in the mass media" to convey the administration's message to the American people.

The strategy recognized, too, the need to target specific American interest groups broken down by geography, religion and ethnic backgrounds. "Themes will obviously have to be tailored to the target audience," the paper stated. An addendum to the paper matched up key members of Congress with their hometown newspapers that would get special attention from the "public diplomacy" operatives. By influencing the newspapers' editorial positions, the administration felt it could bring local pressure on congressional critics.

Pollster Richard Wirthlin discovered one "hot button" to touch off panic among Americans in the Southwest. Using focus groups, Wirthlin learned that anti-communist themes did not resonate well. Many Americans just did not take the alarms seriously. But Wirthlin found that eight out of 10 of those surveyed expressed a "great deal of concern" about the prospect of millions of Central American refugees flooding into the United States.

Reagan's team quickly translated Wirthlin's findings into the "feet people" theme. In a June 1983 speech, Reagan declared that "a string of anti-American, Marxist dictatorships" in Central America could lead to "a tidal wave of refugees, and this time, they'll be 'feet people' and not 'boat people' swarming into our country." Other administration officials claimed, without any documentation, that 10 percent of all Central Americans and Mexicans would be on their way.

The theme proved effective, although the theory that "Marxist dictatorships" caused refugees was never entirely logical. Historically, war and famine have been the two chief forces creating refugees -- both before communism existed and after the Cold War ended. Also, in Central America in the early 1980s, the refugee flow from Nicaragua was one of the lowest in the region. Many more refugees fled the bloody military campaigns of rightist regimes in Guatemala and El Salvador.[27]

Another "public diplomacy" theme was designed to anger American Jews -- an important "target audience." This theme portrayed the Sandinistas as anti-Semitic because much of Nicaragua's small Jewish community, which had close ties to the Somoza government, fled after the revolution in 1979. Edgar Chamorro, a contra director, disclosed later that the anti-Semitism

---

[27] The long-predicted flood of Nicaraguan refugees did not occur until the latter half of the 1980s -- after years of the CIA's covert war and a U.S. economic embargo that devastated Nicaragua's economy. [AP, Aug. 12, 1983]

idea originated with the CIA station in Miami in 1983 as the spy agency was analyzing how to turn parts of the American electorate against the Sandinistas.

However, there was a problem with the theme. The U.S. embassy in Managua investigated the allegations and "found no verifiable ground on which to accuse the GRN [the Sandinista government] of anti-Semitism," according to a July 28, 1983, cable. The Sandinistas' relations with Israel were cool, the embassy said, but that was because many of Nicaragua's Jews had worked closely with Somoza and had helped him obtain weapons from Israel. "The FSLN [Frente Sandinista de Liberacion Nacional] does not engage in anti-Semitic rhetoric per se, and it does not harass Jews who are otherwise of no interest," the cable added.

The administration's response to these unwelcome facts was to keep the cable secret and push the "hot button" anyway. In public speeches, Reagan accused the Sandinistas of "anti-Semitic acts" and for driving Jews out of Nicaragua. The theme succeeded in rallying elements of America's influential Jewish community to support the contras and to pressure leading Democrats, such as Rep. Michael Barnes of Maryland, to denounce the Sandinistas for anti-Semitism.

Beyond putting the Sandinistas on the defensive, the public diplomacy operation worked to neutralize the negative public impressions of the contras, a job that was proving more difficult. From the beginning, U.S. officials knew the contras were an unsavory lot. One senior contra handler was fond of privately comparing the contras to a born-to-be-wild motorcycle gang. "They're always in need of adult supervision," this official chuckled.

But the CIA was working overtime to clean up the contras' image. As the public diplomacy efforts were taking shape in Washington in 1982-83, Duane Clarridge and his CIA team were giving the contras one of their most ambitious makeovers. The CIA changed the name of the chief contra army to the Nicaraguan Democratic Force [or FDN] and brought in spiffier political leadership not tainted by the Somoza dictatorship. To handle the American press, the CIA picked a Jesuit-trained professor, a thoughtful intellectual named Edgar Chamorro.

Though Chamorro fit the bill in terms of a more polished image, his selection would turn out to one of the CIA's worst choices.

Chapter 2
'Perception Management'

For Edgar Chamorro, a handsome man with a hangdog look, his personal crisis came from the constant lying. The brutality and mindlessness of the contra war ate at him, but what sent him over the edge was the bought-and-paid-for mendacity. "The policy of the CIA is buying people's will," Chamorro told me once, with a quiet bitterness in his voice. "They were buying everybody." The CIA bought him for $2,000 a month, plus expenses.

Chamorro sometimes reminded me of the character that William Holden played in the movie "Network," Paddy Chayefsky's masterpiece about the TV news media driven mad by ratings. Holden's character, an aging news executive who remembered the profession's principles but had bent to its commercial demands, is part pushed and part pulled out of his job, neither crass enough to submit anymore nor heroic enough to fight. Like Holden's character, Chamorro's craggy face and thoughtful eyes revealed a man balanced somewhere between expediency and honor.

A professor in prerevolutionary Nicaragua, Chamorro joined other anti-Sandinista nationalists coalescing in Miami in 1980-81. These were more political exile groups than a counterrevolutionary movement. But the CIA, looking for a less bloody image for the fledgling contra army, saw promise. Duane Clarridge -- known to Chamorro by the code name "Dewey Maroni" -- recruited Chamorro in 1982.

Clarridge and his CIA subordinates must have believed in job quotas and diversity. For the seven-member directorate of the Nicaraguan Democratic Force, they picked a woman, a soldier, a businessman, a politician, a doctor, a private-sector representative and an academic. [Later, the CIA would add token Indians and more "moderate" political figures.] The new leadership made its official debut in a glossy, four-language booklet complete with color portraits of the seven, all paid for by the U.S. taxpayers. Chamorro's job was to sell the revamped contras as no longer a bunch of murdering terrorists.

Dividing his time between his family's pleasant stucco home on Key Biscayne, Fla., and contra safe houses closer to the front lines in Honduras, Chamorro cultivated journalists who respected his intelligence and professorial style. But the CIA had picked badly. Chamorro had not overcome his Jesuit training that stresses rationality and truth. Chamorro was a soft-spoken and somewhat pliable man, but he had a core of integrity that was constantly troubled by the hard moral choices confronting him.

Chamorro grew deeply disillusioned over the lies he was ordered to tell. He felt compromised when instructed to claim contra credit for military actions conducted by the CIA. And he was sickened by the brutality of the contra forces, a reality that required ever more lying.

Chamorro's first personal crisis came in late 1982 when the contras kidnapped an elderly Nicaraguan couple, Felipe and Maria Barreda. Chamorro had known the family in prerevolutionary days in Esteli and tried to intervene to protect them. But the couple was executed after allegedly confessing to serving in Sandinista intelligence, a claim the Sandinistas denied. Witnesses said the contras tortured the couple before the executions. As Chamorro knew, there was probably truth in the reported brutality.

At times, Chamorro knew, too, the contra violence was tinged with madness. In 1983, Chamorro arranged for Western reporters to travel with a model contra commander, a rough-and-tumble *hombre* who called himself Suicida. The contra high command saw Suicida as one of the few field commanders with aggressiveness and resolve. But Suicida also was a ruthless killer.

In June 1983, one of Suicida's sweeps through Nicaraguan border villages was especially bloody. Ghastly reports of executions and torture filtered back to CIA headquarters in Langley, Va. Congress, too, began asking about Sandinista government allegations of contra atrocities.

But no one could control Suicida. He fought lustily, raping many of his women captives and sleeping with women under his command. One contra lover was his favorite, La Negra, a willful, tough woman who took her pleasures with other men when Suicida was away. Like many contra field combatants, Suicida resented the far-to-the-rear general staff. "It's me who's burning his balls down here fighting the communists," Suicida complained to reporter Christopher Dickey of *The Washington Post*.

In spring 1983, tensions mounted between Suicida, the star contra, and his superiors back in Tegucigalpa. To argue for his side, Suicida sent La Negra to meet with the high command. After the meeting, as she made her way back to Suicida's camp on the road near Cifuentes along the Honduran border, a bullet fired from a .30-caliber machine gun blasted off part of La Negra's head. Although it was never clear who was responsible for the killing,[28] Suicida suspected the general staff. But he took his vengeance out on the Nicaraguan border towns.

"Suicida's grief was indistinguishable from anger and it quickly engulfed his forces," Dickey wrote in *With the Contras*. "His men died now in numbers they had never suffered before." When the grief-stricken Suicida threw his forces onto the hapless tobacco village of El Porvenir, Suicida had no plan other than fighting and killing. The Sandinistas launched a devastating counterattack, using heavy artillery and mortars that decimated Suicida's troops. Suicida and other survivors fled back to Honduras.

Suicida's crazed behavior and constant disobedience finally grew too much for the high command, its CIA overlords and the Argentine trainers. A Honduran officer whom Suicida trusted lured him to Tegucigalpa where he was taken prisoner. "My life's in danger," he wrote to a friend. "They want to kill me."

---

[28] The Sandinistas later claimed credit for La Negra's death.

According to Dickey's account, Suicida was brought to the contra base camp at La Quinta and court-martialed. The charges ranged from insubordination to rape and murder. Suicida and three subordinates were then taken to the border. The three underlings were executed immediately, but Dickey received a report that Suicida was first stripped naked and tortured for several days. Then, he too was executed, apparently sometime in October 1983.[29]

As the Suicida case suggested, the contras' indiscriminant brutality bordered on war crimes. But Edgar Chamorro told me that he was concerned not just about the brutality inflicted inside Nicaragua. He complained, too, about the rampant violence inside the contra camps: drunken brawls that ended in shoot-outs, the execution of contra rivals and the sexual abuse of women recruits.

One night at his home in Key Biscayne, his voice cracking, Chamorro described to me a visit that he and a doctor made to a hospital in a contra base camp in Honduras. They encountered two hysterical contra women soldiers who were undergoing treatment. Amid screams and tears, they told Chamorro and the doctor how their contra field commander, known as Tigrillo, had raped them at knifepoint.[30]

Back in Washington, the official image of the contra war was not the gruesome conflict that it seemed to Chamorro and others on the ground. Viewed through the filter of the Reagan administration's P.R., the contra war had taken on a celluloid quality. It was the stuff of "Rambo" and "The Green Berets."

The war captured Reagan's imagination as few other government projects did. When the contras were the topic, Reagan was no longer the dozing president or the front man reading three-by-five cards. He would snap to attention and eagerly follow the

---

[29]For the next year, the execution of the model commander was kept a closely held secret. On Oct. 31, 1984, reporter Brian Barger disclosed Suicida's fate in an article for *The Washington Post.*

[30] That commander, Tigrillo, would later rise to the top ranks of the contra command and be touted to visiting journalists as

contras' progress with pins in maps of Nicaragua. "When it came to foreign policy, especially Central America, he was right there and right on top of it," the CIA's Clarridge wrote in his memoirs. "Over time, our guerrillas really became his boys."

Directing the contras on Reagan's behalf, Clarridge saw himself as a kind of master of ceremonies at a three-ring circus, handling one contra crisis after another: picking leaders, planning strategy and holding the army together with the sheer force of his personal will. "Looking back, I sometimes wonder how I managed to keep so many balls in the air at the same time," Clarridge wrote. "I was frequently in Honduras, trying to keep all of the antagonistic factions from ripping the operation apart."

Over those first two years of the CIA's covert war, the contras swelled in number, but never got beyond the military tactic of rampaging through villages along the Honduran border. The contras were falling behind a secret timetable that CIA paramilitary experts had prepared when the president authorized CIA involvement in 1981. The experts had foreseen the contras marching into Managua by late 1983. But by early 1983, the CIA tossed out that optimistic forecast as "pie-in-the-sky," one senior U.S. intelligence official told me.

With growing impatience, Reagan and Casey pressed for clear-cut results. Congress was getting edgy, asking questions about the purpose of the war. The cover story about interdicting arms going north to El Salvador was wearing thin, especially with a new contra army taking shape in Costa Rica, on Nicaragua's southern border.

As the contras floundered, Walter Raymond's public diplomacy boys stepped forward to shoulder more of the burden. While they couldn't improve the contras' fighting trim or seize Managua, they could alter how official Washington "perceived" the Nicaraguan conflict. The trick would be to turn the Washington press corps from skeptics to cheerleaders.

In pursuit of that "perception management" goal, Raymond lectured his subordinates always to stay on message: "in the specific case of Nica[ragua], concentrate on gluing black hats on the

---

another model contra officer. In 1987, however, Tigrillo would be found guilty of murdering one of his contra subordinates.

Sandinistas and white hats on UNO [the United Nicaraguan Opposition, the contras' political arm]," he wrote in one typical memo. There was no room for the fact that both sides wore gray hats. So Reagan's speechwriters dutifully penned descriptions of Sandinista-ruled Nicaragua as a "totalitarian dungeon." The contras were the "moral equals of our Founding Fathers."

As one National Security Council official told me, the campaign was modeled after CIA covert operations abroad where a political goal is more important than the truth. "They were trying to manipulate [U.S.] public opinion ... using the tools of Walt Raymond's trade craft which he learned from his career in the CIA covert operation shop," the official stated.

Another administration official gave a similar description to the *Miami Herald's* Alfonso Chardy. "If you look at it as a whole, the Office of Public Diplomacy was carrying out a huge psychological operation, the kind the military conduct to influence the population in denied or enemy territory," that official explained.[31]

Part of the administration's strategy was to target journalistic "enemies" -- the likes of Raymond Bonner -- while guaranteeing that ideological allies were rewarded. According to one National Security Council memo dated May 20, 1983, U.S. Information Agency director Charles Z. Wick brought private donors to the White House Situation Room for a fund-raiser. The event collected $400,000 for Accuracy in Media, Freedom House and other groups assisting the public diplomacy operations.[32]

As the domestic program moved forward, one of Raymond's recurring concerns was CIA director Casey's insistence that he keep his oar in the water. Given its clear goal of influencing U.S. politics and policies, Raymond fretted about the legality of Casey's continued involvement in what amounted to domestic propaganda. Raymond confided in one memo that it was important "to get [Casey] out of the loop." But Casey would not back off.

---

[31] *Miami Herald,* July 19, 1987.
[32] Walter Raymond later told me that the $400,000 went to support a "public diplomacy" campaign in Europe in support of the deployment of U.S. intermediate-range ballistic missiles. But Accuracy in Media was most active inside the United States, attacking reporters for alleged liberal bias.

In early August 1983, Casey participated in a day of public relations planning on Central America. The balding CIA director hunched over a desk at the Old Executive Office Building next to the White House. He scribbled down notes on the remarks of five P.R. experts who were brainstorming how to sell Ronald Reagan's Central American policies more effectively to the American people.

Earlier that day, a national security aide had warmed the P.R. men to their task with dire predictions that leftist governments in Central America soon would send waves of refugees into the United States -- Wirthlin's "feet people" theme -- and cynically flood America with drugs. The P.R. executives had jotted down some thoughts over lunch and then pitched their ideas to the CIA director in the afternoon.

"Casey was kind of spearheading a recommendation" for better public relations, recalled William I. Greener Jr., one of the ad men. Greener recalled that the ad men sketched out two top proposals: the creation of a high-powered communications operation inside the White House and the raising of private money to finance an outreach program to build support for U.S. intervention.[33]

Raymond already had adopted some of the ideas Casey was hearing from the P.R. men, concepts that echoed the early proposals about the combined public-private backing for Project Truth and Project Democracy. In line with the recommendations, Raymond arranged financing in August 1983 for ostensibly independent groups that endorsed President Reagan's policies.

According to a memo dated Aug. 9, 1983, Raymond reported that USIA director Wick "via [media mogul Rupert] Murdock [sic], may be able to draw down added funds" to support pro-Reagan initiatives. The phrase "draw down" suggested that Murdoch previously had allocated funds for the operation. Raymond

---

[33] Despite concerns about the legality of Casey's role, Raymond continued to send progress reports to the CIA director for three more years. The operation was "the kind of thing which [Casey] had a broad catholic interest in," Raymond shrugged during an Iran-contra deposition. He then offered the excuse that Casey undertook this apparently illegal interference in domestic politics "not so much in his CIA hat, but in his adviser to the president hat."

recommended routing the "funding via Freedom House or some other structure that has credibility in the political center."[34]

Besides avoiding congressional oversight, the use of private money had another benefit: it allowed ostensibly independent groups to advocate administration policies without the public realizing that the group's funding had been arranged by the White House. The group's pronouncements, therefore, were viewed as more objective than those coming from the government. "The work done within the administration has to, by definition, be at arms length," Raymond explained in an Aug. 29, 1983, memo.

Similarly, the CIA funneled covert money to various human rights and church groups to promote criticism of the Sandinistas. The administration and its media allies could then cite this criticism as proof of growing anti-Sandinista sentiments. For instance, contra propaganda chief Chamorro said CIA money was given to Nicaraguan exile Humberto Belli to found the Puebla Institute, another "independent" human-rights group. Puebla also published Belli's book, *Nicaragua: Christians Under Fire,* attacking the Sandinistas' record for religious intolerance.

"Of course, the CIA told us to say that the money for the book and the Institute was from private individuals who wanted to remain anonymous," Chamorro wrote in a 1987 booklet, *Packaging the Contras: A Case of CIA Disinformation.*[35]

Besides covert funding for U.S.-based groups, the administration secretly financed Nicaragua's internal political opposition, too. According to more than a dozen sources I interviewed inside the contra movement or close to U.S. intelligence, CIA money went to virtually every anti-Sandinista group inside Nicaragua, including the Roman Catholic Church, the

---

[34] With Raymond's backing, Freedom House would become a major recipient of U.S. government largesse. The government-funded National Endowment for Democracy, or NED, awarded Freedom House $200,000 in 1984 to build "a network of democratic opinion-makers." Its total bounty from NED would reach $2.6 million by 1988, more than one third of Freedom House's total budget.

[35] The Puebla Institute has denied receiving CIA money, but balked at permitting me to examine the group's financial records.

opposition newspaper *La Prensa,* business organizations and labor groups.

"We've always had the internal opposition on the CIA payroll," one U.S. government official acknowledged. The CIA's budget line for Nicaraguan political action, separate from contra military operations, was about $10 million a year, the sources said. During the early years of the contra war, the CIA paid for *La Prensa's* printing supplies and salaries. Meanwhile, *La Prensa* published harsh attacks on the Sandinistas, who occasionally closed the newspaper on the grounds that it was spreading public discord.

Whenever the Sandinistas did crack down on the CIA-funded political groups, the Reagan administration got another bounce out of the strategy. U.S. officials excoriated the Sandinistas for repression and argued that contra military aid was vital to force them to open the political system. The White House also would demand that contra critics join in the denunciation of the Sandinistas or appear to be Sandinista apologists.

The strategy put the Sandinistas in a whipsaw. They either allowed the CIA's internal front to sow political unrest inside Nicaragua, making the country more vulnerable to contra attacks and sabotage -- or they gave the Reagan administration another argument for contra military aid.

Despite the growing propaganda successes in Washington in 1983, Reagan was anxious over the lack of progress on the ground. After one White House meeting on the need to destroy Sandinista aircraft, Clarridge recalled: "President Reagan pulled me aside and asked, 'Dewey, can't you get those vandals of yours to do this job.'"

Since the contra "vandals" weren't up to the task, Clarridge began substituting direct CIA operations for contra attacks. The CIA bought a freighter for use as a "mother ship." It was adapted to carry two attack helicopters and two high-speed "cigarette boats" that also were modified with armored plating and retrofitted with guns. The CIA trained teams of so-called "unilaterally controlled Latino assets" or UCLAs -- commandos from other nations.

The new sea-based war -- without contras -- was ready by late summer 1983. From the "mother ship," CIA began launching attacks against commercial ports. In October 1983, the seaport town of Corinto was set ablaze by the CIA shelling an oil depot. To create the false image in Washington that the contras were growing into an accomplished fighting force, Chamorro and other contra leaders lied and claimed credit for the attacks.

But Casey and Reagan wanted more. In January 1984, a harried Clarridge was wracking his brain for an answer. "I arrived home from the Agency early enough for once to do something other than fall into bed," Clarridge wrote. "I remember sitting with a glass of gin on the rocks, smoking a cigar (of course), and pondering my dilemma, when it hit me. Sea mines were the solution. ... To this day I wonder why I didn't think of it sooner."

When Clarridge shared his brainstorm about mining Nicaragua's harbors with other Reagan insiders, he recalled that the reaction was overwhelmingly positive. The mines were a "go." Soon, the CIA's UCLAs were salting the international sea lanes through Nicaragua's harbors with explosive mines. The war was escalating.

On March 7, 1984, Sandinista defense forces opened fire on a CIA boat that was dropping mines in the harbor of the Pacific-coast town of San Juan del Sur. When the boat's engine stalled, CIA helicopters, manned by American pilots, swooped in from the mother ship to fire rockets at Nicaraguan coastal batteries. At the time, the Sandinistas were unaware they were fighting Americans. The secret was kept from the U.S. public, too, until I wrote a story about the clash nine months later. [AP, Dec. 20, 1984]

As with the earlier coastal attacks, the contras were assigned only a public relations role in the harbor operation. The CIA ordered FDN spokesmen to take credit for the mining and to warn foreign ships away from the ports. But the mining didn't succeed in frightening off all commercial shipping, as Clarridge had hoped. Many freighters ignored the warnings and plowed ahead into the harbors. The CIA's mines began exploding and damaging ships from around the world.

In an undeclared war against Nicaragua, the Reagan administration was endangering crewmen and cargo in international commerce. When Congress learned of the direct CIA role in the mining, a political furor erupted. An angry Congress stopped all CIA assistance to the contras. The so-called Boland

Amendment, named after Rep. Edward P. Boland, D-Mass., forbade the administration from "directly or indirectly" assisting the contras militarily.

The restrictions were a harsh rebuke to the Reagan administration. Still, Clarridge and his comrades saw nothing wrong with what they had done. "We were proud of the mining," Clarridge wrote. Reagan and his men felt it was Congress and the international community that had gone nuts.

The mining debacle put the administration in a deep political hole. But the Reagan administration tried to climb out by using more "public diplomacy," more "perception management."

In early 1984, a new propaganda theme was a follow-up on a concept heard by the P.R. men who met with Casey: implicate the Sandinistas in the flow of narcotics into the United States. An obstacle to that argument, however, was that the Drug Enforcement Administration knew of no drugs that had transited Nicaragua since the Sandinistas took power in 1979.

The reason had nothing to do with the morality of the Sandinistas. It just made very little business sense for traffickers to smuggle drugs through a country that had limited trade with the United States, especially when the CIA was monitoring all planes and ships leaving Nicaraguan territory. The Reagan administration solved the problem of no drug interceptions by arranging a "sting" operation overseen by Oliver North and the CIA.

In the sting, convicted narcotics trafficker Barry Seal, who was cooperating with the DEA in an investigation of the Medellin cartel, arranged for a plane to fly a load of cocaine into Nicaragua. But the plane was shot down by Sandinista air defenses. Seal then flew in a second plane, a C-123 transport that the CIA had retrofitted with cameras. Seal recovered the load from the first plane and snapped some grainy photos of men, supposedly Nicaraguans and Colombians hoisting bales of cocaine onto the plane. Seal transported the load back to the United States.

In late June, National Security Council aide Oliver North attended at least two briefings on the sting operation. DEA officials later stated that North and the CIA were eager to see the story made public. When the DEA officials refused, they said, the White House leaked the story implicating the Sandinistas to the ultra-conservative *Washington Times,* which is financed by right-wing theocrat Sun Myung Moon. The story appeared on July 17, 1984.

After the disclosure, the federal government slapped together a hasty indictment naming one Nicaraguan, a shadowy figure named Federico Vaughn who allegedly worked for the Nicaraguan Interior Ministry. With the Vaughn charge, the story quickly spread onto front pages across America. Simultaneously, U.S. government sources leaked to major newspapers that other unspecified evidence implicated the top leadership of the Sandinista government. In a TV address, President Reagan accused Sandinista leaders of "exporting drugs to poison our youth."

By this time, however, I had become highly skeptical of the administration's assertions about Central America. I contacted DEA officials and found them less sanguine than the administration's foreign policy operatives. The DEA confirmed that no cocaine had been known to transit Sandinista-ruled Nicaragua prior to the Seal load and that no credible evidence implicated any other Nicaraguan official besides Vaughn.

DEA investigators fumed, too, because they felt the White House had blown the smuggling investigation prematurely. By leaking the Sandinista angle in the run-up to a congressional vote on contra aid, the Reagan administration, in effect, had tipped off the Medellin cartel to Seal's undercover work. Seal barely escaped Colombia as the story was breaking.[36]

"We were in the middle of the most significant investigation of my career," DEA agent Ernst Jacobsen later testified before a House Judiciary subcommittee. "We had a chance to arrest all the cartel members. ... I heard that the leak came from an aide in the White House." But Jacobsen said he could not say for sure that North was the White House official who leaked the information to *The Washington Times.*[37]

---

[36] In 1986, Colombian assassins gunned him down in Baton Rouge, La.

[37] Rep. William Hughes, D-N.J., held hearings on the Sandinista drug case on July 29, 1988, and strongly suggested that North was the prime suspect behind the leak. North did not comment on the suspicions about the Vaughn case.

In a 1988 investigation, the House subcommittee traced the phone number used by Seal to call Vaughn. The phone was located in a house in Managua that had been rented for years by the U.S. or other Western embassies. "Subcommittee staff recently called Vaughn's number in Managua, Nicaragua, and spoke to a 'domestic employee' who said the house belonged to a U.S. Embassy employee," Rep. William Hughes, D-N.J., the subcommittee chairman, told reporters. He added that his investigators were told that the house had been "continuously rented" by the United States or other Western governments since 1981.

The House subcommittee also found references in North's notebook to "Freddy Vaughn," including one July 6, 1984, entry, mentioning "Freddy coming in late July." The impression was that Vaughn might have been a double agent working for the U.S. government in a plot to frame Sandinista leaders. The propaganda would then boost prospects for the congressional resumption of aid to the contras.

Classified U.S. government records also cast doubt on Vaughn's supposed position as a top Interior Ministry official. Instead, he appeared to be a deputy director of the Sandinista government's export-import company, called Heroes and Martyrs Trading Corp., or H&M. Other documents showed that H&M had been infiltrated by Cuban-American operatives, such as Moises Nunez who was working on special intelligence operations for North at the National Security Council.[38]

While eager to implicate the Sandinistas in drug smuggling, the Reagan administration had the opposite feeling about mounting evidence that the contras were the ones knee-deep in the cocaine business. Reagan officials fretted that disclosure of that evidence could sink the contra cause once and for all. In one case, some 50 individuals, including many Nicaraguans, were arrested in the Frogman Case, so called because swimmers in wet suits were caught on Jan. 17, 1983, bringing 430 pounds of cocaine ashore near San Francisco.

---

[38] For more details, see Gary Webb's book, *Dark Alliance*. After the contra war ended in 1990, the U.S.-backed government of Violeta Chamorro took no known action to arrest Vaughn or to turn him over to U.S. authorities.

The problem got worse when a contra political operative in Costa Rica, named Francisco Aviles Saenz, wrote to the federal court in San Francisco and argued that $36,800 seized belonged to the contras. He wanted the money back. In reaction, federal prosecutors decided to expand their investigation to Costa Rica. But CIA lawyers objected.

"There are sufficient factual details which would cause certain damage to our image and program in Central America," CIA assistant general counsel Lee S. Strickland explained to the Justice Department on Aug. 22, 1984. The Costa Rican inquiry was canceled and the $36,800 was returned to the contras.

Another contra drug problem was building around clusters of pro-contra Cuban-Americans who were moving into Central America. The CIA was aware that one prominent Cuban-American, Frank Castro, had close ties to the Medellin cartel and was contributing money for contra training. Facing drug-smuggling charges in Texas in 1984, he also was claiming an affiliation with the CIA. After the Justice Department checked with the spy agency, the charges against Frank Castro were dropped, although it remains unclear whether the CIA made that request.

Out of public view, the Reagan administration also was playing rough with U.S. activists who were trying to build a Vietnam-style movement against US intervention in Central America. Ironically, as Washington accused the Sandinistas of repression inside Nicaragua, the FBI conducted criminal investigations of foreign-policy critics in the United States.

The investigations dated back to 1981 when the FBI started a nationwide probe of the Committee in Solidarity with the People of El Salvador [CISPES] and other advocacy groups that were challenging the Reagan administration's policies. Over four years, the investigation tasked 52 FBI field offices to probe CISPES and 138 related organizations, according to documents later released under the Freedom of Information Act.

As thousands of pages of FBI investigative reports made clear, some enthusiastic FBI agents saw their job as silencing dissent, not enforcing the law. One memo from the FBI's New Orleans office, dated Nov. 10, 1983, said, "It is imperative at this time to formulate some plan of attack against CISPES and specifically against individuals who defiantly display their contempt for the U.S. government by making speeches and propagandizing their cause."

On March 6, 1984, the Philadelphia FBI office cited 12 organizations "actively involved in demonstrations ... regarding U.S. intervention in Central America." Among these groups were the Friends Peace Committee and a hospital workers union. Another FBI report from Cincinnati, Ohio, on Dec. 14, 1984, identified its targets as individuals and groups "involved in activities contrary to the foreign policy of the United States in Central America."

U.S. law enforcement targeted anti-contra activists, too. Tasked by the NSC staff, FBI agents subjected more than 100 Americans to counterintelligence interrogations when they returned from visits to Nicaragua. The FBI investigated groups such as TecNica which assisted Nicaragua on small development projects.

One member of Oliver North's contra-support network, a right-wing security consultant named Philip Mabry of Fort Worth, Texas, said North advocated a strategy of covertly instigating FBI probes of dissidents. Mabry said that in 1984, North urged him and others to request that the FBI open investigations of contra opponents. "Ollie told me that if the FBI received letters from five or six unrelated sources all requesting an investigation of the same groups, that would give the Bureau a mandate to go ahead and investigate," Mabry told *The Boston Globe*.[39]

While the FBI harassed these peace groups, the Reagan administration relied on the most visible arm of the Casey-Raymond "perception management" network to pummel out-of-step journalists. This public arm was a new office opened at the State Department and called the Office of Public Diplomacy for Latin America [S/LPD].

To run the office, The administration selected Cuban exile Otto Reich, a former Miami businessman and city official. The heavy-set Reich was known as blustery, zealous and combative. But one acquaintance described him as "more than anything else,

---

[39] *The Boston Globe,* Feb. 29, 1988.

ambitious." One public diplomacy official told me that Otto Reich acted like a coach of a sports team. If a "favorable" story about the Sandinistas appeared in the U.S. media, Reich would exhort his "players" to get those points back by scoring with some anti-Sandinista stories, the official said.

On one level, Reich's public diplomacy office simply delivered the Central American propaganda messages through as many outlets as possible. In its first year alone, Reich's office booked more than 1,500 speaking engagements, from radio appearances to editorial-board interviews. The office published three booklets on Nicaragua and distributed material to 1,600 libraries, 520 political science faculties, 122 editorial writers and 107 religious organizations.

But Reich's office often used bare knuckles when news organizations crossed the administration's propaganda line. In April 1984, Reich made a trip to the Washington office of CBS News after President Reagan got mad at the network's coverage of El Salvador and Nicaragua. Afterwards, Secretary of State George Shultz sent Reagan a memo describing how Reich had spent one hour complaining to the correspondent involved and two more hours with his Washington bureau chief "to point out the flaws in the information." This was but one example of "what the Office of Public Diplomacy has been doing to help improve the quality of information the American people are receiving," Shultz told the president. "It has been repeated dozens of times over the past few months."

In another case in 1984, Reich and his team complained to National Public Radio about a story describing a contra massacre of farmworkers in northern Nicaragua. The NPR segment covered the funeral of the victims and gave voice to the grief of average Nicaraguans trapped in the violence. "It was a long piece and very, very moving," recalled Paul Allen, NPR's foreign editor. "There was no particular effort to apologize for the contras. This was just a story about a bunch of people who got caught up in the war and were shot up."

But Reich "went ballistic," said Allen, and demanded face-to-face meetings with NPR's executives and reporters. Reich brought along one of his top aides, Jonathan Miller. "It was billed as a brown-bag lunch in [NPR's] editorial conference room," Allen said. Reich's complaint was that the piece "was too emotional, one-sided, not balanced," Allen remembered. "But it was kind of the last straw" for Reich, who had been unhappy with NPR's coverage of the region for some time.

"Reich made the point that our broadcasts were being measured," Allen said. "Miller said some ungodly number of minutes were 'anti-contra.' We said, 'how could you decide what was anti-contra?' But the point was, 'we're monitoring you -- holding a stop watch on you.' The point was, someone was listening and they were doing it with a very critical view."

Bill Buzenberg, NPR's foreign affairs correspondent in Washington, was one NPR staffer in attendance and he described the scene a year later in a speech in Seattle. Buzenberg said Reich informed the NPR editors that he had "a special consultant service listening to all NPR programs" on Central America, analyzing them for possible bias against U.S. policy.

Reich referred to the larger campaign to force changes in U.S. press coverage of Central America. He said he had "made similar visits to other unnamed newspapers and major television networks [and] had gotten others to change some of their reporters in the field because of perceived bias," Buzenberg recalled.

For Allen, who oversaw NPR's coverage worldwide, the intervention by a government official to pressure the radio network to change its coverage was unprecedented. "Never in our coverage of Poland, South Africa, Lebanon, Afghanistan had they chosen to come in and remonstrate with us," Allen said. "We understood what Otto Reich's job was. He was engaged in an effort to alter coverage. It was a special effort."

Given NPR's sensitivity to government strings on its funding, the pressure also worked. NPR executives upbraided Allen about the story in his next job evaluation. A year later, Allen resigned from NPR and left journalism.

While Reich was scoring points with his hardball tactics, the CIA and the contras kept stirring up more trouble for themselves. As soon as one P.R. tempest was brought under control, it seemed another broke loose.

In September 1984, I was given a copy of a Spanish-language manual called *Psychological Operations in Guerrilla Warfare.* Though most of the text was routine advice on making a political case to a target audience, some of the suggestions veered off into violent techniques, apparently drawn from longstanding U.S. counterinsurgency strategies.

Through U.S. government sources, I learned that the CIA had prepared the manual for the contras. I then wrote a story for the AP wires that started as follows:

> The CIA produced a psychological warfare manual for Nicaraguan rebels that instructs them to hire professional criminals for "selective jobs" and says some government officials can be "neutralized" with the "selective use of violence," intelligence sources say. The 90-page manual, written in Spanish, also urges the rebels to create a "martyr" by arranging a violent demonstration that leads to the death of one of their supporters, and it tells how to coerce Nicaraguans into carrying out assignments against their will. [AP, Oct. 14, 1984]

In the story, I quoted FDN political leader Adolfo Calero denying that the CIA had produced the book. But U.S. intelligence sources confirmed that the CIA had. The "murder manual" story was picked up several days later by *The New York Times* and put on the front page. Congressional Democrats lambasted the CIA for publishing a booklet more befitting the traditions of communist Russia than a democracy. "It espouses the doctrine of Lenin, not Jefferson," charged Rep. Edward P. Boland, chairman of the House Intelligence Committee.[40] [AP, Oct. 17, 1984]

In the days after the manual story exploded, Chamorro, the troubled Jesuit-trained scholar, compounded the CIA's P.R. problem. He acknowledged that it was the contras' "practice" to

---

[40] The manual derived much of its advice from earlier U.S. Army special operations manuals, which presumably reprinted material from the Project X counterinsurgency lessons. [For details, see Introduction.]

execute Nicaraguan government officials who were deemed "criminals." Chamorro told me that "in guerrilla war, if you have to exact justice immediately, sometimes you have to do it. We don't have jails. We are in the jungle." Tired of three years of lies, Chamorro spoke bluntly. [AP, Oct. 20, 1984]

The CIA, however, was furious at the violation of the "perception management" code. The CIA also suspected that Chamorro had leaked the manual that had embarrassed President Reagan during his 1984 re-election campaign. Chamorro's days as a contra spokesman were over.

After a flurry of investigations about the manual, the CIA disciplined a handful of mid-level agency officials who had overseen its production. In putting the manual dispute to rest, the CIA mounted an odd defense: that the manual was intended to encourage a greater respect for human rights, by recommending that the contras apply "selective" violence against Nicaraguans. "Selective" killing was deemed preferable to the "indiscriminant" kind. On the campaign trail in 1984, President Reagan pronounced the controversy "much ado about nothing."

I learned later that CIA director Casey personally had ordered the drafting of the manual during a CIA meeting in Honduras in mid-1983, but no action was taken against him. Still, the controversy helped harden congressional resolve to continue the military aid cut-off to the contras.

After splitting from the FDN, Chamorro poured out his CIA experiences in a sworn affidavit to the World Court. He described in detail the CIA's role in uniting the contra movement, paying for Argentine military trainers, creating a special unit for demolitions and funneling money into the hands of CIA-favored leaders. He wrote:

> Some Nicaraguans joined the force voluntarily, either because of dissatisfaction with the Nicaraguan government, family ties with leaders of the force, promises of food, clothing, boots and weapons. Many other members of the force were recruited forcibly. FDN units would arrive at an undefended village, assemble all the residents in the town square and then

proceed to kill -- in full view of the others -- all persons suspected of working for the Nicaraguan government or the FSLN [the Sandinista party], including police, local militia members, party members, health workers, teachers and farmers from government-sponsored cooperatives. In this atmosphere, it was not difficult to persuade those able-bodied men left alive to return with the FDN units to their base camps in Honduras and enlist in the force.

Despite these setbacks, the administration redoubled its public diplomacy efforts after Reagan's landslide reelection victory. On Dec. 20, 1984, Raymond submitted a secret action proposal to national security adviser Robert C. McFarlane. It urged an even greater commitment of manpower to public diplomacy in all areas. Raymond wrote:

I have attempted to proceed forward with a whole range of political and information activities. ... We are engaged in a detailed effort to try to bring USIA into a more direct involvement in a number of public diplomacy and policy areas and we've been reexamining the role of AID in terms of helping fill the infrastructure of democracy. ... There are a raft of ties to private organizations which are working in tandem with the government in a number of areas ranging from the American Security Council to the Atlantic Council, to the nascent idea of a "Peace Institute."

Among the examples of "specific activities," Raymond listed:

significant expansion of our ability to utilize book publication and distribution as a public diplomacy tool. (This is based on an integrated public-private strategy). ... The development of an active PSYOP strategy. ... Regular meetings with the German political foundations concerning programming. ... Meetings (ad hoc) with selected CIA operational people to coordinate

and clarify lines between overt/covert political
operations on key areas. Examples: Afghanistan,
Central America, USSR-EE [Eastern Europe] and
Grenada. ... Meetings with interest groups – Center for
Democratic Institutions, Atlantic Council, Youth for
Understanding, International Rescue Committee,
Freedom House, American Security Council, Woodrow
Wilson Center, Committee for a Community of
Democracies, ... the National Strategy Information
Center (to name a few) to try to stimulate parallel
programs to U.S. foreign policy interests. ...

Provide support to the overall Central American public
diplomacy effort. Otto Reich has the key role, but we
review weekly his thrust and direction, make program
suggestions and utilize our position in the NSC staff as
an instrument to press action and support Reich's
community effort.

To reinforce Reich's forces in the "war of ideas," the
administration actually assigned real warriors. As the public
diplomacy campaign continued to expand, the administration cut
transfer orders for a half dozen psychological warfare experts from
U.S. Special Forces.

One, Lt. Col. Daniel "Jake" Jacobowitz, served as Reich's
executive officer and had a "background in psychological warfare,"
according to Jonathan Miller's Iran-contra testimony. When Reich
asked Raymond for more manpower, the White House transferred
in another five psychological warfare specialists from the 4th
Psychological Operations Group at Fort Bragg, N.C.

Like Gen. Lansdale dissecting the cultural vulnerabilities of
Filipinos and Vietnamese, Reich put his psy-war experts to work
picking out incidents in Central America that would rile the U.S.
public. In a memo dated May 30, 1985, Jacobowitz told Reich that
the military men were scouring embassy cables "looking for
exploitable themes and trends, and [would] inform us of possible
areas for our exploitation."

The public diplomacy office also saw natural allies on the weekend pundit shows. "Correspondents participating in programs such as the 'McLaughlin Group,' 'Agronsky and Company,' 'This Week with David Brinkley' receive special materials such as the report on Nicaragua's Military Build-up expeditiously and have open invitations for personal briefings," according to a Feb. 8, 1985, report of the office's activities.

Oliver North's friends pitched in with their own ideas. On Feb. 19, 1985, Robert W. Owen, a North sidekick, volunteered his thoughts for a "public relations campaign for the freedom fighters." Owen suggested burnishing the contras' fighting mystique by producing a toe-tapping contra version of "The Ballad of the Green Beret."

In early 1985, another internal administration memo fretted about "perception impediments," such as the "idea that U.S. actions violate international law." The memo, dated March 12, 1985, discussed a variety of strategies for countering these "impediments" which presented special problems because they were true.

As part of the March 1985 contra-aid push, Reich's office co-authored a booklet on "the Soviet-Cuban connection" to the Sandinistas. The booklet included maps showing the importance of the Caribbean sea lanes to America's commerce and security. One passage noted that "60 percent of total resupply/reinforcement materiel" to NATO "in the first 60 days [of World War III] sails from Gulf ports through Florida Straits." A caption added: "The Caribbean sea lanes are viewed by the Soviets as the 'strategic rear' of the United States." Presumably, if World War III did not end in a burst of mushroom clouds, there was concern that some Sandinista river patrol boats might bottle up the U.S. fleet in New Orleans.

Despite gains, however, the P.R. plans continued to be disrupted by grisly reports of contra atrocities. In 1985, a human rights report compiled by New York lawyer Reed Brody was released citing 145 sworn affidavits signed by Nicaraguans who had witnessed contra atrocities. Many of the witnesses described contras slitting the throats of captives and mutilating their bodies. After being verified by congressional staff and journalists, Brody's findings received wide play in the national press.

But Brody had made the mistake of accepting transportation from the Nicaraguan government and the use of its office space. His missteps created an opening for the administration's counterattack. On April 15, 1985, in a speech to a pro-contra dinner, President Reagan personally denounced Brody as "one of dictator [Daniel] Ortega's supporters, a sympathizer who has openly embraced Sandinismo."

The administration struck back, too, by planting "white propaganda" in the news media through op-eds secretly financed by the government. In one memo, Jonathan Miller informed White House aide Patrick Buchanan about the administration's success placing an anti-Sandinista piece in *The Wall Street Journal's* friendly editorial pages. "Officially, this office had no role in its preparation," Miller wrote.

Miller also recounted how the office discreetly pushed the positive side of the contras. "Through a cut-out, we are having the opposition leader Alphonso Rubello [sic, the real name is Alfonso Robelo] visit the following news organizations while he is in Washington this week: Hearst Newspapers, *Newsweek* magazine, Scripps-Howard newspapers, *The Washington Post* (editorial board) and *USA Today*," Miller wrote in the May 13, 1985, memo to Buchanan.

But Miller added that time and discretion would limit his updates. "I will not attempt in the future to keep you posted on all activities since we have too many balls in the air at any one time and since the work of our operation is ensured by our office's keeping a low profile. I merely wanted to give you a flavor of some of the activities that hit our office on any one day," Miller wrote.

As busy as the public diplomacy office was, it could not keep pace with another spark plug in the administration's drive to build a pro-contra majority in Congress. This gung-ho Marine also worked to keep the contras from falling apart in Central America. As the political battle lines were drawn in Washington, President Reagan found himself relying more and more on this young Marine officer assigned to the National Security Council staff, Oliver North.

Chapter 3
Containment

The clubby, dark-wood Hay Room restaurant at the Hay-Adams Hotel belonged to an earlier age, a time of cigar smoke and men-only conversations. In the 1980s, the room's stone hearths, medieval tapestries and quiet alcoves seemed almost quaint. Yet, the restaurant still attracted a bustling lunchtime power crowd. The stately Hay-Adams was just a stroll across Lafayette Park from the White House.

Many from the younger power set preferred the Adams Room, the hotel's other main-floor restaurant, with its light, yellow, airy look, matching the trendy nouvelle cuisine. But even the men who favored the dark recesses of the Hay Room often picked from the menu's lighter fare and sip iced tea or possibly a white wine. Their forebears would have devoured blood-red steaks and downed scotches and manhattans.

On a warm midsummer day in 1983, I was waiting at a table in the Hay Room for my first meeting with a National Security Council aide, a young Marine major named Oliver North. With me was a conservative acquaintance who had been touting the virtues of this brash, new, behind-the-scenes activist in President Reagan's national security establishment. North arrived a few minutes late. He wore a dark suit, but his crisp appearance and straight bearing had the air of a military man even at first sight. He and I both ordered salads.

As the lunch progressed, North told me that he had done some checking on my work for *The Associated Press*. He had heard bad things about me, he said, without being specific. I imagined he meant my articles on the continuing human-rights abuses in El Salvador, but I also had written about the Reagan administration's broad expansion of intelligence powers and William Casey's tangled finances.

Though leery of me, North was not hostile. Over lunch, he talked expansively about his hopes for President Reagan's reelection in 1984. North said his feelings were not partisan -- Republican or Democrat -- just a strong belief that the country needed the continuity of a two-term presidency. And, North said, the president had some important business to finish.

When a comment was made about the recent assassination of Lt. Cmdr. Albert Schaufelberger in El Salvador, North launched into a personal recollection of the Navy officer who had been second in command of the U.S. military group in that Central American war zone.

In the calm, matter-of-fact tone of a military officer who had seen it all, North recounted how he and Schaufelberger had, just months before, flown over a battle between the Salvadoran army and a band of guerrillas. Immediately after the firing stopped, North said, he and Schaufelberger landed their light, propeller-driven plane on a dirt road near the army's positions.

Between bites of his salad, North said he and Schaufelberger had wanted a fast after-action report on the fighting. They wanted to evaluate how well the Salvadoran army had performed. North said they waited for the shooting to stop before landing, but he winked as if I really wasn't supposed to believe that.

After the plane rolled to a halt on the dirt road, North said, he and Schaufelberger hopped out and soon found themselves pinned down under renewed firing. The Americans spotted two Salvadoran soldiers lying on the ground bleeding from their wounds. North said he and Schaufelberger carried the wounded men back onto the plane. Schaufelberger administered CPR to one.

North climbed behind the controls, turning the plane onto the dirt road for takeoff. Just then, North continued, a Salvadoran guerrilla jumped out from behind a bush and opened fire with an automatic rifle. North said the bullets blew out the windshield showering him with glass. The plane picked up speed down the dirt road and managed to lift off, rising above the trees and hills. The damaged plane fluttered back to El Salvador's Ilopango military airbase and landed, North added with no special excitement in his voice.

Once on the ground, North said, he and Schaufelberger pulled the two soldiers from the plane. One was already dead and the other died soon afterwards on a desk at the airfield. North added that he returned to Washington and told the story to President Reagan.[41] As a response, North said, Reagan dispatched a special medical training team to El Salvador along with evacuation helicopters.

I knew at least the part of the story about sending the medical training team was true. I thought the rest could have been either real or bravado. With Schaufelberger dead, there seemed to be no simple way to corroborate exactly what North had done on the flight.

But the calmly told tale revealed more about North than about conditions on the ground in El Salvador. His many admirers would see in it and in his other action stories North's courage, commitment, his flair for adventure and his gift for spinning a dramatic anecdote that elevated dirty, brutal jungle wars into the stuff of heroism. His detractors would point to his tendency toward recklessness that could do more to destroy a policy than make it succeed. Some simply would call him a liar.

I filed the derring-do away in my memory. My chief discovery from the luncheon was that here was a government official to keep an eye on -- he was either going to do great things or make some horrendous mistakes.

---

[41] Like many North stories, this one would change somewhat in its retelling by his friends after North became a household name in 1986. Those versions would have North on a daring mercy mission to rescue wounded Salvadoran soldiers. But that was not exactly what North recounted over lunch that day in the Hay Room restaurant.

As the focus of U.S. attention in Central America shifted from El Salvador to Nicaragua in 1983-84, I would hear bits and pieces about Oliver North's continuing adventures. One senior U.S. intelligence official told me that North was at Ilopango again when a contra plane took off for a foolhardy assault on Managua airport on Sept. 8, 1983.

The plane, with two 500-pound bombs strapped under the wings, reached Managua but was shot down by defenders and crashed into the control tower. The pilot and co-pilot died along with an airport worker on the ground. The crash occurred just minutes before a plane carrying two influential U.S. senators -- Gary Hart, D-Colo., and William Cohen, R-Maine -- was scheduled to land. If their plane had arrived a few minutes early, the senators might have been casualties of a bizarre attack, carried out by a CIA airplane.

With the cut-off of CIA assistance in 1984, I also began to hear rumors that North was filling in as the contras' surrogate adviser. He also was lending a hand on the administration's political campaign to overturn the Boland Amendment and secure more military aid for the contras. North understood how perceived contra successes in the field could boost their chances for a congressional victory in the spring.

In one 14-page memo, dated March 20, 1985, Oliver North informed NSC adviser Robert McFarlane about more than 80 planned publicity events for influencing public and congressional opinion for an upcoming congressional vote.

"In addition to the events depicted on the internal chronology," North wrote, "other activities in the region continue as planned -- including military operations and political action. Like the chronology, these events are also timed to influence the vote: planned travel by [contra leaders Adolfo] Calero, [Arturo] Cruz and [Alfonso] Robelo [and] special operations attacks against highly visible military targets in Nicaragua. ... You should also be aware that Director Casey has sent a personal note to [White House chief of staff] Don Regan on the timing matter" of the contra-aid vote.

According to North's timetable, in the two months before the vote, U.S. intelligence would research and publicize Sandinista war violations; "public diplomacy" officials would review opinion polls "to see what turns Americans against Sandinistas"; a "dear colleague" letter would be prepared "for signature by a responsible Democrat which counsels against 'negotiating' with" the Sandinistas; the Justice Department would prepare a "document on Nicaraguan narcotics involvement"; interviews with contra fighters would be arranged for the press; and in one ironic entry, the State Department would "release [a] paper on Nicaraguan media manipulation."

By spring 1985, I heard other stories about North helping the contras raise money. My first hard information about this activity came in two terse phone interviews with retired Maj. Gen. John K. Singlaub. The general was a grudging interview subject, but he acknowledged reporting to North about the fund-raising and receiving indirect guidance about what to do. Singlaub's World Anti-Communist League and its U.S. affiliate had been scratching around to raise money for the contras.

"I say [to North], 'This is what I'm going to do,'" Singlaub told me. "'If it's a dumb idea, send me a signal.' Nobody has called me and told me, 'You're screwing up'." Singlaub's account, of course, was only a small part of the story.

I also tracked down an administration official who had sat in on White House meetings where schemes were debated for keeping the contras afloat in late 1983 or early 1984. The money crunch was a problem by then because Congress had capped the funds in fall 1983 at $24 million. The official CIA contra accounts were expected to run dry by early 1984.

This source described how NSC adviser McFarlane brought Reagan a memo -- called a "non-paper" -- that North had written about recruiting private individuals and third countries to supplement the contras' finances. The source said McFarlane returned the next day and told the small group that the word back from Reagan was go ahead. The White House began secretly to solicit funds and arrange other assistance for the contras.

Later, I located a third source who had been inside the NSC staff and who described the peculiar comings and goings in North's office, a pattern of visits that suggested that North was meeting with key figures in the contra support network. There were also anecdotal comments about North's management role from contra sources, including Edgar Chamorro. I was close to writing a story and AP management seemed interested.

One impetus for the AP's North investigation came from my second-place showing in the Pulitzer Prize competition for national reporting in 1984. My articles on the CIA's activities in Nicaragua, particularly the "murder manual," had reached that level, but in early 1985, the selection board opted for a politically safer series of articles on the dangers of farm equipment.

AP executive editor Walter Mears, a crusty political writer and past Pulitzer winner himself, had pushed the AP entry in the jockeying that goes on among the top national news organizations for these honors. After the Pulitzer board picked the farm safety series, Mears grumbled that all those stories proved was that "it's dangerous to fall off a tractor." He encouraged me to keep on the CIA-Nicaragua story so he could "shove it back down their throats" next year.

My proposal back to Mears was to investigate how North was running a secret operation to sustain the contras. I recommended that the AP hire Brian Barger, who had worked as an editorial assistant for *The Washington Post* but was then freelancing. Fluent in Spanish, tall and rangy, the son of a U.S. Foreign Service officer, Barger had developed excellent contacts among the various mercenaries and lowlifes who were drawn to the contra war.

In a pattern that would repeat itself over the next year, however, the AP executives turned hesitant. Mears agreed to take Barger on as a "maternity leave" fill-in but with the bureaucratic proviso that he would be treated as a general-assignment reporter and not be allowed to concentrate on the contra project. This edict would hamper the investigation. But even part-time, Barger brought prodigious skills to our reporting.

As Barger was coming on board, I began to compose the first article about North's contra network. On May 31, 1985, I contacted NSC press officer Karna Small and asked her to put a question to McFarlane. She wrote down my query as "it's my understanding that some day at the end of 1983 or the beginning of 1984, Reagan instructed McFarlane orally to arrange for private and other outside, non-USG fundings for contras. Is that true? And what comment does McFarlane have about it?"

Small also sketched my journalistic background for McFarlane. "Bob Parry, AP (who can be <u>tough</u> but has awfully good sources) is working on a big piece on 'the national security council involvement in Nicaragua with respect to funding by private, outside groups'."

McFarlane's scrawled answer at the bottom of the page read, "It is absolutely untrue -- in fact, the guidance was firmly to the contrary, that there would be no solicitation by any USG official." North also got hold of Small's inquiry and fired off a warning memo to deputy NSC adviser John Poindexter.

"For several weeks now there have been rumors of stories being prepared which allege an NSC connection to private funding and other support to the Nicaraguan resistance," North wrote. "The rumors originally surfaced with a reporter Alfonso Chardi [sic] from the *Miami Herald* and now seem to focus more [on] an *Associated Press* reporter named Robert Parry. Parry is the reporter who 'broke the story' on the so-called CIA 'murder manual'."

North claimed that Chardy had been threatened with a cutoff of access to contra base camps if he printed the story and that "Chardi [sic] promised to drop the story" – a claim that Chardy later flatly denied. North continued, "The attached note from Karna is, however, more disturbing. Parry is an avowed liberal with very close connections in the Democratic party. ... It is also reported that he has a personal relationship with one of the NSC staff."

When North's memo surfaced during the Iran-contra scandal, some reporters asked me to comment about the accusations. Though both charges are false -- I am not an avowed anything and have never had a personal relationship with anyone on the NSC staff -- denying such charges always seemed silly. But North's accusations were the kind of remark that could circulate around Washington and damage a reputation.

As North fumed to his boss, Small called back to steer me away from the NSC-contra article. She offered no on-the-record response, but a State Department spokesman continued the administration's flat denial of my information. Still naive about how dishonest the government had become, I softened the lead slightly to avoid a direct challenge to the administration's statements.

The story ran on the AP wires on June 10, 1985 and started: "The White House gave advice -- at least initially -- to individuals involved in private fund-raising for Nicaraguan rebels despite a public stance that it doesn't encourage or discourage those efforts, according to sources." The story quoted one source as saying, "The National Security Council staff handled contacts with private groups, including the World Anti-Communist League, a conservative organization headed by retired Maj. Gen. John K. Singlaub." Singlaub was then quoted saying his White House contact was Oliver North. It was the first time North's name had surfaced publicly.

Though the scandal story of the decade was taking shape, the Washington news media mostly shied away. There were follow-up stories in *The New York Times* -- which omitted North's name -- and in *The Washington Post* -- which included North's name because the AP already had. But the combination of senior news executives who sympathized with Reagan's hardline foreign policy and the ubiquitous public diplomacy teams limited the coverage.[42]

So, with the major newspapers spun, it fell to *The Associated Press*, a news organization with little reputation for investigative journalism, to do most of the digging. In September 1985, Barger and I laid out what we saw as the next phase of the North story. In a memo to Washington bureau chief, Charles Lewis, we wrote:

> We have a story about National Security Council aide North's involvement in assisting, indirectly, with the shipment of weapons, ammunition and other military supplies from ... the United States to Nicaraguan rebels. ... We have evidence of the active involvement of officials from the National Security Council, the CIA,

---

[42] By early 1986, when the *Times* and *Post* did lengthy articles on the inner workings of Reagan's NSC, both papers failed to mention Oliver North at all. When I asked a friend at the *Post* about the omission, he told me that the newspaper's White House sources had given assurances that North was an inconsequential figure.

State Department and DOD [Department of Defense] in the not-so-private effort. ... Concerned early last year [1984] that Congress would ban contra aid, even before revelations that the CIA was mining Nicaraguan ports, White House officials began looking for ways to continue the contra operations, even if that meant bypassing Congress. ...

One former top NSC official has told us the order came directly from President Reagan through Bud McFarlane. Contra leaders have described to us in detail, meetings with senior CIA and NSC officials where creation of this operation was discussed. ... Building an "old boys" network of former military colleagues, North encouraged and oversaw creation of a sophisticated "private aid" network. It involved money laundering through offshore banks, public fund-raising events, shipping military supplies from the United States to Honduras and Costa Rica in apparent violation of the Arms Export Control Act and the Neutrality Act, enlisting third-country support for the contra pipeline and using American "volunteers" to replace CIA trainers in the field.

The memo also detailed the roles of North's courier Robert Owen and the participation of Israel and other U.S. allies.

Yet, while we pushed our editors to move ahead, NSC adviser McFarlane was stamping out the last embers of congressional interest in the initial press disclosures. "I can state with deep personal conviction that at no time did I or any member of the National Security Council staff violate the letter or spirit" of the congressional contra-aid ban, McFarlane wrote. "I am most concerned ... there be no misgivings as to the existence of any parallel efforts to provide, directly or indirectly, support for military or paramilitary activities in Nicaragua. There has not been, nor will there be, any such activities by the NSC staff."

Beyond the White House's increasingly brazen lying, the public diplomacy team was getting nastier, too. Otto Reich and his operatives were spreading rumors about the sex lives of reporters who had offended the administration. At cocktail parties, the public diplomacy boys would talk about American female journalists "sleeping with Sandinistas." They also spread a scurrilous story from a Sandinista defector that male reporters received prostitutes in return for pro-Sandinista stories. "It isn't only women," Reich asserted in the July 29, 1985, issue of *New York* magazine. For gay journalists, Reich claimed, the Nicaraguans provided men.

Brian Barger and I had begun to refer to the State Department's "P&D" shop not as "the office of public diplomacy" but as "the office of propaganda and disinformation."

As 1985 wore on, more controversies played out behind the scenes in Washington. In the fall, congressional intelligence committees discovered that the CIA had been covertly sending Nicaragua's Catholic Church hundreds of thousands of dollars to finance anti-Sandinista political activities. The panels insisted that this funding be cut off for fear it would compromise the church. The CIA grudgingly complied, but that only meant switching the church programs to North's private slush fund. He earmarked $100,000 to go to Cardinal Miguel Obando y Bravo for more anti-Sandinista activities.

Still, by December 1985, the administration saw light at the end of the "public diplomacy" tunnel. "Informed Americans ... have become disenchanted with the Sandinistas," declared a classified "90-day plan" for action. Still, the action plan advised that another breakthrough was needed before the spring 1986 votes on contra aid if Congress was to reverse itself.

Again, the action plan called for public opinion polls to pick out "buzz words" that would excite the American people. In a section on "themes," the paper played a medley of old and new propaganda favorites: "Sandinista chic -- Commandantes living a high life style while speaking of the poverty of their people; Corruption and drugs; Ties with PLO, Libya and terrorists."

One section matched themes with U.S. interest groups. "Sandinista repression of civil rights of: Church groups -- Catholic, Protestants (Evangelicals, Moravians), Jews; lawyers who defend persons charged with violating law for maintenance of public order and security; Nicaraguan employees of American embassy in Managua; press, radio, TV; unions; private enterprise." The hum of "buzz words" was deafening.

When Barger was not busy with his "general assignment" work -- that is, whatever the AP needed a warm body to go cover -- we would team up on Central America. Barger introduced me to some of his sources. One of the stranger ones was a former contra trainer named Jack Terrell, whom Barger had met in Central America.

Terrell was a tough-talking fellow who spoke in a slow southern drawl and wore a black .380 Walther pistol strapped to his calf. He had grown up in youth reformatories and lived in the French Quarter of New Orleans. He wore his blond hair cropped close to his head. Tall and trim, he went by the code name El Flaco, "the thin man."

Terrell had joined up with a paramilitary outfit called Civilian-Military Assistance [CMA] to help the contras after Congress cut off CIA support. Though the CMA cultivated an image of good ol' boy amateurs, it drew some genuine training expertise from the Alabama National Guard's reserve special-forces units. Terrell lacked that kind of formal experience, but he talked a good game and went to assist the contras in Honduras. Before long, however, he and his men gained a reputation for trouble and were booted out.

After his expulsion, Terrell began opening up to Barger -- and later to me. One of his gripes about the contras was the "class separation" that divided the contra bases sharply between poorly fed peasants who camped in squalor and the pampered commanders who lived comfortably behind wire fences. Another of his concerns was the rampant brutality.

"The contras were slaughtering people like hogs," Terrell said. "It was like living in a slaughterhouse. They [the contras] would bring in the people who were 'fleeing from communism' sometimes in handcuffs. They would take away their shoes and beat them with canes. ... One old man -- they had found a newspaper article folded up in his pocket that mentioned the Sandinistas. They said these were his 'Sandinista credentials.' They made him dig his own grave and then they stuck him in the neck to kill him. They said, 'We have to find a way to stop infiltrators.' This 68-year-old man, they murdered him as an example. He was too old to fight."

Other times, Terrell said he witnessed "almost ritualistic" killings. One method, he said, was called the "Colombian necktie," in which the victim's throat is cut open and his tongue is pulled through the opening. To carry out these executions, he said, the contra commanders used high-quality K/Bar knives.

Terrell admitted taking part in one mass execution, the close-quarter shooting of a half-dozen captured Sandinista soldiers. He said he was ordered to kill them or face execution himself. "The oldest one couldn't have been 18 years old," he said. "It sickened me. I still have nightmares about it. I'll never forget the gun going off, the bone chips and blood hitting me in the face. I ran to a creek and couldn't get the blood off me."

Terrell also talked about the NSC's secret role in support of the contra war: giving orders, arranging the flow of weapons, lining up trainers. Terrell's account fit with other information that Barger and I had been hearing from other sources. But Terrell made another startling charge: that drug trafficking was occurring inside the contra movement.

Though skeptical of that last claim, Barger and I began examining the contra-drug lead in late 1985. We got clearance for a trip to Miami, where much of the contra hierarchy lived. In Miami, we heard more about contra-drug trafficking. We met with Panamanians who linked the contra smuggling to Panamanian strongman Manuel Noriega. They also saw a connection to the murder of Hugo Spadafora, a former Panamanian health minister who had joined the contra army of Eden Pastora on the so-called Southern Front in Costa Rica.

By mid-1985, Spadafora, a romantic revolutionary, had grown disillusioned with Pastora and his ARDE forces. Spadafora concluded that the contras were wallowing in corruption and cocaine. Spadafora threatened to return to Panama and denounce the contras as well as Noriega. At the time, however, Noriega was an important U.S. ally. He also was receiving visits from Oliver North and other U.S. officials seeking help for the contra war.

North reportedly met with Noriega in June 1985 on a boat anchored off Panana City.

Despite the risks, Spadafora was determined to blow the whistle. On the morning of Sept. 13, 1985, he boarded a bus for Panama City. That afternoon, he crossed into Panama. At the first check point manned by the Panamanian Defense Force, soldiers boarded the bus and questioned Spadafora but let him continue.

When the bus reached the town of La Concepcion, however, he was apprehended and escorted off by a member of Panama's G-2 military intelligence unit. A day later, Spadafora's headless body was found stuffed into a U.S. mail bag on the bank of a river on the Costa Rican side of the border. The body showed signs of torture and was carved with the initials "F-8" -- an apparent reference to a Panamanian intelligence hit team.

In the weeks that followed, CIA operatives tried to divert the Spadafora murder case away from Noriega and the contras. A later Costa Rican prosecutor's report would allege that a German living in Panama and working for Joe Fernandez, the CIA station chief in Costa Rica, had spread a false cover story to pin the murder on leftist Salvadoran guerrillas. Authorities wasted time checking out that lead while the trail of the real murderers turned cold.

Despite the Spadafora murder and the drug suspicions, Noriega continued to enjoy friends in high places. On Nov. 1, 1985, CIA director William Casey met with Noriega face-to-face. Casey made no mention of Noriega's suspected drug trafficking. Indeed, according to a Casey memo later cited in a U.S. Senate report, Noriega felt "reassured" by Casey's comments at the meeting. Inside the U.S. government, other officials felt that Casey had "let Noriega off the hook," according to testimony to the Senate by Francis McNeil, a former U.S. ambassador to Costa Rica.

Besides the Spadafora mystery, Barger and I were examining allegations that drug-connected Cuban-Americans had joined the contra cause, partly out of anti-communist ideology and partly for business reasons. One lead went to a Miami-based shrimp importing company, called Ocean Hunter. We were told that the company was suspected of smuggling cocaine frozen in shrimp from Costa Rica. A sister firm in Costa Rica was called Frigorificos de Puentarenas.

The Miami trip had proved valuable, but we concluded that to nail down the contra-drug story, a trip to Costa Rica was necessary. With some difficulty, we persuaded the AP hierarchy to permit it.

San Jose, a city of old Spanish architecture and mountainous surroundings, had a Casablanca feel in the mid-1980s. There was a blend of licentiousness and intrigue in the air. Prostitutes worked the streets and the bars, finding business brisk from the many American adventurers, soldiers, spies and journalists. Costa Rican officials seemed apprehensive, distrustful, maybe frightened. Even from our short stay, it was clear that Costa Rica was a country in political turmoil.

Years later, a Costa Rican prosecutor's report would detail how deeply the CIA had penetrated Costa Rican intelligence. One CIA-trained unit, known as "The Babies," was used to spy on Costa Rica's democratically elected officials because they favored neutrality in the conflict in neighboring Nicaragua.

Formed in 1984, "The Babies" got their nickname because they were trained by a CIA officer known as Dimitrius Papas, or "papa." According to the prosecutor's report, the unit developed a strong loyalty to the Americans, who paid the bills, gave the intelligence operatives their own building, and supplied them with cars and equipment.

"The Babies, who lost loyalty to their [Costa Rican] superiors, were used to run surveillance" on top officials, including President Luis Alberto Monge, the Costa Rican report stated. As proof, the report cited declarations by two senior officials from the Ministry of Public Security. It appeared that the CIA was looking for any kind of edge to induce the Costa Ricans to take the contras' side.

The Costa Rican investigation also determined that Papas built ties to the police through antiterrorism training taught to the Organization of Judicial Investigations, the OIJ, Costa Rica's FBI. The report said "a close bond" developed between Papas and the OIJ's Office of Special Affairs, which handled all state-security crimes. With CIA money, the office obtained telephone-tapping equipment, recorders and photographic equipment, creating "a true economic dependency."

Though Barger and I did not have those details at the time, we couldn't miss how Costa Rican security and narcotics officials spoke to us nervously. They seemed under intense pressure to overlook what the powerful U.S. embassy was up to, particularly in the north along the Nicaraguan border. Most American officials also were circumspect.

We did interview the U.S. embassy's senior DEA official, Robert Nieves, who described meetings he had with Hugo Spadafora in the days before Spadafora's ill-fated return trip to Panama. Nieves said Spadafora seemed sincere about his contra-drug allegations but short on the kind of specifics that the DEA needed to conduct a full-scale investigation. Given the web of relationships that existed in Costa Rica, Barger and I suspected that Spadafora might have added to his personal danger by talking to Nieves. Word of the meeting probably reached the CIA station and possibly its intelligence allies in Costa Rica and Panama.

Though we encountered many obstacles in San Jose, some officials did take chances to help us. One American official met us secretly at a bar near our hotel. Over several beers, he confirmed much of the information we already had about contra-protected drug operations in northern Costa Rica.

This official described contra soldiers guarding clandestine air strips while drug planes refueled. Some contras, he said, transported loads of cocaine into San Jose and then to the coast for transshipment by freighter to the United States. The evidence implicated virtually all the contra groups, including the Honduran-based FDN, which had opened its own second front in Costa Rica.

On the last day of our trip, Barger and I drove out to a Costa Rican prison where two contra mercenaries were incarcerated. These out-of-luck soldiers-of-fortune -- British Peter Glibbery and American Steven Carr -- added more pieces to the puzzle about how the contras were sustaining their operations. They described weapons flights from Miami to a Costa Rican landing strip controlled by John Hull, a U.S. farmer with close ties to the CIA. They claimed that Hull's contra operation was getting $10,000 a month from the National Security Council.

Carr also said he saw a large quantity of cocaine at the Miami home of one Cuban-American arms supplier, Francisco Chanes.

Carr said he made the discovery in March 1985, when he was sent to Chanes's home to pick up weapons for a contra supply flight being arranged by another Cuban exile, Rene Corvo. Chanes was involved in the suspicious Costa Rican shrimp operation, Frigorificos de Puntarenas. Corvo also was a close associate of Cuban-American Frank Castro, an alleged contact between the Medellin cartel and the contras.

When we boarded the plane back to the United States, Barger was thrilled. "We got it," he exulted. But my experience with the AP bureaucracy tempered my enthusiasm. "The trouble's only just begun," I grumbled.

B ack in Washington, our contra drug story received a mixed reception. Bureau chief Charles Lewis liked it, but objections came from AP's New York headquarters. To bolster the reporting, I got a senior White House official on the phone. He tried to steer me away from implicating the FDN and Hull. But the official admitted that a CIA analysis on narcotics trafficking had found that Pastora's contra group, ARDE, had used cocaine profits to pay for a $250,000 shipment of a helicopter and weapons.

Lewis felt the new confirmation was enough to finish up the story. He instructed me to send the story to the Washington General Desk for final editing. Putting Lewis's initials at the top so the story would go to his personal attention, I transmitted the story by computer. The paper copy was torn off the printer and taken into his office.

But concerns of the New York editors were not over. Later that afternoon, Lewis summoned me to his office and dejectedly told me that New York was insisting that we obtain on-the-record confirmation from a government official. The trouble was that any official insane enough to attach his name to drug allegations against the contras would be fired. Lewis felt the story was dead.

Over the next two days, Barger and I interviewed officials at the Drug Enforcement Administration, trying to satisfy New York's concerns. DEA officials stated that northern Costa Rica had grown into a large-scale transit point for cocaine, but they said they had no idea about the political connections of the smugglers.

After returning from one interview, Barger received a call from an old acquaintance. The man complimented us on our story about contra-drug trafficking. Barger exploded, demanding to know how the person had seen the article. The perplexed caller responded that it had been in newspapers all over Latin America. Ashen faced, Barger approached my desk. Somehow the contra-drug story, held up by the New York editors, had gone out to AP subscribers in Spanish-speaking countries.

In a panic, I checked back through the computer records. We discovered that the story I had sent to Lewis's attention had popped up in another computer at AP's World Services. It was routinely translated and sent out to newspapers that take AP's Spanish-language wire. The story had gone out by accident.

Over the next several hours, AP editors worked anew on the English-language version, which finally moved on Dec. 20, 1985. The lead read:

> Nicaraguan rebels operating in northern Costa Rica have engaged in cocaine smuggling, using some of the profits to finance their war against Nicaragua's leftist government, according to U.S. investigators and American volunteers who work with the rebels. The smuggling activity has involved refueling planes at clandestine airstrips and sometimes helping transport cocaine to other Costa Rican points for shipment to the United States, said U.S. law enforcement officials.

The official U.S. government response came the next morning from State Department spokesman Charles Redman. "We are not aware of any evidence to support those charges," he said at the daily press briefing.

When other news organizations showed little interest in pursuing the story, chills went through AP management worried that we had gone out too far on a shaky limb. Early in 1986, when I approached Lewis with ideas about following up the contra-cocaine connection, he lowered his voice and advised, "New York doesn't want to hear any more about the drug story."

Barger and I were losing management's ear on the broader North-related stories, too. Our new story memos were largely ignored. In my computer, I started slugging the proposals "deepsix1," "deepsix2," etc. During one lull in the contra debate, Lewis encouraged me to move on to other stories, that the AP had never intended for me to focus so much on one issue. "Nicaragua isn't a story anymore," he added.

Still, Barger and I pushed onto the AP wire other stories challenging the administration's cheery pro-contra P.R. One in January 1986 gave voice to the complaints of anti-Sandinista Nicaraguans who felt their dreams of retaking their homeland had been tarnished by contra misconduct and clumsy interference from Washington. Another in March examined how congressional investigators could not account for most of the contras' "humanitarian" aid money.

Our stories sparked the interest of a freshman senator from Massachusetts, Democrat John F. Kerry. He assigned members of his personal staff to investigate contra corruption and prodded the Republican-controlled Senate Foreign Relations Committee to demand internal government records about alleged contra-cocaine trafficking.

With crucial contra-aid votes expected in spring 1986, the public diplomacy teams weren't sitting idly by, either. They were tuning up their Mighty Wurlitzer for a crescendo of buzzwords against the Sandinistas and heroic strains about the contras.

The administration's campaign benefitted enormously from the growing influence of conservative journalists. Pro-contra *New Republic* writer Fred Barnes was one of many who rallied to the contras' defense against the never-ending accounts of contras torturing and murdering civilians and prisoners of war.

In an article dated Jan. 20, 1986, and entitled "The Sandinista Lobby," Barnes tried to throw the human rights community onto the defensive. The story attacked leading human rights groups as hypocritical for criticizing the contras while going soft on the Sandinistas. Barnes countered Reed Brody's report of Nicaraguan eyewitnesses to contra atrocities by referencing the findings of a secret U.S. investigation that had absolved the contras of many charges. Barnes's article marked the human rights groups as politically suspect, communist dupes who no longer deserved the trust of the Washington press corps.

Again, skeptical of the administration's information on Nicaragua, I tracked down the secret report that had been leaked to Barnes. I found that it had been written by the CIA and was based on the word of the contras themselves. One of the CIA's chief defenses, debunking the slitting-throat allegations, was that the contras could not have slit throats because they "are normally not equipped with either bayonets or combat knives." The CIA failed to note that photographs of the contras from that period showed them slouching off to battle carrying a variety of machetes and other sharp objects.

The report admitted to some of Brody's findings, but tried to rationalize or minimize the events. For instance, the CIA did acknowledge the kidnapping of the elderly Nicaraguan couple, Felipe and Maria Barreda, on Dec. 28, 1982. The Barredas had traveled from their home in Esteli to the countryside over the Christmas holidays as volunteers picking coffee. But they were captured by the contras and force-marched to a contra base camp. There, they were tortured -- according to other coffee pickers who survived the ordeal -- and executed.

Instead of simply denouncing this atrocity, the CIA tried to justify it. The CIA report poked fun at Brody's description of the couple as active in their church parish and "deeply religious." The CIA stated that "the 'deeply religious' Barreda couple were senior officers of the Directorate General of State Security in Esteli, and after finally confessing to this fact, were executed on [contra commander] Suicida's orders. ... They were not tortured."

The CIA repeated the contra panel's other quibbling with Brody's "false statements" about the Barredas. They were not handcuffed during the march, the report declared. As with the knives, it was an equipment shortage. The contras have "few or no handcuffs in inventory," although the panel added "the Barredas may have been handcuffed at the camp." Somehow, a couple of handcuffs had materialized. And the panel insisted that the couple was not kept in a tent. "There were no tents in any of Suicida's camps," the CIA report argued.

Beyond the niggling over handcuffs and tents, the CIA report didn't explain why the Barredas would voluntarily admit to working for Sandinista security when that would seal their doom. Still, the CIA insisted that the Barredas "were not tortured" because that would have been against contra policy. For its part, the Sandinista government denied that the Barredas were senior state security officials.

Another administration strategy to neutralize human rights reports about contra abuses was to subsidize pro-contra activists who would pose as human rights experts. They would then challenge the findings of Americas Watch and other independent human rights groups. A Brigham Young University student named Wesley Smith released two reports alleging Sandinista atrocities and challenging accounts of contra abuses. Smith's reports were treated seriously in the mainstream media -- and he sometimes was put on network TV as a coequal expert with established human rights investigators.

But Smith provided few specifics that could be cross-checked. He claimed to have interviewed hundreds of Nicaraguans, but withheld the names, he said, for security reasons. No one he spoke with had heard a word about contra abuses, only Sandinista ones. Though a secret at the time, his expenses were paid by North's White House slush fund, according to Iran-contra documents that surfaced later.

Another one of North's private surrogates, Thomas Dowling, dressed up as a Roman Catholic priest and gave testimony on alleged Sandinista human rights abuses to the House Foreign Affairs subcommittee on the Western Hemisphere. Dowling began: "I am Father Thomas Dowling, a Catholic priest." The burly Dowling, his Irish blue eyes flashing, then told the House panel about inspirational visits to the contra camps in Honduras and Costa Rica.

"There are people in Washington today who can give direct testimony to the fact that the Sandinistas do put on contra uniforms and commit atrocities," Dowling declared. "The only other thing I can tell you is that the contras are overwhelmingly religious. One sees tremendous artifacts of Christianity, both Catholic and Protestant, tremendous amounts of Bibles, crucifixes, etc."

When the Iran-contra scandal exposed North's financial network, subcommittee members discovered that Dowling was not an ordained Roman Catholic priest but belonged to an unofficial sect called the Old Catholic Church. Iran-contra records also showed that Dowling had received $2,500 in traveler's checks from North's White House safe and tens of thousands of dollars more from contra leaders.

Rep. Sam Gejdenson, D-Conn., a panel member, complained that Dowling had been dispatched by the White House "public diplomacy" team to mislead the Congress. "Mr. Dowling testified dressed in a clerical collar and stated, for the record, that he was a Catholic priest who had ministered to contra combatants," Gejdenson declared. "This man is not a Catholic priest. He has never been a Catholic priest."

As the pro-contra lobbying heated up in February 1986, CIA director Casey personally lent a hand. At two White House meetings with 60 members of Congress, Casey showed up carrying a brown paper bag. The bag contained a classified report that the CIA director claimed detailed a Sandinista "disinformation campaign" aimed at the American people, the U.S. press and Congress.

With drama in the air, the report was passed around for some of the members to get a closer look. Presumably, the members thanked heavens that they were not identified by name as Sandinista pawns. Sen. David Durenberger, R-Minn., chairman of the Senate Intelligence Committee, rebuked Casey for the stunt. Durenberger called the ploy an "outrageous" attempt "to portray every senator and congressman who votes against lethal aid as a stooge of communism."

But the political hardball was working. The perception managers were gaining ground. In one memo in March 1986, Reich boasted to Raymond that the public diplomacy office was taking "a very aggressive posture vis-à-vis a sometimes hostile press." Declaring that his office "did not give the critics of the policy any quarter in the debate," Reich added that the Washington press corps now understood that "attacking the president was no longer cost free." His report bragged about having "killed" many purportedly "erroneous" news stories.

In another memo submitting his office for a government commendation, Reich credited his team with whipping Congress and the press into line on the contra war. "S/LPD [his office initials] has played a key role in setting out the parameters and defining the terms of the public discussion on Central America policy," Reich stated.

The New Republic, a longtime left-of-center publication which had veered to neo-conservative in the 1980s, demonstrated how right Reich was. The magazine emerged as an influential voice in Washington as it parroted the administration's public relations themes. In the March 24, 1986, issue, the magazine reprised the many anti-Sandinista arguments in an editorial entitled "The Case for the Contras."

The editors wrote that if contra military aid were not restored, the Sandinistas would crush the rebels and "then, just as certainly, the unarmed resistance, demoralized and abandoned, will follow, leaving the Sandinistas in total, permanent control of Nicaragua. ... If in Nicaragua transition to democracy were possible without war, we too would oppose any fighting. But that option does not exist. Does anyone believe that the Sandinistas will ever peacefully transfer power or permit free allocation of power by election?"

On April 7, 1986, Fred Barnes had another story in *The New Republic,* a glowing first-hand account of the contras in their base camps. As new contra-aid votes loomed, the former St. Alban's prep school student went south to play the unlikely role of "Contra for a Day," the title of his article about "roughing it with the freedom fighters." He used the dateline "on the Nicaraguan border" and offered his readers "some of the flavor" of his adventure.

"My companion and I had to ford five streams," Barnes wrote. "Yes, we had a four-wheel vehicle, but it didn't take the bumps in what passed for roads too smoothly. Some bumps were so bad I hit my head on the roof."

But bad roads were only part of the ordeal. "I had to settle for standard contra food," Barnes wrote, adding:

It wasn't too bad if you like rice, beans and mystery meat for breakfast, lunch and dinner. I ate hearty. The coffee wasn't hot enough, but it was sweet and strong. And the chow was better than the overnight accommodations at a training camp 15 miles inside Nicaragua. I was told to bring a sleeping bag, heavy boots, water, bug spray, malaria pills, flashlight, toilet paper. I needed all of them. My bed in the Hospedaje Visita, the place for visitors, consisted of a plywood slab on legs. I've slept better.

For three days, contra commanders ferried Barnes around "contraland," as he called it. He reported back images of a well-motivated guerrilla force, "freedom fighters" battling against the odds. Though he had criticized human rights groups for not thoroughly investigating alleged Sandinista abuses, Barnes insisted that he lacked the time to check out the human-rights complaints that had been lodged against the contras.

Barnes did, however, record denials from contra commander Enrique Bermudez. Barnes wrote: "The stories of continuing atrocities by his troops are untrue, he said. To prove it, he presented a commander named Tigrillo, who he said was blamed in a recent report for murder. The man was in the hospital at the time, Bermudez said."

A year later, Tigrillo would be convicted by the contras themselves of murder, the slaying of one of his own men. The *Los Angeles Times* reported that Tigrillo was suspected of killing 16 more contras under his command and of murdering an unknown number of unarmed prisoners of war.[43] But Barnes presented Tigrillo as a wrongly accused man.

By 1986, Barnes and *The New Republic* were important cogs in the Reagan-Bush propaganda machine. The magazine was all the more important because of its long history as a thoughtful left-of-center publication. But like a once fine restaurant that had been taken over by contra cooks serving "mystery meat," *The New*

---

[43] *Los Angeles Times,* Jan. 24, 1987.

Republic was no longer dishing out honest journalism. The magazine had been on that course since it was purchased by Martin Peretz in the 1970s, but by 1986, the transformation was complete.

The change brought rewards aplenty. With its irreverent writing style and its inside track with the White House, *The New Republic* was one of the decade's "hot mags," a magazine that Washington insiders had to read. The political journal carried great weight with top editors at larger publications, such as *Newsweek*. But *The New Republic's* greatest reach came when its star columnists -- Barnes, Morton Kondracke and Charles Krauthammer -- amplified their and the government's views through redundant appearances on the TV chat shows and with columns published in *The Washington Post.*

The New Republic also marked a more general shift in the Washington news media, away from careful reporting to a judgmental style with a safely conservative edge. Just as Raymond Bonner represented the disappearing standards of the Watergate-era press and its readiness to question the national security rules, *The New Republic* and its many copycats marked a transformation to sneering punditry journalism that puts a writer's career advancement above all else.

Reporters who bucked the trend increasingly found their jobs in jeopardy. In 1986, ABC News' Karen Burnes did a creditable job following leads about contra corruption. But she found herself with no choice but to devote extraordinary care whenever she dealt with a story that put the contras in a negative light. "It takes months and months to do this story," she said. Because her editors wanted more minutes on the air, she was marked down for taking that time.

The toll became so heavy that reporters reached the point that they psychologically wanted to submit to the administration's propaganda themes. "It's easy to become co-opted," Karen Burnes told *Rolling Stone* magazine. "At times you are so desperate and tired that you want to believe anything you hear." Finally, for a break, she volunteered to cover a civil war in Ethiopia. "It was a relief," she said. "I'll take a civil war any day before working in this city."[44]

I also was taking my share of hits, although most were delivered with whispers to other journalists. One day in 1986, I had drinks with the *Miami Herald's* Alfonso Chardy at Bullfeathers, a dark-wood-and-brass bar on Capitol Hill. "They're trashing the hell out of you," Chardy warned. The public diplomacy operatives were quietly challenging my journalistic integrity, he said.

Another journalist told me that when he called State Department spokesman Greg Lagana for a comment about one of my stories, Lagana went beyond denying the facts to attacking my professionalism. "That's what happens when you have a wire service reporter who should be writing for the advocacy press," Lagana said over the phone. "Bob Parry, he's contra obsessed."

Barger and I continued our reporting, however. We learned that some federal investigators were taking an interest in the same evidence we were finding. Jeffrey Feldman, an assistant U.S. attorney in Miami, had started to look at the allegations of contra gunrunning and drug smuggling. One of the witnesses was our old source, Jack Terrell. The former mercenary was visited in New Orleans by Feldman and FBI agents.

Behind the scenes in Washington, Feldman's fledgling investigation was raising alarms among Reagan's legal advisers, according to documents that surfaced in the Iran-contra scandal. "Please get on top of this," came the worried message from Stephen Trott, then head of the Justice Department's criminal division. "DLJ [deputy attorney general D. Lowell Jensen] is giving a heads-up to the NSC." That briefing of NSC adviser John Poindexter occurred on March 24, 1986.

Later that same month, Feldman flew to Costa Rica to interview participants in North's network. He already had put together many of the pieces. But he did not seem to realize the political danger that was closing in around him. At the U.S. embassy, he discussed his suspicions with U.S. Ambassador Lewis

---

[44] Rolling Stone, Sept. 10, 1987.

Tambs and CIA station chief Joe Fernandez. The information was promptly reported back to Oliver North.

One alarm about Feldman was sounded by North's private courier, Robert Owen. In an April 7, 1986, memo, Owen warned North that Feldman had outlined a contra support network headed by North. "Feldman looks to be wanting to build a career on this case," wrote Owen. "He even showed ... the Ambassador a diagram with your name underneath and John [Hull]'s underneath mine, then a line connecting the various resistance groups in C.R. [Costa Rica]. Feldman stated they were looking at the 'big picture' and not only looking at a possible violation of the neutrality act, but a possible unauthorized use of government funds."

Eight months before the official Iran-contra scandal broke, Feldman had outlined the actual lines of authority from the White House to the field. But Feldman's investigation did not go much further. On April 4, after Feldman returned from Costa Rica, another assistant U.S. attorney, David Leiwant, claimed to overhear Miami's U.S. Attorney Leon Kellner saying he had been told to "go slow" on the probe because of upcoming congressional votes. Kellner later would deny Leiwant's account.

At AP, Barger and I got wind of the federal investigation and made another trip to Miami to confirm it. On April 10, we published a story disclosing that the U.S. Attorney's office in Miami was examining allegations of contra gunrunning and drug trafficking. The AP story rattled more nerves inside the Reagan administration. On a trip to Miami, Attorney General Edwin Meese III pulled Kellner aside and asked about the story of the contra probe.

Back in Washington, the major newspapers started sniffing around the story, but mostly went off in wrong directions. A *New York Times* reporter interviewed Meese's spokesman Patrick Korten who dismissed the contra allegations by claiming that "various bits of information got referred to us. We ran them all down and didn't find anything. It comes to nothing."[45]

---

[45] Though the article does not identify Korten by name, Meese's P.R. assistant later admitted to me that he was the source. *The New York Times,* May 6, 1986.

In Washington, the inaccurate *Times* story put another damper on our investigation. In Miami, however, Feldman and the FBI agents actually were finding a lot of corroboration. On May 14, 1986, Feldman recommended to his superiors that the evidence of contra crimes was strong enough to justify taking the case to a grand jury. Feldman's boss, Kellner, scribbled on the memo, "I concur that we have sufficient evidence to ask for a grand jury investigation."

But on May 20, less than a week later, Kellner met with his top aides and reversed the recommendation. Without telling Feldman, Kellner rewrote the memo to state that "a grand jury investigation at this point would represent a fishing expedition with little prospect that it would bear fruit." Kellner then signed Feldman's name to the mixed metaphor, again without telling Feldman, and sent the memo to Washington on June 3. The doctored memo was slipped to congressional Republicans who leaked it to the conservative media and used it to discredit Kerry's early contra-drug investigation. Back in Miami, Kellner reassigned Feldman to far-flung investigations, including one in Thailand, effectively suspending the contra probe.

Years later, senior CIA officer Alan Fiers Jr. told Iran-contra investigators that North personally kept a nervous eye on the Miami probe. Fiers, who ran the CIA's Central American Task Force, said North brought his influence to bear to block the Feldman probe as well as the AP reporting. Fiers also testified that North specifically encouraged the FBI to "do something" about me.

The Iran-contra report on the Fiers interview stated that the CIA officer "also has a recollection that Feldman's investigation had been put on hold." But Fiers said he did not know precisely what the Justice Department or the White House might have done to obstruct the probe. "The only activity Fiers is aware of by anyone in the government to in any way influence this case was North telling him [Fiers] that he [North] was going to call Oliver 'Buck' Revell at the FBI and have him 'do some things'," the report said.

"Fiers recalls that North on two or three occasions told him he was having Revell either do something or not do something," the interview report continued. "Fiers thinks one of the calls from North to Revell was about North's concern about him [North] being hounded by Bob Parry, the reporter. Fiers [also] thinks he has a vague recollection that North was going to ask Revell to shut down the Feldman investigation. ... He does recall North talking about contacting Revell and having him do something about these kinds of things."

Fiers gave his statement to the Iran-contra investigators on Aug. 1, 1991, after special prosecutor Lawrence Walsh had broken through the long-running Iran-contra cover-up and gained Fiers's cooperation. I discovered the interview report in declassified records at the National Archives in late 1996. I then tracked Fiers down at his job with a Wisconsin-based subsidiary of the W.R. Grace Co.

I left three messages before he finally called back in January 1997. But he was not inclined to be helpful. After some small talk about the merits of life in Wisconsin vs. Washington, D.C., he told me bluntly that he had returned my call only out of courtesy. He did not talk with reporters, he said, even when approached by national TV anchors, such as NBC's Tom Brokaw.

I appealed to Fiers on a personal basis. I noted that since he had mentioned me by name to the Iran-contra investigators, it only seemed fair that he give me some clarification of what his cryptic remarks meant. I asked what the FBI might have done to stop me from investigating the "hounded" Oliver North.

My question apparently rang a bell in his memory as he recalled who I was. "That's right," the gravelly voice growled over the phone as my name registered, "you were the enemy."

Though not entirely surprised by his comment, I responded that I did not consider myself "the enemy." What I thought I had been doing in my reporting was alerting everyone to the fact that North's contra-support activities were careening toward a major scandal. I argued that if the White House had learned from my stories -- rather than trying to bury them -- it might have been a lot better off.

But Fiers was not persuaded by either my personal appeal or my reasoning. He would not break his rule of silence about talking with the press. "Whatever's there [in the statement] is there," he answered. "Whatever is in there is all I know."

Still, I wasn't quite ready to hang up. I told Fiers a story that I had heard in the mid-1980s. North was claiming to some administration colleagues that Barger and I were "Sandinista agents" who had somehow poisoned North's dog. North was apparently reaching for any sort of criminal "predicate" that would justify an FBI counter-intelligence investigation of us.

I told Fiers that beyond the fact that I didn't know where North lived at the time or that he had a dog, Iran-contra investigators had determined that the dog had died of natural causes, a combination of old age and cancer. But Fiers was still not willing to help.

After hanging up with Fiers, I contacted Revell, the former FBI official who sat with North on some of the Reagan administration's high-powered counter-terrorism task forces. In January 1997, I read Revell the relevant portion of the Fiers statement. The ex-FBI man emphatically denied that he had ever authorized an investigation of me or any other reporter.

"Ollie would sometimes say things for effect," Revell maintained. "North never called me on anything like that. ... It's not true about him talking about you or any other reporter. They couldn't initiate even a preliminary investigation of a reporter without approval of the attorney general." Revell, however, did recall North mentioning "about someone poisoning his dog."

I next tried to contact Oliver North. The former Marine lieutenant colonel was a talk-radio host in the Washington area and an executive at Guardian Technologies in Sterling, Va., a company that manufactured bulletproof vests. I faxed North two relevant pages from Fiers' statement and a request that he clarify what he had asked Revell to do about me, if anything. I was not surprised that North did not respond. I assumed that unlike Fiers, he had not forgotten who I was.

Yet, whatever the truth about North's misuse of the FBI, Fiers did make clear that the CIA was closely following official investigations into the secret Central American operations in 1986. According to Fiers's statement, the CIA kept track of both the Feldman investigation in Miami and Kerry's inquiry in Washington.

"Fiers was also getting a dump on the Senator Kerry investigation about mercenary activity in Central America from the CIA's legislative affairs people who were monitoring it," the Fiers statement read. "Fiers also knew that there was a 'pissing contest' between the U.S. attorney in Miami [Kellner] and AUSA [assistant U.S. attorney] Feldman over this investigation. Fiers recalls that Feldman wanted to more actively pursue it."

Chapter 4
A Breakthrough, of Sorts

By spring 1986, Brian Barger and I felt we had an abundance of detail -- and sourcing -- for a full-scale article on how Oliver North was running this contra support operation through cut-outs. But AP's top editors remained nervous and wanted more authoritative confirmations.

While we scratched for more evidence, we also prepared two stories in late May. One revealed the CIA's role in forcing renegade contra leader Eden Pastora to quit the war and the other disclosed how the contras had exchanged their "humanitarian" aid dollars at "black market" rates and then sank the profits into weapons accounts.

Both were expected to run around the Memorial Day weekend when a hiatus in official government business would give AP investigative stories a better chance for wide usage in newspapers around the country. After those stories, we planned to push again for publication of the comprehensive article on how North's network operated. We were hearing from some of our sources that the *Miami Herald* was pursuing the same story and gaining ground on us.

The Pastora and black-market stories, however, were encountering more delays with AP editors. Early one evening after most of the AP staff had left the office, I confronted bureau chief Charles Lewis about the story holdups. Lewis, a tall, gangly man,

then in his early 40s, looked exhausted. His face was drained of
color. His eyes were bloodshot.

I knew that besides handling the pressures of managing the
large AP bureau, Lewis served as the AP's point man with the
administration over negotiations to gain the release of Terry
Anderson, an AP correspondent who had been kidnapped in Beirut
on March 16, 1985. AP management was very tight-lipped about
those talks, but Lewis would meet periodically with Anderson's
sister, Peggy Say, who was energetically lobbying for more
aggressive U.S. action.

When I broached the contra stories, Lewis began describing
the inside of North's NSC office on the third floor of the Old
Executive Office Building. He had just met with North there to
discuss the Anderson situation. Lewis marveled at North's bank of
telephones that rang with distinctly different sounds. North would
grab one receiver and then the next, fielding calls from the nation's
most sensitive intelligence agencies. North confided, too, that his
windows were coated with a special substance to block enemy
electronic spying.

I came away from the strange discussion with Lewis
wondering if North might be playing a double game. Certainly,
Lewis was in a tight spot, meeting with North about Anderson while
Barger and I were preparing investigative stories suggesting that
North was violating the law. One of Lewis's secretaries noted that
Lewis was getting so many calls from North's office that she
started to suspect that he was having an affair with a woman
named Fawn, since North's secretary, Fawn Hall, placed many of
the calls.

For his part, Lewis stated that North's assistance on the
Anderson case did not interfere with the AP's investigative work on
North's contra network. But the story delays around Memorial Day
did correspond with North's trip to Teheran -- when he was
bringing the Iranian mullahs a Bible inscribed by President Reagan
and a chocolate cake as a sign of U.S. goodwill. One of the goals of
that mission was Anderson's freedom and our stories likely would
have been a major distraction to North's travel plans.

Not until the end of that week -- after the Teheran meetings
had collapsed on May 27 -- was a watered-down version of the

Pastora story released by the AP. The next week, the "black-market money" story moved, although Lewis released the story at 8:15 p.m., a decision that guaranteed the story would get very little use. The comprehensive North story was still on hold.

Only after the *Miami Herald* ran its version of the North piece -- with far fewer sources than we had -- did the AP agree to publish our account. Finally, on June 10, 1986, the AP story ran citing two dozen sources. It began:

> The White House, working through outside intermediaries, managed a private aid network that provided military assistance to Nicaraguan rebels during last year's congressional ban, according to government officials, rebel leaders and American supporters. The American intermediaries helped the rebels with arms purchases, fund raising and enlistment of military trainers after Congress, in October 1984, barred U.S. officials from "directly or indirectly" aiding the contra war against Nicaragua's leftist government. ... Lt. Col. Oliver L. North, deputy director for political-military affairs at the National Security Council, oversaw the work of the intermediaries, including conservative activist Robert W. Owen and retired Army Gen. John K. Singlaub.

The AP story, with its multitude of sources, pushed the issue to a new level. But Congress still was hesitant to confront a reality that was becoming painfully obvious.

The administration's public diplomacy had pounded Congress as it had the news media, like a hurricane surging ashore. Each wave of propaganda swelled up along the surf line, rose, crested and crashed upon those opinion circles. The erosion of rational thought was undeniable.

Faced with the extraordinary lobbying campaigns and Washington's now-dominant pro-contra punditry, Congress finally buckled in spring 1986. In House and Senate votes, Congress agreed to resume $100 million in mostly military support for the contras. The long-running public diplomacy campaign had achieved its principal objective. But the final touches were not put on the contra-aid provision until fall, keeping the administration nervous that some new scandal might break in the meantime.

Without doubt, trouble continued to surround the contra operation. On June 27, 1986, the World Court ruled by a lopsided margin that the United States had broken international law and violated Nicaraguan sovereignty through the contra war. Nevertheless, the finding -- the first ever World Court condemnation of the United States -- was treated as a one-day story in most of the American press.

Continuing press inquiries and Sen. Kerry's investigation caused other worries. On one front, North's allies continued working at discrediting the witnesses, especially Jack Terrell. North assigned one of his operatives, a former CIA officer named Glenn A. Robinette, to investigate and entrap the ex-mercenary. As "security officer" for what North called Project Democracy, Robinette was paid $4,000 a month.

When Terrell traveled to Washington to tell his story to Congress, Robinette contacted Terrell, took him out for expensive dinners and dangled a business venture in front of him. On July 17, 1986, Robinette explained his goals in a memo to North. Through the phony business deal, Robinette hoped to silence Terrell and stop him from being "dangerous to our objectives." Robinette also used the meetings as a pretext to pump information out of Terrell.

Though Terrell didn't fall for the business ploy, he allegedly made some comment over the phone to someone else that he could "get the president." The remark had been intercepted by U.S. intelligence and was being interpreted as a threat against President Reagan's life. To feed the flames of suspicion, Robinette passed on other derogatory material about Terrell to the FBI.

Seeing an opening, North escalated the anti-Terrell campaign inside the White House. On July 17, 1986, North wrote to NSC adviser John Poindexter that a special unit set up to counter international terrorism was assisting in the Terrell investigation. North said the high-powered Terrorist Incident Working Group [TIWG] had turned over "all information" on Terrell to the FBI.

Further, North said the TIWG "operations sub-group" would review an FBI "counter-intelligence, counter-terrorism operations plan" aimed at Terrell. North added that "the FBI now believes that Terrell may well be a paid asset of the Nicaraguan Intelligence Services [DSGE] or another hostile intelligence service. ... It is interesting to note that Terrell has been part of what appears to be a much larger operation being conducted against our support for the Nicaraguan resistance."

Eleven days later, North wrote another memo entitled, "Terrorist Threat: Terrell," which was initialed as read by President Reagan. In that July 28, 1986, memo, North suggested that his chief worry about Terrell was his public criticism of the contras, his "anti-contra and anti-U.S. activities." North called Terrell:

> an active participant in the disinformation/active measures campaign against the Nicaraguan Democratic Resistance. Terrell has appeared on various television "documentaries" alleging corruption, human rights abuses, drug running, arms smuggling and assassination attempts by the resistance and their supporters. Terrell is also believed to be involved with various congressional staffs in preparing for hearings and inquiries regarding the role of U.S. government officials in illegally supporting the Nicaraguan resistance.

In August 1986, FBI and Secret Service agents hauled Terrell in for two days of polygraph examinations before concluding that Terrell had no plans to assassinate President Reagan. Terrell told me later that the investigation had chilled his readiness to testify about the contras. "It burned me up," he said. "The pressure was always there."

Years later, I raised the Terrell issue with Oliver "Buck" Revell, who represented the FBI on the TIWG's "operations sub-group." Revell said he was always suspicious of North's anti-Terrell vendetta, so suspicious that he ordered two FBI agents to watch North and his associates to determine if they were engaged in some kind of "plumbers" operation. "I actually had some surveillance run against them to see if they were running an investigation" of Terrell, Revell said. "I just wanted to see what the hell was going on."

Whatever Revell's suspicions, they did not stop the FBI from hassling Terrell over the bogus assassination plot. During the same time frame, there were other unexplained incidents suggesting that North's allies were digging for dirt on his "enemies." One day, Barger spotted photographic surveillance of his townhouse on Monroe Street, just off 16th Street in northwest Washington.

Barger chased one man who fled rather than answer questions. Barger then notified District police who investigated and confirmed that an apartment on 16th Street had been used by two men to photograph comings-and-goings at Barger's house. But the men had cleared out and the police never determined who was behind the surveillance.

T he AP story about North's contra activities finally spurred members of the House Intelligence Committee to do something. Although the Republicans were hostile toward any inquiry and the Democrats were scared, the panel's members finally trooped over to the White House Situation Room for a face-to-face meeting with North.

On Aug. 11, 1986, in polite give-and-take, North insisted that "he did not in any way, nor at any time violate the spirit, principles or legal requirements of the Boland Amendment," according to minutes of the meeting. At the end, Rep. Lee Hamilton, D-Ind., the committee chairman, "indicated his satisfaction in the responses received."

Afterwards, I got a call from a congressional staff aide telling me that the panel had investigated the North operation and concluded that my story "didn't check out." With the Democrats now joining with the Republicans in disparaging our work, it appeared that the AP investigation of North's network had failed. Barger and I had had enough trouble explaining to our editors why the Reagan administration would lie so blatantly. Now, we faced a much tougher argument: Why would the Democrats so easily go along, unless our stories were indeed wrong?

As Congress turned its back, the internal AP situation grew grimmer. Lewis had moved Barger to the AP overnight shift and told him that he would remain there well into the fall. A single parent with a school-aged daughter, Barger decided that he had no choice but to resign. While my job was not in jeopardy, I saw myself deep inside the AP doghouse.

By late summer 1986, the administration could breathe a sigh of relief. Congress and the press had fallen into line. But Casey and other principals realized how fragile their situation remained. From his CIA perch, Casey still kept a close eye on the delicate political situation and prodded the public diplomacy team to stay active. In August 1986, Walter Raymond prepared a memo for NSC adviser Poindexter to sign reporting to Casey on even routine bureaucratic changes inside the public diplomacy team.

But Casey was not placated. He continued to pepper Raymond with suggestions, some carried by Casey's CIA counselor, former ad man Peter Dailey. On Aug. 26, 1986, Raymond reported in a computer message to Poindexter that Dailey "invited me to breakfast" and expressed concerns about the future:

> What he thought was missing was the immediacy of the problem from the American domestic perspective. He believes that we are operating with a relatively narrow window in which to turn around American perceptions re Contras -- and particularly Nic[aragua] -- or we will be chewed up by Congress. We discussed the obvious, which is part of our strategy, including such things as: the need to convince people of the key importance of contras to our national security; the need to glue white hats on our team, etc. ... The key difference is that he thinks we should run it more like a political/presidential campaign. ...
>
> Later, in talking to Ollie [North] and Bob Kagan [Otto Reich's successor as head of the State Department's public diplomacy office], we focused on what is missing and that is a well-funded independent outside group -- remember the Committee for the Present

Danger -- that could mobilize people. Peter suggested 10 or 12 very prominent bipartisan Americans. Added to this would need to be a key action officer and a 501-c-3 tax-exempt structure. It is totally understanding why, for discreet political reasons, it was not included in the memo to Bill Casey. I told Pete he was right but we need a "horse" and money!

CIA counselor Dailey, who had worked for Casey on the 1980 Reagan presidential campaign, later defended his intervention to me. "You don't give up your rights when you go to work for the CIA," Dailey argued, adding that his advice "had nothing to do with advertising" nor with "public diplomacy."

Besides working through Dailey, Casey personally cornered NSC officials to express his concerns. "Bill Casey was in this morning," reported Poindexter in a Sept. 13, 1986, computer message to North, "and amongst other things he said that he still felt that we needed somebody in the WH [White House] full time on Central America public affairs. ... I think what he really has in mind is a political operative that can twist arms and also run a high-powered public affairs campaign."

Raymond remained skittish about the legality of Casey's personal role, however. "Although Pete Dailey, Bill Casey and Clif White [a prominent GOP political operative] have all been involved in general discussion of what needs to be done, we are going to have to be sure that Pete and Bill are not involved. Pete is getting very nervous on this item," Raymond wrote to Poindexter. "The problem with all of this is that to make it work it really has to be one step removed from our office and, as a result, we have to rely on others to get the job done."

"Rely on others" was a watchword for the administration's efforts to defeat troublesome Democrats at the polls. Starting in summer 1986, Oliver North's cut-outs mounted negative political campaigns against contra critics. Rep. Michael Barnes, D-Md., chairman of the House Foreign Affairs subcommittee on the Western Hemisphere, was a particular target since he had made pointed inquiries about North's activities.

When Barnes ran for the U.S. Senate in 1986, one North operative named Kris Littledale told Iran-contra investigators that "we all, of course, wanted to nail Barnes's ass." Undated notes taken by one participant at a strategy session made clear the intent: "destroy Barnes [and] use him as [an] object lesson to others"; "Barnes -- wants [to] indict Ollie. Watergate babies -- want to get at the Pres. through Ollie. Want another Watergate. Put Barnes out of politics. If we get rid of Barnes we get rid of the ring leader and rid of the problem."

To punish Barnes and make him an example, North's operatives placed ads on Washington-area TV stations and in local newspapers. The ads portrayed Barnes as a Sandinista sympathizer who was soft on communism. When Barnes lost the Democratic primary, North operative Carl "Spitz" Channell sent North a telegram proclaiming "an end to much of the disinformation and unwise effort directed at crippling your foreign policy goals."

On another front, AP's management continued to appeal for North's help in winning Terry Anderson's freedom. On Sept. 8, 1986, North reported to John Poindexter by computer message that AP executives understood the value of secrecy in the difficult hostage talks. AP general manager Louis D. Boccardi "is supportive of our policy on terroprism [sic] and on the hostage issue," North wrote. "He made a cogent observation that I think is relevant: 'I sure hope that you are dealing with someone regarding Terry and the others in Lebanon -- and that you can keep it quiet -- that's the only way that any of this will work'."[46]

B y early fall 1986, another danger arose for the administration's fragile pro-contra consensus. Sen. John Kerry's Senate investigators were finding witnesses who were filling in details about contra-drug smuggling. But the Reagan administration balked at the release of documents that might corroborate the drug connections.

Years later, one of Kerry's investigators, Jack Blum, would complain publicly that the Justice Department had actively

---

[46] Terry Anderson remained a captive in Lebanon for five more years. He was freed on Dec. 4, 1991.

obstructed the congressional probe. Blum fingered for particular criticism William Weld, who took over as assistant attorney general in charge of the criminal division in September 1986. Blum called Weld and his assistants an "absolute stonewall" blocking the Senate's access to evidence linking the contras to cocaine smuggling.

"Weld put a very serious block on any effort we made to get information," Blum told the Senate Intelligence Committee a decade after the fact. "There were stalls. There were refusals to talk to us, refusals to turn over data." Weld denied the charges. He insisted that he conscientiously pursued the allegations. But the evidence undercuts him and supports Blum.

When Weld arrived at the Justice Department in September 1986, Senate Foreign Relations Committee requests for contra-cocaine evidence were pending. Kerry had persuaded Sen. Richard Lugar, R-Ind., and Claiborne Pell, D-R.I., the chairman and ranking minority member respectively, to support the investigation. In letters to Justice, Lugar and Pell requested information on more than two dozen individuals connected to the contra operation and suspected of drug trafficking.

One of Weld's top deputies, Mark Richard, was worried about the Justice Department's failure to respond to that request. "In the September [1986] time frame, a new assistant attorney general [Weld] comes on board," Richard testified in a deposition. "I must confess I was concerned. I was concerned not so much that there were going to be hearings [about contra-connected drug trafficking].

"I was concerned that we were not responding to what was obviously a legitimate congressional request. We were not refusing to respond in giving explanations or justifications for it. We were seemingly just stonewalling what was a continuing barrage of requests for information. That concerned me to no end."

Richard said he raised his worries with Weld directly. "I impressed upon the new assistant attorney general that this, in my judgment, was an issue that had to be addressed. We had responsibility across section lines. ... To my knowledge, we just were not saying we're not going to give it. We're not saying we're going to give it. We're just not saying anything."

On Sept. 26, 1986, Kerry made another move to prod action by the Justice Department. Kerry brought Weld an 11-page "proffer" statement from a 31-year-old female FBI informant. The informant, Wanda Palacio, had broken with the Medellin cartel. Besides talking to the FBI, she approached Kerry with an account about Colombian cocaine kingpin Jorge Ochoa bragging that he had made payments to the contras.

As part of this contra support operation, Palacio asserted that pilots for a CIA-connected airline, Southern Air Transport, were flying cocaine out of Barranquilla, Colombia. She claimed to have witnessed two such flights, one in 1983 and the other in October 1985. She quoted Jorge Ochoa as claiming the flights were part of an arrangement to exchange "drugs for guns."

According to contemporaneous notes of the "proffer" meeting between Weld and Kerry, Weld chuckled that he was not surprised about the allegations of "bum agents, former and current CIA agents" involved in corrupt dealings with the cartel. Weld indicated that he would give serious consideration to Palacio's charges.

After Kerry left, however, the Justice Department started looking for holes in Palacio's story, anything that would allow the testimony to be dismissed. Like other contra-cocaine witnesses, she may have been credible when the FBI was using her on other matters, but she was judged to lack credibility when she mentioned the contras and the CIA.

On Oct. 3, 1986, Weld's office informed Kerry that it was rejecting Palacio as a witness on the grounds that there were some contradictions in her testimony. The discrepancies apparently related to such minor points as which month she had first talked with the FBI. But the Palacio case was about to have some new twists, as was the larger administration campaign to protect the contra secrets.

By October 1986, the Reagan administration appeared to have the contra situation pretty much in hand. At the CIA, Casey still fretted over the thin congressional majority supporting lethal aid to the contras. Administration officials groused, too, that House Speaker Thomas P. "Tip" O'Neill, D-Mass., a strong contra critic, was dragging his feet on an appropriations bill that would deliver the $100 million in CIA assistance to the rebels. But that bill finally was nearing completion. The money -- and the weapons -- would start flowing in weeks, if not days.

Oliver North's little air force was wrapping up its secret mission. Despite disclosures about other facets of the operation, North's flyboy activities had largely escaped the attention of a browbeaten national press corps. Between the public diplomacy operatives and the influential pro-contra pundits, the space for critical journalism about the contras had all but disappeared.

On the morning of Oct. 5, a sleepy Sunday, one of North's four-member flyboy teams boarded a C-123 cargo plane, the same aircraft that the CIA had retrofitted for Barry Seal's 1984 drug flight to Nicaragua. Piloted by two Americans, the plane and its supply of military equipment took off from Ilopango airport in El Salvador. It crossed to the Pacific and headed south along Nicaragua's coastline. After reaching southern Nicaragua, the plane banked eastward and sliced over the lush jungle terrain.

The plane was nearing one of its drop points. An unemployed Wisconsin construction worker and onetime CIA cargo handler named Eugene Hasenfus opened the cargo door and was preparing to kick out boxes of AK-47 automatic rifles. Since his job required him to work near the open door, Hasenfus, a big bearish man, was wearing the only parachute on board.

On the ground, watching the lumbering plane was a young Sandinista soldier, a teen-age draftee with a Russian-made surface-to-air missile on his shoulder. The soldier had never fired a SAM missile and wasn't sure what to expect. He aimed the missile, fired and watched amazed as the missile headed right at the plane. The missile struck below the wing, near an engine. The plane spun wildly out of control.

On board, Hasenfus was knocked off his feet by the explosion. But he somehow struggled to the open door. He climbed through the opening and pushed himself clear of the doomed plane. Hasenfus yanked at the ripcord and parachuted safely to earth. The only survivor, he was quickly captured by Sandinista soldiers.

The plane crash sent a jolt through the small community of journalists who had followed North's secret operations. My ex-AP colleague Brian Barger had landed a contract with a CBS News show called "West 57th Street." Immediately after the shootdown, he was pressing the Nicaraguan government's representatives in Washington for access to Hasenfus. Barger thought he had convinced one of them that the Sandinistas should grant a joint interview to the AP and his program. He called me with a suggestion that we hop a plane to Managua. After some consultations with AP management, my trip was cleared. Barger and I flew to Managua, the center of so much American political and military interest.

Although I had traveled to other countries in Central America, this trip was my first to Nicaragua. When we landed, I was struck by how poor and pathetic the country was. Surrounded by volcanic mountains and situated on a polluted lake, Managua had never recovered from an earthquake that shattered the city in 1972 nor had it come back from the violent revolution that brought the Sandinistas to power in 1979.

Many buildings were still in ruins, grass growing up around the wreckage. One reporter I met referred to Managua as a city with no more than two working elevators at any one time. The idea that Nicaragua was somehow a military threat to the United States seemed all the more absurd.

When we reached our hotel, Barger began calling around to Sandinista officials hectoring them about access to Hasenfus. He found the Sandinistas unsure exactly how they wanted to handle the international press crush on Hasenfus. But our chances of getting the first crack did not look good. Barger's contact in Washington was unable to deliver on his promises.

The Sandinistas did, however, offer us a kind of consolation prize. They invited us to the headquarters of Nicaraguan military intelligence for a briefing, an offer we accepted. That evening, we took a cab to the low-rise, open-air compound in Managua. We were cleared through armed checkpoints, mostly casual young soldiers sitting behind metal desks examining our credentials. We were then led to a large office and invited to sit on chairs around a wooden coffee table.

The office belonged to Ricardo Wheelock, the chief of Nicaraguan military intelligence. He arrived in military khakis, welcomed us and began chatting with Barger in Spanish. One of Wheelock's aides brought a manila envelope that Wheelock said contained the documents found in the plane's wreckage. The aide emptied the envelope onto the table.

Wheelock assured us that photocopies would be made available to the international press corps the next day at a news conference featuring Hasenfus. But not trusting the Sandinistas' assurances, I began copying as much as I could into my notebook. For the next few hours, as Barger and Wheelock talked, I scribbled.

While the documents included a wealth of data -- from business cards to ID's to phone numbers -- I spent most of the time copying the flight records of the co-pilot Wallace "Buzz" Sawyer. His two flight logs listed hundreds of flights over the past 16 months, as well as the crews and the tail numbers of the planes. But the notations were hard to decipher. The career pilot had written his departures and landings in four-letter international airport codes. A few I recognized but most were unfamiliar.

At the end of the evening, my hand was cramped and my head was spinning with all the details. The hour was late, so Wheelock offered us a ride to our hotel. We accepted. Wheelock climbed behind the wheel of his military four-wheel-drive vehicle. We jumped in the back and sat on benches across from young Sandinista soldiers armed with AK-47s. Wheelock then drove us back to our hotel.

The next day, Hasenfus was featured at a news conference before the international press corps. He said he had been working for a CIA operation, with close ties to the office of Vice President George Bush. Hasenfus said two Cuban-Americans, named Max Gomez and Ramon Medina, "worked for the CIA [and] did most of the coordination of these flights."

After the news conference, the Sandinistas handed out photostatic copies of some of the plane's records but not a complete set. I felt that my scribbling might have been worthwhile after all. So, with only part of our mission accomplished, Barger and I returned to Washington.

Back at the AP office, I located a book that listed international airport codes. I also contacted the Federal Aviation Administration for help identifying the planes that Sawyer had listed only by their tail numbers. From the letters and numbers on Sawyer's logs, I could show him crisscrossing the globe from one curious location to another, from flights to Angola to trips to U.S. military bases out West. But most of his flights were to airstrips in Central and South America.

While I was busy following the new leads, the Reagan administration was busy keeping the lid on the Hasenfus story. In response to Hasenfus's allegations about the CIA and Bush's office, the administration issued a flat denial. President Reagan, Vice President Bush and a host of subordinates declared that there was "no U.S. government connection" to the downed aircraft.

On Oct. 11, 1986, assistant secretary of state Elliott Abrams brazenly went on CNN and duped the conservative pundits Rowland Evans and Robert Novak. "I can say first of all there's no Max Gomez," declared Abrams. His presentation suggested that Hasenfus had invented the character who supposedly was running the Ilopango operation.

Evans and Novak fell for the deception. "I've seen a lot of cover-ups in this town, Rowland," Novak noted sagely, "but this doesn't look like a cover-up, and it doesn't because there's no equivocation. ... The so-called Max Gomez, the CIA operative supposedly hired by the CIA or Vice President Bush, doesn't even exist."

But "Max Gomez" did exist, as Abrams surely knew. "Max Gomez" was the cover name for Felix Rodriguez, a Cuban-American CIA veteran who indeed was placed in Central America by Bush's office. Max Gomez's real identity slipped out in the days that followed, as Congress finally began asking more pointed questions about Oliver North's mysterious operations.

There was also another development in the Wanda Palacio case. In the week after the Hasenfus plane was shot down, Palacio was sitting in the office of one of Sen. Kerry's staff investigators. A photo of the dead co-pilot, Wallace Sawyer, flashed onto a TV screen. Palacio grew excited, exclaiming that Sawyer was one of the pilots she had seen loading cocaine onto the Southern Air Transport plane in Barranquilla, Colombia, in early October 1985. Her claim stunned members of Kerry's staff. The identification seemed too convenient. Now, Kerry's investigators had their own doubts about Palacio's credibility.

Though I didn't know about Palacio's contra-cocaine accusations at the time, I was putting the finishing touches on my AP article about Sawyer's many travels. It focused on Sawyer's dozens of flights in Central America and Africa. In the final paragraph, I noted that Sawyer also had made three flights to Barranquilla, Colombia. The dates were Oct. 2, 4, 6, 1985, and he was piloting a Southern Air Transport plane. [AP, Oct. 17, 1986]

Shortly after the article moved on the AP wires, I received a phone call from a member of Kerry's staff. The investigator sounded shocked and asked for more details about the last paragraph of the story. The investigator wouldn't say why he wanted to know more and I didn't press him for a full explanation.

Without me knowing, Sawyer's logs had corroborated a key element of Palacio's testimony. She also passed a polygraph exam. But Weld still was not persuaded to trust Palacio or accept her as a credible witness.

Palacio also grasped how unwelcome her testimony was. "When I was telling that story, it was like a time bomb coming down or something," Palacio stated in a Senate deposition. "It was like this man, Richard Gregorie [an assistant U.S. attorney] was okay until I got to that point. [Then] he didn't say anything. But he just started like not putting much interest on it. ... Everytime, I would mention CIA and guns for drugs, it was like he would just talk about the guns and how did they go, but the drugs were hardly mentioned."[47]

---

[47] In 1996, when Weld was governor of Massachusetts and challenging Kerry for the Senate, the contra-drug allegations were back in the news. I called Weld's office to ask about Palacio, and Weld still put her down. His Justice Department aides, he said, "felt her credibility was roughly that of a wagon load of diseased blankets."

Under Weld's leadership, the criminal division also continued to withhold contra-drug information requested by the Senate in fall 1986. According to Justice Department records, Weld and his subordinates were confronting new demands from Sens. Lugar and Pell, two of the most mild-mannered members of the U.S. Senate. On Oct. 14, 1986, the two senators complained that they had been waiting more than two months for information that the Justice Department had promised "in an expeditious manner."

"To date, no information has been received and the investigation of allegations by the committee, therefore, has not moved very far," Lugar and Pell wrote. "This has led to concern about Justice's willingness to provide information, its responsiveness to our requests and its readiness to cooperate with our investigation. We're disappointed that the Department has not responded in a timely fashion and indeed has not provided any materials."

That bipartisan volley got the Justice Department's attention, but Weld continued to delay. Weld called two meetings that bogged down over peripheral issues, according to Weld's deputy, Mark Richard. "I remember being frustrated because he [Weld] was spending so much time on one [contra-connected fraud] case," Richard explained in a deposition.

Though still not forthcoming with the Senate, Weld was getting nervous. On Oct. 16, 1986, he sent a memo to another assistant, Victoria Toensing, ordering her to "get me a copy of Sen. Kerry's stmt re DOJ not investigating Nicaragua." By Nov. 6, another memo indicated that Weld had opened a special "Nicaragua" file. He wrote in still another memo that "Nicaragua is front burner."

By Nov. 11, Weld was lamenting to his staff that "delay looks awful." He wanted to know where court records from a major San Francisco contra-cocaine criminal case were. That was the so-called Frogman Case, which had caught contra-connected Nicaraguans smuggling cocaine by sea into the Bay Area. Though the Frogman records were among the files sought by Congress, a Kerry investigator told me that Weld's office never delivered those records to the Senate.

Later in November 1986, Weld personally edited a letter to Kerry denying federal protection to Wanda Palacio. "The

Department ... does not provide protection for an informant," the letter read. "It protects a person providing information who agrees to become a witness." But by rejecting Palacio as not credible, Weld had blocked her attempts to become a federal witness and left her exposed to possible retaliation.

The Reagan administration's long pattern of protecting the contras' image at all costs was entering a new phase. With so many secrets threatening to leak out, the president's men were working overtime at the business of cover-up. But for once, their best wasn't enough.

Chapter 5
'Good for the Country'

One of the AP's office assistants looked pained as he approached my desk. I had been on the phone and a persistent caller was demanding that the switchboard put him through to my line. The caller's name was Andy Messing, the office assistant said.

By fall 1986, I had known Messing for four years. A conservative expert on counterinsurgency warfare, Messing was a solidly built, Vietnam veteran who traveled the globe visiting Third World trouble spots. His organization, the National Defense Council, delivered medicines to war zones while Messing collected information that made him a valuable source for government officials and reporters back in Washington.

Messing also was a boisterous admirer of Oliver North. It was North, Messing said, who "was at the cutting edge of the Reagan Doctrine. Reagan talked about anti-communism, but ... it was Ollie North who put meat on the bones of rhetoric."

Normally, Messing exuded confidence, if not bravado, but not that morning. When his call was put through on Nov. 25, 1986, his voice had an edge of urgency bordering on panic. "They've hosed Ollie," Messing exclaimed. National security adviser John Poindexter was also out, he said. I lost my breath at the news.

It was clear that a crisis had been building at the White House since Oct. 5 when the plane carrying Eugene Hasenfus was shot down in Nicaragua. The situation worsened with the Nov. 3

disclosure by a Beirut newspaper that the Reagan administration had been shipping arms to Iran, trading weapons for American hostages held in Lebanon.

But Messing's urgent message meant that the White House bloodletting had begun. I peppered Messing with questions about how and why, but Messing insisted he knew little more and advised simply, "Call Fawn."

The names "Ollie" and "Fawn" had yet to become household words across America, but to those of us who had followed the White House intrigues in Central America, the names had the familiarity that police investigators feel toward subjects of long, frustrating investigations. Indeed, Messing once told me that Oliver North compared my pursuit of his secret network to the old-time TV series, "The Fugitive." In that show, a plodding police detective obsessively pursues a wrongly accused man. In the show's last episode, the fugitive, played by the handsome David Janssen, is vindicated. In North's mind, of course, I was the unappealing detective and he was David Janssen.

After hanging up with Messing, I called the direct line to North's NSC office. North's secretary, Fawn Hall, answered. Her voice was quavering. She seemed to have lost her normal composure. I had met Fawn only once, several months earlier, when Messing and I dropped in at a bar called Portner's in Old Town Alexandria. Hall, a long-legged pretty blonde, was sitting at a tall table with another woman. She seemed startled to meet me on that occasion, but was cooly polite throughout the conversation.

When I reached her on Nov. 25, however, she was not the haughty young woman I had encountered. She sounded flustered, hesitant. Haltingly, she confirmed Messing's account.

It was mornings like this that made work at the AP worth the many frustrations. I rushed the information I had to the national desk where we began to file an urgent series. The story led with the departure of national security adviser Poindexter, but we also included the lesser-known North up high. There was a presumption that the firings were connected to the disclosures about missile sales to Iran. But I argued that we needed to insert North's reported role in secretly arming the Nicaraguan contras, too. President

Reagan was expected to make a formal announcement around noon.

When Reagan finally appeared in the White House press room, he looked stricken and suddenly old, as if some terrible event had pierced his actor's detachment. Reagan briefly announced the departure of Poindexter and North before abruptly turning over the press conference to Attorney General Edwin Meese III. Looking almost jovial, Meese divulged that an internal investigation had discovered that proceeds from the clandestine weapons sales to Iran had been diverted to Central America. The Iran-contra scandal was officially born.

I n the weeks that followed, the major Washington news media tried to make up for lost time on the North stories. Lengthy articles appeared on the front pages. Congress geared up for hearings. A special prosecutor -- an experienced Republican lawyer, Lawrence Walsh -- was named to examine possible crimes, including North's "shredding parties" to destroy incriminating evidence. To get his own handle on events, Reagan appointed a three-member investigative board headed by former Sen. John Tower, R-Texas.

The administration was in retreat, but it was not a rout. Immediately, the administration sought to limit the damage by laying the blame at the feet of North, Poindexter and Robert McFarlane -- while protecting Reagan and other senior officials. Besides the NSC team, it looked like CIA director Casey might have to take a fall, too. But that problem was resolved in December when Casey collapsed with brain cancer. He was unable to answer detailed questions about his activities.[48]

Despite the investigations, the White House also still hid key facts. The president's investigators on the Tower Commission initially concluded that there was no organized contra-support network, a senior investigator for the board told me. But in January 1987, a computer expert accessed hundreds of secret computer messages that White House officials thought had been deleted. The

---

[48] Casey died five months later.

messages established beyond any doubt that North's network indeed had existed. The commission was forced to request a one-month delay to examine the new evidence.

The spreading investigations threatened the CIA, too. The spy agency kept insisting that it was not involved with North's operations. On Feb. 1, 1987, however, one of my AP stories jumped the firebreak that had protected the spy agency. The story stated:

> The Central Intelligence Agency, acknowledging that one of its officers helped funnel weapons to the Nicaraguan rebels despite a congressional ban, is forcing the station chief in Costa Rica to accept early retirement, intelligence sources said. The sources, insisting on anonymity, also said the station chief sent secret messages to then White House aide Oliver L. North and to the aid network over sophisticated encoding devices that North obtained from the National Security Agency, the U.S. government's top-secret communications arm.

The scandal was spreading to the CIA. But the story connecting CIA station chief Joe Fernandez to North's network was my last at the AP. After the Iran-contra scandal broke, I was approached by *Newsweek's* bureau chief Evan Thomas with an offer to become one of the magazine's national correspondents.

Though I had my misgivings about *Newsweek's* commitment to serious journalism, I felt that it was time to leave the AP and all the conflicts that had grown up around the contra reporting. I also thought, naively, that the Iran-contra story might shake the Washington press corps out of its long lethargy and restore the Watergate-style skepticism about national security secrets.

I didn't know at the time, but my arrival at *Newsweek* in February 1987 also coincided with what I now regard as the height of the Iran-contra scandal. Though it might not have seemed like it then, the White House slowly was regaining control. President Reagan shook up the NSC staff, bringing in steadier hands, the likes of Frank Carlucci and Colin Powell. The administration's talented P.R. apparatus resumed its damage control. Reagan's allies in the news media mounted a vigorous rear-guard defense. But most importantly, the six years of "perception management" and "public diplomacy" had sapped the will of leading news organizations and key congressional offices to pursue the Iran-contra investigation diligently.

Cleverly, too, the administration lured the press into a dead-end question: Did Reagan authorize the Iran-contra diversion? There was no clear evidence that he had. So, by framing the issue that way, the White House guaranteed that the congressional hearings would fall flat. Less attention was devoted to the other questions: arms export violations to both Iran and Central America, misuse of government funds to support the contras during the Boland Amendment, the cover-up of contra atrocities and -- possibly the most politically dangerous of all -- contra-drug trafficking.

T o me, the interlocking cover-ups -- the containment of the scandal -- had become the central story by February 1987. In my first week at *Newsweek,* I discovered that the White House was battling to build a new firebreak to prevent the Iran-contra scandal from reaching Reagan. The president's men were especially worried about the illegal arms shipments to Iran in 1985, deals that some senior officials felt could lead to Reagan's impeachment.

As that first week wore on, I supplied the lead reporting for the article that was featured on *Newsweek's* cover. The headline read: "Coverup: To protect the president, NSC staffers say [White House chief of staff] Don Regan ordered them to conceal the early approval of arms sales to Iran by Ronald Reagan." The story began:

> The word was out from Donald Regan himself: "Protect
> the president." So lights burned late in a bustling,
> paper-strewn office in the White House last Nov. 18 as
> Oliver North and his colleagues in the Iran arms deal
> tried to massage the record of the complex weapons-
> for-hostages negotiations into a chronology that would
> minimize Ronald Reagan's role. As no fewer than three
> witnesses described it last week, the challenge was to

portray Reagan as not knowing what he had done until
five months after he actually did it.[49]

The story broke important new ground, moving the criminal
actions to the door of the Oval Office. But the overall press reaction
to the *Newsweek* cover story was negative. Many reporters,
especially those who relied on Don Regan as a source, dismissed it
as an example of amateurish overreaching. The Washington press
corps was already buying into that other kind of cover story -- that
North and his friends had been "cowboys" off on some "rogue"
operation, that Reagan's inner circle didn't know very much about
either the secret contra war or the early Iran arms sales.

I noticed that this press reaction already was starting to
influence attitudes inside *Newsweek.* At the magazine, I heard from
one of my colleagues that the *Newsweek* brass was so ashamed of
the "coverup" cover -- and the hostile reaction it received -- that
extra copies lying around the Washington office were collected and
thrown away.

Congressional Democrats also were shying away from a fight.
In early 1987, fearful of the political fall-out from another
Watergate-style crisis, their leaders decided that the Iran-contra
investigation should avoid an impeachment drama. Since Reagan
was entering the last two years of his term and remained politically
popular, the Democratic leadership told staff investigators that the
scandal should not lead to the Oval Office.

Some of the staff investigators told me that they were
offended by the political limitations that were placed on the
inquiry. "We were never given a green light to go at the White
House," said Tom Polgar, a former CIA officer who worked on the
congressional investigation. "The committees had no heart to take
action that would lead to impeachment or even talk of
impeachment." Years later, former House Speaker Jim Wright
confirmed to me that the Democrats had chosen not to pursue
Reagan out of a mixture of personal sentimentality and political
practicality.

---

[49] *Newsweek,* March 2, 1987.

The major newspapers lacked the stomach, too, for a thorough examination of the most disturbing allegations seeping out of the Iran-contra swamp, especially reports of contra-connected cocaine smuggling. The notion that the U.S. government would sanction the drug trade was more than could be tolerated.

On Feb. 24, 1987, Keith Schneider of *The New York Times* wrote a dismissive story about Sen. Kerry's ongoing contra-drug investigation. Schneider quoted "law enforcement officials" as saying that the contra allegations "have come from a small group of convicted drug traffickers in South Florida who never mentioned contras or the White House until the Iran-contra affair broke in November" 1986.

The *Times'* information, of course, was false and clearly contradicted by the public record. The AP contra-drug story had appeared almost a full year before the Iran-contra scandal broke. Kerry's initial witnesses had surfaced in early 1986. Wanda Palacio's proffer was made in September 1986 -- not after November 1986. Many of the witnesses, including Palacio, also were not "convicted drug traffickers." But the *Times* seemed not to care about the facts.

When the *Times* reporters interviewed Palacio, she immediately sensed their hostility. In her Senate deposition, Palacio described her experience at *The New York Times* office in Miami where, she said, Schneider and a "Cuban man" rudely questioned her story and bullied her about specific evidence for each of her statements. The Cuban man "was talking to me kind of nasty," Palacio recalled. "I got up and left, and this man got all pissed off, Keith Schneider."

The limits of the Iran-contra investigation were being set. On Feb. 27, 1987, the Tower Commission report was released. It criticized President Reagan's "failure of responsibility" and his inattention to detail. "The NSC system will not work unless the President makes it work," the report stated.

Beyond that, the commission accepted Reagan's assurances that he knew nothing about North's efforts to ship military aid to the contras. The president was cleared of any role in a cover-up, too. "The Board is convinced that the President does indeed want the full story to be told," the report read. The commission essentially accepted the notion of high-level misjudgment but not a systemic problem and no serious criminality.

The commission's findings meshed neatly with a secret "plan of action" drafted by chief of staff Regan in the days before Meese's Nov. 25 news conference. That draft plan recommended that "tough as it seems, blame must be put at NSC's door -- rogue operation, going on without President's knowledge or sanction. When suspicions arose, he took charge, ordered investigation, had meeting with top advisers to get at facts." While Regan's summary was untrue -- Reagan would later blurt out that the contra-aid scheme was "my idea to begin with" -- the damage control was working.

How quickly the investigative space was closing down hit home to me on March 10, 1987. I had been asked to attend a dinner at the home of bureau chief Evan Thomas in an exclusive neighborhood in northwest Washington. The guests that night were retired Gen. Brent Scowcroft, who was one of three members of the Tower Commission, and Rep. Dick Cheney, R-Wyo., who was the ranking House Republican on the congressional Iran-contra committee.

At the table also were some of *Newsweek's* top executives and a few of us lowly correspondents. As the catered dinner progressed and a tuxedoed waiter kept the wine glasses full, the guests were politely questioned. Scowcroft, a studious-looking man, fidgeted as if he wanted to get something off his chest. "Maybe I shouldn't say this but," he began with a slight hesitation. He then continued, "If I were advising Admiral Poindexter and he had told the president about the diversion, I would advise him to say that he hadn't."

I quietly put down my fork. Not fully cognizant of the etiquette of these affairs, I asked with undisguised amazement in my voice: "General, you're not suggesting that the admiral should commit perjury, are you?" My question was greeted with an embarrassed silence around the table.

Scowcroft hesitated as if contemplating his answer. But *Newsweek* editor Maynard Parker came to his rescue, tut-tutting my impertinence. "Sometimes," Parker boomed, "you have to do what's good for the country." From around the table, a chorus of guffaws ended the uncomfortable moment. Scowcroft never answered my question.

I dug my hole deeper at *Newsweek* a few months later. I learned that for years, the CIA had sent covert financial assistance to the Nicaraguan Roman Catholic Church and its cardinal, Miguel Obando y Bravo. The purpose of the covert aid was to help Obando and his subordinates undermine the Sandinista government. The instability had the secondary effect of pushing the Sandinistas into more repressive policies and thus strengthened the political case in the United States for more contra military aid.

Several U.S. intelligence sources told me that the money was slipped to Obando and his subordinates through a maze of cutouts in Europe. Some sources thought that Obando might not know precisely where the money originated. But one well-placed Nicaraguan exile told me that he had spoken with Obando about the money and the cardinal had expressed fear that his past receipt of CIA funding would be revealed.

Though I was hesitant to expose a CIA operation inside Nicaragua, Evan Thomas seemed interested in the story. So, I sent a list of questions down to Joseph Contreras, the *Newsweek* correspondent in Central America. After receiving my query, Contreras outlined the questions to the cardinal's aides.

Later, Contreras went to Obando's home in a posh suburb of Managua to deliver the letter with my formal questions. As Contreras waited at the gate, it suddenly swung open and the cardinal, sitting in the front seat of his burgundy Toyota Land Cruiser, blew past the reporter. Contreras made eye contact with the cleric and waved the letter. Obando's driver gunned the engine. Contreras jumped into his own car and followed.

Contreras lost sight of Obando's vehicle, but the reporter guessed correctly that Obando had turned left at one intersection and was headed north toward Managua. Contreras caught up to the cardinal's vehicle at the first stoplight. Obando's driver apparently spotted the reporter and, as the light changed, sped away, veering from lane to lane. The Land Cruiser again disappeared from view.

At the next intersection, Contreras turned right and spotted the vehicle pulled over, with its occupants presumably hoping that

Contreras would turn left. Quickly, the cardinal's vehicle swerved back onto the road and sped back toward Obando's house. Contreras gave up the chase, fearing that any further pursuit might be seen as harassment.

Several days later, having regained his composure, the cardinal met with Contreras. Obando denied receiving CIA money. But Contreras told me that he found Obando's denial unconvincing.

When *Newsweek* published the story of the CIA's covert money in June 1987, Nicaragua's Catholic bishops issued an angry denial. Accuracy in Media, the right-wing media watchdog group secretly funded by the White House, demanded that *Newsweek* conduct an internal investigation of me. Behind the scenes, I learned that assistant secretary of state Elliott Abrams began lobbying *Newsweek's* senior editors to silence my reporting.

But the story was true. Later, the congressional Iran-contra report would refer to $80,000 of a $100,000 payment funneled from North's slush fund to an unnamed "humanitarian organization" in Nicaragua. I subsequently obtained a classified congressional document that identified the "humanitarian organization" as the Roman Catholic Church.

More confirmation came years later in 1996 when former CIA director Robert Gates published his memoirs, *From the Shadows.* Gates acknowledged that the CIA did funnel money through Nicaragua's Catholic Church to finance anti-Sandinista political operations. In an offhand comment about why CIA director Casey lost credibility with Congress, Gates wrote that Casey "did, apparently, cross the line on several occasions, such as continuing to provide covert funding for the Catholic Church in Nicaragua after he promised Congress he would stop."

As summer 1987 wore on, the Iran-contra hearings and their limited goals soon bored the American public. The timid Democrats, who accepted the justifications for the contra war while quibbling about its implementation, framed the debate narrowly: "Is it right to lie to Congress?"

By July, when Oliver North testified, the stage was set for the nation to feel sympathy for anyone who looked like he believed in what he was doing. By standing up to Congress, North did emerge as the star of the hearings. He gave no ground on the rightness of promoting the contra cause -- and the Democrats did not challenge him. North did admit that he lied to Congress during the Aug. 11, 1986, meeting. "I misled the Congress," North conceded. "I misled ... at that meeting ... face to face."

But the dark underbelly of the contra war was still off-limits. When two demonstrators stood up during North's testimony and demanded that the committee "ask about the cocaine," they were dragged off to jail and the panel politely evaded the question of the drug trafficking.

That same month, *The New York Times* was back at the job of discrediting the contra-drug charges. On July 16, 1987, correspondent Schneider reported that except for a few convicted drug smugglers from Miami, the contra-cocaine "charges have not been verified by any other people and have been vigorously denied by several government agencies."

Four days later, Schneider and the *Times* added that "investigators, including reporters from major news outlets, have tried without success to find proof of ... allegations that military supplies may have been paid for with profits from drug smuggling."[50] The *Times* was wrong again, of course. The original AP story in December 1985 had found proof, citing a CIA report describing the contras buying a helicopter with drug money.

But the *Times* had set the tone, writing off the drug allegations as unfounded. The congressional Iran-contra committee followed that lead. Staff investigator Robert A. Bermingham submitted a contra-drug report on July 23, 1987, claiming that "hundreds of persons" had been questioned and vast numbers of government files reviewed, but that no "corroboration of media-exploited allegations of U.S. government-condoned drug trafficking by Contra leaders or Contra organizations" was found. The report, however, listed no names of any interview subjects nor any details about the files examined.

In a 1987 interview with *In These Times,* Schneider seemed more preoccupied with protecting the image of the contras and the U.S. government than getting at the truth. "This story can shatter a

---

[50] *The New York Times,* July 20, 1987.

republic," Schneider said. "I think it is so damaging, the implications so extraordinary, that for us to run the story, it had better be based on the most solid evidence we can amass."[51]

By the end of summer 1987, the Iran-contra scandal was fading fast and the contra-cocaine allegations had become, in the lexicon of Washington's conventional wisdom, "a nutty conspiracy theory." When *Newsweek* hosted new CIA director William Webster at another dinner party in late September 1987, one concern expressed by *Newsweek* executives was that the lingering scandal should not force major changes in the intelligence community.

One senior editor told Webster that the CIA's obligations to inform Congress about its covert actions were intrusive enough. "These procedures seem so elaborate and isn't one of the dangers after something like the Iran-contra business that there'll be all sorts of pressure, particularly from Congress but perhaps from the executive himself, to set up new procedures?" the editor asked. Before Webster could respond, the editor answered his own question: "These things are self-correcting to a great degree. The publicity, the appointment of someone like yourself." Webster did not disagree.

During the Iran-contra hearings, however, I began finding documents about the public diplomacy operations stuck in the press packets, the piles of declassified documents released each day before the hearings. In the testimony, the papers were rarely mentioned and they received little notice from a Washington press corps not eager to highlight how it had been manipulated. But I kept track of the curious documents, setting them aside in a special file. The evidence suggested that the public diplomacy pressure was far more organized than I had understood.

It also was clear that there were some congressional investigators who considered the public diplomacy issue important. On Sept. 30, 1987, a legal opinion by the congressional General Accounting Office concluded that the Public Diplomacy Office's "white propaganda" operation amounted to "prohibitied

---

[51] *In These Times,* Aug. 5, 1987.

covert propaganda activities designed to influence the media and the public to support the administration's Latin American policies."

In October 1987, as the congressional Iran-contra committee wrote its final report, I learned that a draft chapter was prepared on the CIA's role in manipulating U.S. public opinion. But Republicans fought hard to exclude the story about the public diplomacy apparatus. The GOP had leverage because the Democrats hoped to convince three moderate Republicans -- Sens. Warren Rudman, William Cohen and Paul Trible -- to sign the majority report and thus give the findings a gloss of bipartisanship. One of the demands from the GOP moderates was that the draft chapter on public diplomacy be deleted.

As a compromise, some parts of the draft chapter were inserted in the executive summary, but the full chapter with a detailed explanation of the public diplomacy operation was left on the editing room floor. The American people were thus spared the draft chapter's troubling conclusion: that a domestic covert propaganda apparatus had existed, run by "one of the CIA's most senior specialists, sent to the NSC by Bill Casey, to create and coordinate an inter-agency public-diplomacy mechanism [that] did what a covert CIA operation in a foreign country might do. [It] attempted to manipulate the media, the Congress and public opinion to support the Reagan administration's policies."

Though the public was denied the full story, Otto Reich's old office at the State Department became the only institutional casualty of the Iran-contra scandal. S/LPD was shut down. Afterwards, however, one senior public diplomacy operative told me wryly, "they can shut down the public diplomacy office, but they can't shut down public diplomacy."

The measure of public diplomacy's success could be seen, too, in the weakness of the Washington press corps little more than a decade after Watergate. In October 1987, when the congressional Iran-contra report was released, bureau chief Evan Thomas said *Newsweek's* New York editors were not interested in doing much on it. "We don't want more than two sentences on the report," Thomas told me as we walked toward the office elevators.

Thomas didn't even want me to read the report, but he added that a story could be done if I found something new that the report had missed. I wasn't quite sure how I would know what was not in the report if I didn't read it, but I kept that concern to myself. By the end of the week, I had cajoled the magazine editors into expanding the story of the Iran-contra findings to one page.

T he year 1987 had proved to be a pivotal one for American journalism. The year started with the prospect that the Iran-contra scandal had blown open a route back to the serious work of the 1970s, when reporters challenged government secrecy and informed the public about issues important to the democratic process.

But six years of the Reagan administration's "perception management" proved too much. The relentless propaganda, supported by a growing right-wing news media and influential conservatives in the mainstream press, prevailed. The timidity of the congressional Democrats made the work all the easier. By year's end, those of us who had pushed the Iran-contra stories were more embattled and more in jeopardy than ever.

In 1988, however, there was still hope. Sen. Kerry was pressing his contra-drug investigation. Special prosecutor Lawrence Walsh was pushing the Iran-contra probe. Facing indictment, North and several other administration officials could be expected to disclose more information as part of their courtroom defenses.

The presidential campaign was another potential forum for seeking the truth. Vice President Bush was ducking questions about his involvement in Iran-contra as well as the contra-cocaine controversy. Bush's Iran-contra defense -- that he was "out of the loop" -- had never sounded very plausible, especially given the evidence that his office had placed Felix Rodriguez in Central America and that Rodriguez had been briefing Bush's national security adviser Donald Gregg, another former CIA man.

Rodriguez and Gregg acknowledged talking regularly but insisted that they never discussed contra re-supply. That claim was undercut, however, by a memo that listed "resupply of the contras" as one meeting topic. But the two former CIA men -- and Bush, the former CIA director -- stuck to their stories.

Other contra-connected sources told me that Bush's office had an important early role in the contra re-supply operations, that the early lines of authority actually went through Gregg even before North emerged as a key player. The sources connected the early Bush pipeline through Rodriguez and other Cuban-Americans to a mysterious arms warehouse set up in San Pedro Sula, Honduras, where millions of dollars in weapons from communist Eastern Europe were stockpiled for the contras. Documentary evidence, including North's notebooks, indicated that U.S. officials suspected the warehouse was financed from drug proceeds.

My investigation of the warehouse led to some testy interviews with Bush's aides, but eventually the story ran in *Newsweek's* edition of May 23, 1988. The story began:

> From outside, they were three anonymous warehouses in San Pedro Sula, the steamy industrial capital of Honduras. Inside, they were stacked high with cases of weapons from the East bloc -- $20 million worth, by one estimate, originally destined for the Nicaraguan contras. That's what remains of an enterprise called the Arms Supermarket, and it is generating new and potentially damaging questions about the role of Vice President George Bush and his staff in keeping the contras supplied during the congressional aid cutbacks of 1984-86, before Oliver North set up the Iran-contra connections. The Arms Supermarket was an unlikely partnership involving longtime CIA arms merchants, agents of the Israeli Mossad secret service and the intelligence arm of the Honduran military. And according to government documents and high-level administration officials, it was financed at least in part with drug money.

The Bush camp was furious with the story and complained bitterly to senior *Newsweek* editors about me. One day, I arrived at work and ran into Evan Thomas in the corridor that connects the *Newsweek* offices. He pulled me aside and told me that editor Maynard Parker was livid. At a dinner party hosted by Richard Holbrooke the night before, Parker sat next to Donald Gregg, who spent much of the evening denouncing me. I had ruined the editor's evening.

K erry's contra-cocaine investigation was faring little better. His public hearings with drug smugglers and U.S. officials from Central America drew P.R. attacks from administration loyalists who repeated the same theme over and over: that the traffickers were inventing their contra-drug allegations to get reduced sentences.

The theme worked because Washington-based reporters never seemed to question the logic of the get-out-jail-fast argument. If anyone had bothered to think for a minute, the theory would have made no sense. Since Reagan's Justice Department controlled the prisons, convicts who did implicate the contras were likely to receive no leniency and, in fact, no witness did benefit from linking the contras or the CIA to the drug trade. Still, reporters accepted the administration's claim and buried the contra-drug stories.

That pattern continued even when Kerry issued his final contra-drug report on April 13, 1989. Kerry's report was a remarkable historical document. It established that the Reagan administration gave contra-supply contracts to four companies that were either under indictment for drug trafficking or listed as suspected smugglers in law enforcement computers. Kerry's probe also confirmed that pilots used for contra arms flights carried cocaine into the United States as well as guns to Central America. And Kerry found that drug kingpins had contributed heavily to the contra cause, in hopes of currying favor with Washington.

"It is clear that individuals who provided support for the contras were involved in drug trafficking, the supply network of the contras was used by drug trafficking organizations, and elements of the contras themselves knowingly received financial and material assistance from drug traffickers," the Kerry report said. "In each case, one or another agency of the U.S. government had information regarding the involvement either while it was occurring, or immediately thereafter."

Never before had an official U.S. government report leveled direct charges that a U.S. intelligence operation had collaborated with drug smugglers. But instead of front-page treatment, *The New*

York Times, The Washington Post and the *Los Angeles Times* all wrote brief accounts about the Senate findings and stuck them deep inside their pages. The *Times* article, 850 words long, landed on page 8. The *Post* put its kiss-off article by Michael Isikoff on A20. The *Los Angeles Times* chose page 11. The findings earned Kerry a reputation around Washington as a nut case. In a "Conventional Wisdom Watch," *Newsweek* dubbed him a "randy conspiracy buff."

When Oliver North went on trial in 1989, Evan Thomas made clear once more that *Newsweek* had little interest. I was told that senior editors did not deem the North trial a story worthy of first-person coverage. Again, it appeared to me that the top editors in New York were letting their ideological sympathies cloud their journalistic judgments. Other major news organizations, I knew, were planning coverage.

I recognized, too, that the New York decision put me in a tough spot. I sensed that whatever happened, I would lose out. If I challenged the no-coverage ruling, I would invite more antagonism from New York. If I went along with their call and the North story came to dominate the daily news, I would get blamed for missing it.

My solution to the dilemma was to work on other stories during the day but arrange to have the daily North-trial transcripts delivered to my house every night. Usually, a motorcycle messenger would arrive with the packet at about 10 p.m. I would then read the transcripts and look for leads that other reporters might have missed.

The North trial did become a big story with most major news organizations playing it on page one or leading their evening newscasts with developments. *Newsweek* was one of the few national news organizations not in attendance. The transcripts proved handy, however, because they not only gave me the full flavor of the testimony but they included bench conferences between the judge and the lawyers that could not be heard in the courtroom. From the written record, I was able to develop several stories about the collapsing Reagan cover stories. I also managed to convince *Newsweek* editors to run at least brief articles on the

Periscope page. But my enterprise did not help me with the magazine's top management.

In early 1990, Evan Thomas told me that Maynard Parker would start yelling whenever my name was mentioned. Thomas said I had become a disruption to *Newsweek's* Washington office. He said he no longer wanted me around. I told Thomas that it made no sense for an investigative reporter to work for a company that wasn't interested in his stories. I agreed to leave *Newsweek.*

But beyond my personal disappointment, I was troubled by what I saw happening to the Washington news media. I concluded that the battle for the truth about the 1980s -- and in a larger sense, the struggle for a principled press corps -- had been lost. "Perception management," it seemed to me, had won.

Chapter 6
Tale of Two Scandals

In crucial ways, Watergate, the signature scandal of the 1970s, and Iran-contra, the signature scandal of the 1980s, were opposites. Watergate showed how the national institutions of American democracy -- the Congress, the courts and the press -- could check a gross abuse of power by the Executive. A short dozen years later, the Iran-contra scandal demonstrated how those same institutions failed to protect the nation from serious White House wrongdoing.

Watergate had been part of a brief national awakening which exposed Cold War abuses -- serious presidential crimes, lies about the Vietnam War and assassination plots hatched at the CIA. The Iran-contra cover-up marked the restoration of a Cold War status quo in which crimes, both domestic and international, could be committed by the Executive while the Congress and the press looked the other way.

The last significant hope that the story might turn out differently rested with the man who put himself in the way of the cover-up, Iran-contra independent counsel Lawrence Walsh. A tall and formal man then in his 70s, Walsh was an unlikely candidate for the job of exposing wrongdoing by a GOP administration. He was a lifelong Republican who had served in President Eisenhower's Justice Department and was a supporter of President Reagan's foreign policies.

But for Walsh, the Iran-contra experience was a life-changing one, as his investigation penetrated one wall of lies only to be confronted with another and another – lies not just from Oliver North and his cohorts but lies from nearly every senior administration official who spoke with investigators.

In *Firewall: The Iran-Contra Conspiracy and Cover-up,* Walsh detailed his six-year battle to break through the "firewall" that White House officials built around President Reagan and Vice President Bush. According to Walsh, the cover-up conspiracy took formal shape at a meeting of Reagan and his top advisers in the Situation Room at the White House on Nov. 24, 1986, the day before the Iran-contra diversion was announced.

The meeting's principal point of concern was how to handle the troublesome fact that Reagan had approved illegal arms sales to Iran in fall 1985, before any covert-action finding had been signed. The act was an apparent felony -- a violation of the Arms Export Control Act -- and possibly an impeachable offense.

Though virtually everyone at the meeting knew that Reagan had approved those shipments through Israel, Attorney General Edwin Meese III announced what would become the cover story. According to Walsh's narrative, Meese

> told the group that although [NSC adviser Robert] McFarlane had informed [Secretary of State George] Shultz of the planned shipment, McFarlane had not informed the president. ... [White House chief of staff Don] Regan, who had heard McFarlane inform the president and who had heard the president admit to Shultz that he knew of the shipment of Hawk [anti-aircraft] missiles, said nothing. Shultz and [Defense Secretary Caspar] Weinberger, who had protested the shipment before it took place, said nothing. [Vice President George] Bush, who had been told of the shipment in advance by McFarlane, said nothing. [CIA director William] Casey, who [had] requested that the president sign the retroactive finding to authorize the CIA-facilitated delivery, said nothing. [NSC adviser John] Poindexter, who had torn up the finding, said

nothing. Meese asked whether anyone knew anything else that hadn't been revealed. No one spoke.

When Shultz returned to the State Department, he dictated a note to his aide, Charles Hill, who wrote down that Reagan's men were "rearranging the record." They were trying to protect the president through a "carefully thought out strategy" that would "blame it on Bud" McFarlane.

As part of that strategy, virtually all of Reagan's top advisers gave false and misleading testimony to Congress and prosecutors. Shultz prefaced his misleading testimony by telling Congress that he lived by the principle that "trust is the coin of the realm."[52] The administration accounts essentially blamed the illegalities on Oliver North and his bosses at the National Security Council, McFarlane and Poindexter. Pretty much everyone else -- at the CIA, Defense Department, the Vice President's Office and the White House -- claimed ignorance of any crimes.

By summer 1987, Congress was so eager to accept the theory of a rogue operation that it rushed ahead with televised hearings designed to make North and his NSC superiors, McFarlane and Poindexter, the primary culprits, the so-called "men of zeal." Without even questioning North ahead of time, the Iran-contra committee granted the charismatic Marine officer and his pipe-smoking boss, Poindexter, limited immunity. North then testified that he was the "fall guy" in the White House scheme. The Democrats, however, still fell for it.

Indeed, the story might have stopped there but for the work of Walsh and his small team of lawyers. Yet Walsh's investigation was hampered from the start by the earlier congressional mistakes, hostility from key elements of the news media and Executive Branch manipulation of national security secrets. White House claims of national security forced Walsh to narrow his cases to more technical issues, such as lying to Congress and destruction of

---

[52] In 1991, when Iran-contra prosecutor Walsh confronted Shultz with documentary evidence of his false testimony, Shultz "repeatedly admitted that significant parts of his testimony to Congress had been completely wrong." [See Walsh's *Final Report of the Independent Counsel for Iran/Contra Matters.*]

documents. On May 4, 1989, however, Walsh won North's conviction on three counts of obstruction and accepting an illegal gratuity.

Still, Walsh's larger investigation was in trouble. In fall 1989, Walsh unsuccessfully pleaded with President Bush to loosen the "standards for the release of information to the courts." Otherwise, Walsh wrote, "we face the likelihood that former high officials cannot be tried for crimes related to their conduct in public office. ... It seems clear that if we continue in this effort to withhold this information we lose a much more important national value – the rule of law."

A year later, the congressional immunity came back to haunt Walsh's hard-won conviction of North. Conservative judges on the federal appeals court, Reagan loyalists Laurence Silberman and David Sentelle, exploited the immunity opening to reverse North's conviction. Sentelle, a protégé of Sen. Jesse Helms, R-N.C., also joined in another decision in 1991 to wipe out Poindexter's conviction.[53]

In his book, a frustrated Walsh described the GOP majority on the U.S. Appeals Court for the District of Columbia as "a powerful band of Republican appointees [who] waited like the strategic reserves of an embattled army, ... a force cloaked in the black robes of those dedicated to defining and preserving the rule of law."

Still, despite the legal and political obstacles, Walsh's investigation broke through the White House cover-up in 1991. Almost by accident, as Walsh's staff was double-checking some long-overdue document requests, the lawyers discovered hidden notes belonging to Weinberger and other senior officials. The notes made clear that there was widespread knowledge of the 1985 illegal shipments to Iran and that a major cover-up had been orchestrated by the Reagan and Bush administrations.

---

[53] In 1992, Chief Justice William Rehnquist appointed Sentelle to run the three-judge panel that selects independent counsels. Sentelle then named Kenneth Starr and other conservative lawyers to investigate President Clinton and his aides.

The belated discovery led to indictments against senior CIA officials and Weinberger. Congressional Republicans, led by Sen. Bob Dole, R-Kan., reacted by angrily denouncing Walsh and calling for an end to his investigation. Dole's eruption surprised Walsh, who claimed to have long respected Dole as a Republican leader.

"I had once felt a certain kinship with Dole as a fellow mainstream Republican," Walsh wrote. "Perhaps because of my previous favorable impression of Dole, I was doubly shocked that he would so openly intrude in a federal prosecution. ... This type of influence-peddling is generally left to party fixers, who are important within a political organization itself but not usually the public party leaders."

By 1991, the Washington press corps also had grown hostile, complaining that Walsh's probe had taken too long and had cost too much. The conservative *Washington Times* and the *Wall Street Journal's* editorial page fired near-daily barrages at Walsh often over trivial matters, such as his spending on first-class air fare and room-service meals. Key columnists and editorial writers -- along with television pundits David Brinkley and Christopher Matthews -- joined in the Walsh bashings.

Some journalists mocked Walsh as a modern-day Captain Ahab from *Moby Dick*. In his own book, however, Walsh compared his trying experience to another maritime classic, Ernest Hemingway's *Old Man and the Sea.* In that story, an aging fisherman hooks a giant marlin and, after a long battle, secures the fish to the side of his boat. On the way back to port, sharks attack the marlin, devour its flesh and deny the fisherman his prize. "As the independent counsel, I sometimes felt like the old man," Walsh wrote, "more often, I felt like the marlin."

More seriously, the congressional and media attacks effectively limited Walsh's ability to pursue what appeared to be other false statements by senior administration officials. Those perjury inquiries could have unraveled other major national-security mysteries of the 1980s and helped correct the history of the era.

For instance, the Walsh team had strong suspicions that Bush's national security adviser, ex-CIA officer Donald Gregg, had lied when he testified that he was unaware of North's contra resupply operation. Gregg's close friend, Felix Rodriguez, was working with North in Central America and called Gregg after each contra delivery.

There already had been problems with Gregg's story, including the discovery of a vice presidential office memo describing a planned meeting with Rodriguez about "resupply of the contras." In 1989, Gregg tried to explain the memo away as a typo that should have read, "resupply of the copters."

In *Firewall*, Walsh disclosed that Gregg's stonewall suffered another crack when Col. James Steele, U.S. military adviser to El Salvador, flunked a polygraph test when he denied his own role in shipping weapons to the contras. Confronted with those results and incriminating notes from North's diaries, "Steele admitted not only his participation in the arms deliveries but also his early discussion of these activities with Donald Gregg," Walsh wrote. Gregg also failed his own polygraph when he denied knowledge of the contra supply operation.[54]

Walsh encountered other problems when he interviewed former President Reagan in Los Angeles on July 24, 1992. Reagan, known to be suffering from Alzheimer's disease, claimed to have forgotten virtually every fact about the Iran-contra scandal, according to a transcript of the deposition. "It's like I wasn't president at all," Reagan said in response to one inquiry.

Walsh accepted that Reagan's memory loss was a consequence of the disease, although Reagan answered in rich detail when questioned about coincidental events not connected to alleged Iran-contra crimes. Despite Reagan's unresponsive Iran-contra answers, the deposition did offer a look at unreleased Reagan diary entries that were read into the record. The diary demonstrated that Reagan was intimately involved with the Iran-contra operations and fully aware that some of his actions violated the law.

Yet, when Walsh and his prosecutors questioned Reagan about even basic facts that connected to the scandal, the ex-president

---

[54] Gregg flunked, too, when he denied involvement in the so-called October Surprise operation in 1980, an alleged secret CIA-GOP operation to undermine President Carter's Iran hostage negotiations and secure Reagan's election. [For more details on Gregg's alleged October Surprise role, see Robert Parry's *Trick or Treason*.]

asserted a near-total lack of memory. Asked if George Shultz was secretary of state in Reagan's second term, Reagan answered, "I think so, but I can't swear anymore."

"During your second term was Bud McFarlane the national security adviser?" asked a prosecutor.

"I can't tell you or remember when Bud left that job," Reagan responded. Robert "Bud" McFarlane resigned on Dec. 5, 1985, nearly a year into Reagan's second term.

On more substantive questions, Walsh's team read entries from Reagan's diary to refresh his memory about the Iran-contra arms-for-hostage deals, but that didn't help. Walsh asked about a Feb. 26, 1985, entry in which Reagan wrote, "Assad seems to be making effort to get four kidnap victims back from Hezbollah."

Reagan answered, "You know something? I'm trying to remember now who was Assad." Hafez Assad, of course, was the president of Syria.

At another point, Reagan was reminded that "you had a task force on counter-terrorism. Do you remember? I think Vice President Bush headed it."

Reagan answered, "I had forgotten about that."

When asked a question about a late July 1985 diary entry about "P.M. Nakasone sending emissary, very hush hush," Reagan needed to be reminded that Yasuhiro Nakasone was then prime minister of Japan.

"I don't know what that would have been about," Reagan said.

"All right, sir," Walsh said.

"I'm very embarrassed," responded Reagan. "I'm sorry. ... It's like I wasn't president at all."

Reagan, however, did admit that he approved a plan to have Israel ship U.S. weapons to Iran and then have Israel restocked by the United States, a key question in the legal issue of whether Reagan violated the Arms Export Control Act in 1985. "I have a dim memory of, through Israel, they would make available the weapons to the Iranians, but we would replace the weapons to Israel," Reagan said. "I do remember that we did something of that kind and we replaced with Israel what they had sent the Iranian people."

But Reagan's memory was clearer about non-Iran-contra events that occurred in the same time period. When Walsh tried to question Reagan about a key Iran-contra discussion in Geneva in mid-November 1985, Walsh set the stage by mentioning the summit there with Soviet leader Mikhail Gorbachev.

The ex-president suddenly launched into a detailed account of the Gorbachev meeting. Gorbachev "replied to our people in the invitation that no, he wanted it in a neutral country." Reagan continued about Gorbachev:

> He didn't say no to a summit meeting, but he wanted it neutral. We said yes and he was the one that then said by virtue of that, in Switzerland we have the meeting and so we agreed on that. We had quite a meeting there with him and his people. I can remember a few things about that because of the oddity of it. We decided that the subject of the summit meeting would be mutual reduction of armaments and he agreed on that ...

> Then the first meeting with him, real meeting, it was going to be the first meeting in a big home along Lake Geneva and at a table like this only a little longer he and his team on one side and me and my team on the other to deal with the weapons. I told my people what I was going to do so they wouldn't be surprised. As everybody started to sit down, I looked across the table at him and I said, 'Why don't we let our two teams start this discussion about the reduction of the weaponry and all, and why don't you and I get some fresh air? He was out of his chair before I finished that sentence, and there he was. So, he and I left and we walked about a 150 yards down across the lawn to the lake where there was a beach house, and again I had told our people about this.

> It was cold, a real wintry day and that beach house had a big roaring fire going in the fireplace. We entered and in there were the two translators. I stopped him before we even sat down and looked right at him and I said,

'I'm going to give you a quotation that's not mine.
Someone else has said that we mistrust each other
because we're armed.' I said, 'I believe we're armed
because we mistrust each other.' Then I said, ...
'wouldn't it be fine if we would spend just as much
time trying to find out the reasons for our mistrust?'...
I said to him that we should do this and I said, 'The
only alternative to this is we resume the arms race.'
Then, looking him right in the eye, I said, 'That is a
race you can't win. There is no way we're going to
permit you to be superior to us in weaponry.'

So he took that and we sat down and the meeting went
under way for an hour and a half. Then, I figured that
we'd better get back up to the rest of our people, so we
got up and we started back up the hill.

Finishing his detailed account of the summit, the ex-president
assured the lawyers that his fuzzy memory about Iran-contra was
not simply convenient. "I'm not fooling when I say that when I
started reading the diary the other day, I couldn't even remember
writing the things that I was writing about." Then, when the
questioning turned to the key Iran-contra meeting held during the
same Geneva trip, Reagan responded, "I don't have a memory of
that."

After Reagan returned to Washington from the Geneva
summit, the possible release of hostages dominated White House
meetings. The diary reflected Reagan's close personal involvement.
"We have an undercover thing going by way of an Iranian which
could get them [the hostages] sprung momentarily," Reagan wrote
on Nov. 22, 1985. "Still sweating out our undercover effort to get
hostages out of Beirut," he wrote the next day. When asked about
those entries, Reagan stated, "I just don't have a clear-cut memory
of the specific meetings or anything on it."

On Dec. 5, 1985, Reagan noted in his diary a sensitive national
security briefing: "Subject our undercover effort to free our five
hostages held by terrorists in Lebanon. It is a complex undertaking
with only a few in on it. I won't even write it up in this diary what

we are up to." But in the deposition, Reagan asserted no memory of this operation.

One of Reagan's few acknowledged Iran-contra recollections came from his anger over the law prohibiting him from selling weapons to Iran, a predicament that he blamed on Congress. "I was just madder than the devil about them [the Congress] and their doing this to us," Reagan testified. "This was why something like in this-and-that supposed law about sending the arms, I felt that as far as being the president that a thing of this kind to get back five human beings from potential murder, yes, I would violate that other -- that law."

Yet, when asked about the famous May 1986 trip to Iran by McFarlane and Oliver North, Reagan replied, "What?"

"Do you remember McFarlane going to Teheran?"

"No, I can't say that I do."

Walsh also read diary entries that Reagan wrote in November 1986 when the Iran-contra story broke. Strangely, the private diary entries tracked with the false cover stories that Reagan and his advisers were spreading publicly. On Nov. 7, Reagan wrote, "there is a discussion of how to handle the press who are off on a wild story built on an unfounded story originating in Beirut that we bought hostage [David] Jacobsen's freedom with weapons for Iran."

Asked about that entry during the deposition, Reagan responded: "Well, I don't remember it, but I agree with it."

In his diary entry on Nov. 12, 1986, Reagan lashed out again at the press coverage of the Iran arms-for-hostages deal. "The whole inescapable bilge about hostages and Iran has gotten totally out of hand," he wrote. "The media looks like it's trying to create another Watergate."

In 1992, when Walsh's questioning turned to secret funding for the Nicaraguan contra rebels, Reagan again denied any specific memories. He said he could not even recall the name of the Boland Amendment that barred U.S. military aid to the contras. "I don't remember the details at all," Reagan testified. But he added that he remembered how angry the legal restriction had made him. "I'm still a little mad right now," Reagan testified.

After the deposition, Walsh decided not to pursue any legal action against the ailing ex-president. The imponderable question from Reagan's testimony was whether the Alzheimer's disease truly had erased his recollections of the Iran-contra crimes or whether Reagan was taking advantage of his deteriorating memory to recall only the facts that he chose to.

Nevertheless, his limited responses and the diary entries left little doubt that Reagan was aware that his decision to ship missiles secretly to Iran through Israel was illegal. But the wily ex-president also made the correct calculation that even if he were caught, he still would be able to fight -- or to finesse -- any legal consequences.[55]

Feeling pressure in 1992 to bring the investigation to a conclusion, Walsh concentrated on the pending perjury cases against Weinberger and CIA officials, Clair George and Duane Clarridge. But as those cases moved forward, anti-Walsh attacks multiplied in Congress and in the Washington media.

The Republican independent counsel also infuriated the GOP when he obtained a second indictment of Weinberger on the Friday before the 1992 elections. The indictment contained documents revealing that President Bush had been lying for years with his claim that he was "out of the loop" on the Iran-contra decisions. The ensuing furor dominated the last several days of the campaign and sealed Bush's defeat at the hands of Bill Clinton. Walsh had discovered, too, that Bush had withheld his own notes about the Iran-contra affair, a discovery that elevated the president to a possible criminal subject of the investigation.

After the election, Dole was madder than ever. In a Nov. 9, 1992, letter, Dole demanded that Walsh fire James Brosnahan, a San Francisco lawyer who had been brought in to try the Weinberger case. Dole attacked Brosnahan's past involvement in

---

[55] In his final report, Walsh criticized Reagan's role in overseeing "the creation of a false account of the Iran arms sales to be disseminated to members of Congress and the American people." Reagan's deposition was one of scores of Iran-contra documents that I requested that the National Archives process and release. Initially, my request was turned down on the unusual grounds that Reagan's performance was so embarrassing that it would constitute a violation of his privacy. The National Archives reversed that decision in spring 1999 and made the deposition available in its entirety.

Democratic politics. When Walsh refused, Dole's spokesman Walt Riker said Walsh's response did "not address the active, liberal agenda of Mr. Brosnahan and, obviously, it is politics at its worst."

On Nov. 11, four GOP senators followed Dole's urging and demanded a special prosecutor to investigate Walsh, the special prosecutor, particularly over whether the new Weinberger indictment had been timed for political reasons, though there was no evidence that was the case.

"It is time for Mr. Walsh and his staff to plead guilty to playing politics for their taxpayer-funded inquisitions," Dole declared in one speech. "As of August [1992], Walsh had billed taxpayers for more than $5.6 million for office space, $881,000 for incidental expenses, $401,000 for maintenance, $698,000 for contractual services, and a whopping $665,000 for per diem and subsistence, including $300,000 for personal living expenses and an estimated $65,000 in room-service meals."

By December 1992, Dole was demanding a list of all Walsh's employees so the Republicans could mount personal investigations and judge each "employee's objectivity and impartiality." The senator also obtained information about the staff's pay levels. "With the election over, maybe the Walsh political operatives will decide to pack it in," Dole wished. "The only mischief left for them is more humiliating courtroom defeats."

Facing an expanding Iran-contra probe that finally looked to be breaking through six years of lies, Bush resorted to the final weapon in his arsenal. On Christmas Eve 1992, Bush destroyed the Iran-contra probe once and for all by pardoning Weinberger and five other convicted or indicted defendants, including CIA men Duane Clarridge, Clair George and Alan Fiers.

"George Bush's misuse of the pardon power made the cover-up complete," Walsh wrote. "What set Iran-contra apart from previous political scandals was the fact that a cover-up engineered in the White House of one president and completed by his successor prevented the rule of law from being applied to the perpetrators of criminal activity of constitutional dimension."

The pardon strategy also succeeded because some leading congressional Democrats, including House Speaker Tom Foley, and influential members of the Washington news media signaled acceptance of the Weinberger pardon before it was granted. Even supposed "liberals" in the media hailed the decision to spare Weinberger, who was a popular figure within the Washington Establishment.

Washington Post columnist Richard Cohen spoke for many of the capital's insiders. Cohen described how impressed he had been that Weinberger would push his own shopping cart at the Georgetown Safeway, often called the "social Safeway" because so many members of Washington's Establishment shopped there. "Based on my Safeway encounters, I came to think of Weinberger as a basic sort of guy, candid and no nonsense -- which is the way much of official Washington saw him," Cohen wrote in praise of the pardon. "Cap, my Safeway buddy, walks, and that's all right with me."[56]

Bush's decision also spared other Republican superstars, such as Colin Powell and possibly Bush himself, from the embarrassment of testifying in court and opening themselves to possible perjury charges. After Bush left office in 1993, the ex-president reneged, too, on an understanding that he would submit to a full-scale interview with Walsh about Bush's real involvement in the scandal. Walsh had postponed the questioning until after the presidential election to spare Bush from the distraction. But once out of office, Bush refused to cooperate. Signaling the widespread disdain for Walsh's long Iran-contra probe, the nation's newspapers barely mentioned Bush's non-testimony.

After Bush ducked the full-scale interview, "my immediate instinct was to use the grand jury and subpoena Bush," Walsh wrote. "In this I was alone. The staff unanimously opposed the use of the grand jury, arguing that to do so would exaggerate public expectations and would appear retaliatory. ... I gave up. We then turned our full attention to our final report."

With Walsh's battered staff unwilling to press forward, the Iran-contra cover-up had finally succeeded. But the concealment could not have worked if the other institutions of Washington -- Congress, the courts and the press -- had not helped.

---

[56] *The Washington Post,* Dec. 30, 1992.

By early 1993, the Washington press corps flaunted a strange pride in defiantly not wanting to know the truth about the Iran-contra scandal. *The Washington Post* Sunday magazine summed up the feelings of the national media insiders. Writer Marjorie Williams explained, "In the utilitarian political universe of Washington, consistency like Walsh's is distinctly suspect. It began to seem ... rigid of him to care so much. So un-Washington. Hence the gathering critique of his efforts as vindictive, extreme. Ideological. ... But the truth is that when Walsh finally goes home, he will leave a perceived loser."[57]

The Iran-contra cover-up marked a historic reversal for the Washington press corps -- from protecting the Constitution in Watergate to protecting government criminality in the Iran-contra scandal. The hip sneering tone that *The New Republic* popularized in the 1980s could now be heard and read everywhere.

In the years that followed, bits and pieces of the real history would slip out in memoirs or in documents. I would spend many hours at the National Archives in College Park, Md., poring through recently declassified papers, piecing together new parts of the story. They would become grist for articles in *The Consortium* on the Internet or in *iF Magazine*. I learned about more unsavory connections, more about contra-connected drug trafficking, more about terrorists working for the U.S. government.

But these intriguing stories were of little or no interest to the new Washington press corps. In the early days of the Clinton administration, the media was all "edge" and "attitude." Still, to me, the pulling together of these scattered pieces of evidence was a chance to salvage some of the "lost history" and make some sense of what I had witnessed. They also would lead to new evidence about one of the worst crimes from the Reagan-Bush era, the U.S. government's complicity in drug trafficking.

---

[57] *The Washington Post,* April 11, 1993.

Chapter 7
Cuban Connections

The Money Launderer

On the afternoon of Oct. 2, 1987, Cuban-American John F. Molina and a Panamanian companion, Enrique DelValle, had finished clearing up business with lawyers at the firm of Sucre y Sucre in Panama City. Molina, a 46-year-old with the looks of a Latin Sean Connery and a fondness for pretty women, was tired of his work as a money launderer for the Nicaraguan contras. He wanted out.

The process of extricating himself from the complex arrangements had brought him to Sucre y Sucre, the firm that had created shell corporations for the contra arms supply network. Molina and DelValle spent the morning closing down the shell companies. By the afternoon, their work done, the two men sauntered out of the firm's stylish Panama City offices. They stepped out onto the busy street and climbed into Molina's red Mitsubishi four-wheel drive vehicle.

Without their noticing, a young bushy-haired man with a moustache darted toward the car. The young man raised a .32-caliber pistol, pointed it at Molina's head and fired three times. Molina slumped across the front seat. For a moment, DelValle thought Molina was reaching toward the opposite side door. Then, DelValle realized that John Molina was dead.

The gunman fled on foot. He was chased and cornered by an armed bystander, and was arrested by Panamanian police. In custody, the killer identified himself as Maximillano Casa Sanchez, a Colombian hit man. Casa Sanchez told police that Colombian narcotraffickers had sent him to Panama to rub out Molina over a drug debt.

In the following days, *La Republica,* a newspaper allied with dictator Manuel Noriega, played up the drug angle -- and Molina's ties to the Cruzada Civilista, an organization of upper-and-middle-class citizens critical of Noriega. The newspaper noted that in the 1970s, Molina was president of UniBank, or the Union de Bancos, the Panamanian outpost for the WFC Corp., a shadowy money-laundering network run by Miami-based Cuban-Americans with close ties to the CIA.

But the Molina case had a more contemporary CIA connection. At the time of his death, Molina was the financial architect behind a mysterious arms warehouse in the Honduran industrial center of San Pedro Sula. The warehouse, sometimes called the Arms Supermarket, was stacked high with millions of dollars in guns and ammunition earmarked for the contras. In that operation, Molina had told family members that he worked for the CIA.

To this day, the mystery of the Arms Supermarket's money remains one of the most intriguing questions of the Iran-contra scandal and its connection to drug trafficking. Molina's death as the shooting victim of a Colombian hit man does support the notion that someone with connection to the cocaine trade wanted Molina dead. But the Molina case shed light into another dark corner of the Reagan administration's contra war: how, in a variety of cases, the funding for that covert operation was closely tied not only to guns-for-drugs but to the even-murkier world of drug money laundering.

Since the mid-1980s, drug pilots and cocaine-cartel operatives have asserted that contras assisted in transshipping cocaine to the United States in exchange for money and guns. Others stated that cartel kingpins contributed cash to the contras to curry favor with the Reagan administration and buy some protection from U.S. law enforcement. The Molina case was a doorway to a slightly different question: how much did the contra war benefit from dirty money.

The CIA would neither confirm nor deny the claim that Molina worked for the CIA. "This is not something I can really, really give you a definite answer on," said CIA spokesman David Christian. "We just don't have the resources to check all inquiries of this sort."

The Drug Enforcement Administration also failed to respond to repeated requests about Molina. A senior government official, however, confirmed that Molina's name had been linked to drug smuggling and was mentioned in a number of DEA criminal files, including some cases that were still active 10 years after Molina's murder.

U.S. government records also showed that the money for the Arms Supermarket's guns was always suspect. The Iran-contra files included Oliver North's handwritten notes. On July 12, 1985, he scribbled down a warning from one CIA officer in the field that "$14M [million] to finance came from drugs."

But Ronald Martin, the Arms Supermarket's principal owner, vehemently denied any drug connection and denounced the charge as a lie spread by North and other business rivals who wanted to horn in on contra arms profits. "All they were trying to do was taint us and push us out of any business that might be forthcoming," Martin told me. Martin acknowledged, however, that Molina did arrange the Arms Supermarket's money through banks in Panama. Martin also would not say exactly who put up that money.

Though the Arms Supermarket may have had some powerful enemies, it also had some influential friends. According to a contra-supply flow chart that I found in the Iran-contra records at the National Archives, the Arms Supermarket was part of a complex arms network ultimately reporting to Felix Rodriguez, the anti-Castro Cuban and former CIA officer who used the pseudonym, "Max Gomez." Through Rodriguez, the arms network connected to the office of then-Vice President George Bush and his national security adviser Donald Gregg, the chart indicated.

The text accompanying the chart described "Max Gomez" as the Bush-Gregg man on the ground in Central America. "Max Gomez" connected to another former CIA Cuban exile named, Mario Dellamico, who held "a position of authority with Honduran officers and the FDN [contra] camp," the text stated. Dellamico, in turn, set up the "Arms Warehouse/Supermarket" in Honduras, with a corrupt Honduran officer, named "Col. Aplicano."

"The 'Arms Warehouse' was started with 'seed money' of approximately $14 million, from the CIA," the chart read. "Later, it was believed that funds relating to narcotics traffic found its way into inventory in the warehouse." Although the authorship of the flow chart was unclear, it matched information supplied to investigators by another contra arms broker, Barbara Studley, who worked closely with retired Gen. John K. Singlaub and CIA director Casey.

In a deposition in a related civil case, Studley testified that "General Singlaub informed me that he had been briefed by Oliver North that the Supermarket had been funded by drug money." Asked if she had heard those allegations from anyone else, Studley responded, "numerous conversations with numerous people, ... this item came up."

But the Arms Supermarket drug suspicions were never resolved. William Hassler, a lawyer who handled the issue for special prosecutor Walsh, explained that the Martin group was not a focus of the Iran-contra probe. "I'm not sure we considered it a part of our investigation," Hassler told me.

Still, the answer to the larger question of whether the Reagan administration knowingly worked with -- and protected -- drug money launderers appeared to be "yes." Little-noticed Iran-contra evidence demonstrated that the Reagan administration repeatedly turned to criminal money laundering to finance contra activities.

While serving as a White House national security aide, Oliver North tapped into one money-laundering network that collected hundreds of thousands of dollars in untraceable cash in New York City. The cash was pulled together by the husband of a Republic National Bank officer, named Nan Morabia. When North would need cash, his Swiss financial adviser, Willard Zucker, would pass an order to Morabia, according to Morabia's admission to Iran-contra investigators.

Morabia testified that her husband and son then would deliver bags filled with hundreds of thousands of dollars in cash to North's operatives in New York hotel rooms. Sometimes, to identify themselves to the money launderers, North's men would be required to display matching halves of torn dollar bills.

At the European end of this money-laundering scheme, Zucker would make equivalent transfers from North's Swiss bank accounts, containing profits from U.S. arms sales to Iran into the Swiss accounts of the money launderers. That way, the money launderers could turn their "dirty" money in the United States into "clean" money in Europe.

Morabia, who was granted immunity from prosecution in exchange for her cooperation, acknowledged that the so-called "cash drops" were designed to circumvent federal currency laws. Those anti-money-laundering statutes require federal reporting of any cash transfer of $10,000 or more into or out of the United States. Walsh's final report in 1993 stated that the cash transfers through Zucker's operation totaled $2.7 million.

Similarly, Walsh's probe found that another $467,000 went in bags from Southern Air Transport's petty cash fund in Miami to pay salaries and buy gas for North's contra air resupply operations based at El Salvador's Ilopango airport. SAT, a onetime CIA-owned airline, was then reimbursed through money transfers from North's Swiss accounts, Walsh report stated.

Again, the cash deliveries flouted federal requirements to report the removal of more than $10,000 in cash from the United States. But given the strong political pressures on Walsh to wrap up his long-running investigation, the independent counsel chose not to prosecute the participants in the money-laundering schemes. The money laundering also received almost no media attention. Southern Air Transport was the airline that Wanda Palacio fingered back in 1986 as the owner of planes loaded with cocaine in Barranquilla, Colombia.

The Reagan administration's collaboration with drug traffickers and money launderers also was far from isolated. In 1986, the Reagan administration paid $806,401 to four companies to supply the contras with non-lethal aid despite documentary evidence of drug trafficking by all four companies.

One of the contra contractors, the Costa Rican seafood company called Frigorificos de Puntarenas, was created as a cover for drug money laundering, according to sworn testimony by two of the firm's principals, Carlos Soto and Ramon Milian Rodriguez, an accountant for the Medellin cartel. Still, the State Department put $261,937 into a Frigorificos bank account controlled by Cuban-American Luis Rodriguez. In 1987, Luis Rodriguez was charged in federal court as a major marijuana smuggler.

The State Department has never explained how the four drug-smuggling and money-laundering companies were selected, although Ambassador Robert Duemling who oversaw contra "humanitarian" aid recalled that North wanted continuation of "the existing arrangements" that had been set up for the contras.

Those "existing arrangements" were maintained despite even earlier drug warnings from some of North's field operatives. In June 1984, North's courier, Robert Owen, passed on information that Cuban-Americans working with the contras are "involved in drugs." Another North aide, Lt. Col. Robert Earl, recalled that in 1986, CIA officers on the ground were worried because these Cuban-Americans were knee-deep in "corruption and greed and drugs." But the DEA has stated that it has no record that North or his associates passed on evidence of contra-drug trafficking.

S till, the case of John Molina may represent the most provocative link between the contra supply operation and drug money launderers. And like so much other intrigue that has plagued Latin America for nearly four decades, it is a story dating back to the hottest days of the Cold War, when Fidel Castro's revolutionary forces ousted Mafia-connected dictator Fulgencio Batista in 1959.

For John Molina's family, Fidel Castro's victory in 1959 was good news. Molina's uncle, Frank Pais, had helped Castro organize international support for his guerrilla bands in the Sierra Maestra mountains of Cuba. After being killed by Batista's forces, Pais was enshrined as a revolutionary hero.

But Castro's embrace of communism sent young John Molina and other family members into the stream of refugees flowing to the United States. A bright and ambitious young man, John Molina moved to Atlanta, where he landed a job in the mail room of a bank. To improve his earning potential, Molina went to school nights to earn a bachelor's degree in business administration.

Molina's future, however, would soon be caught up in events unfolding to his south, in Miami. There, the CIA station had landed another kind of job: presidential orders to remove Fidel Castro by virtually any means necessary. Hundreds of exiles were signing up with a CIA-trained army that would be landed on Cuba's coast to spearhead an uprising to overthrow Castro and stop the spread of communism.

One of those exiles -- who would play a part in Molina's life story -- was Guillermo Hernandez Cartaya. Along with hundreds of other Cubans, Cartaya traveled to Central America for training in Brigade 2506, the core assault force for the invasion.

On April 14, 1961, under CIA direction, the 1,400-man brigade landed at the Bay of Pigs. Quickly, however, the Cuban army pinned down the invaders and captured 1,189 of them, including Cartaya. Months later, the U.S. government ransomed Cartaya and the others with $53 million in medicine, tractors and other equipment.

But the Bay of Pigs soldiers did not simply fade away. Many stayed with the CIA and carried the anti-communist crusade to far-flung corners of the globe. Some fought with special counterinsurgency teams in Vietnam. Others signed up with intelligence agencies throughout South America.

By the 1970s, Cartaya was hitting it big in politics and banking, too. According to Jonathan Kwitny's *Endless Enemies,* Cartaya parlayed his anti-Castro credentials into powerful relationships, even joining Nelson Rockefeller on hunting and fishing trips. Then, in the mid-1970s, Cartaya launched his most ambitious endeavor, an international financial holding company called the World Finance Corp., later renamed WFC Corp. The firm's maze of banks reached to the United Arab Emirates, Switzerland, London, the Caribbean, Miami, Colombia and Panama.

To head the crucial Panama bank, known as UniBank, Cartaya recruited another Cuban exile whom Cartaya had met during travels to Atlanta. That Cuban exile was John Molina. Taking up Cartaya on his job offer, Molina moved to Panama City to run UniBank. With Molina at the helm, UniBank began steering Cartaya's money from all over the world into untraceable accounts. Molina also oversaw Cartaya's extensive financial dealings in Colombia and other South American countries. Millions of dollars were going in and out of major Colombian agricultural projects.

But Cartaya's banking empire encountered troubles in South Florida. Responding to a routine call, Dade County police found large quantities of marijuana residue in a Miami dumpster. Along with the marijuana residue, police discovered business records of corporations connected to WFC. As the investigation developed, authorities uncovered other corporate links between WFC and Aerocondor, a South American airline that had been caught smuggling drugs. Police also discovered that WFC agents had contacts with the Mafia drug syndicate of Santo Trafficante, Jr., whose lucrative narcotics operations had dominated Cuba prior to Castro's revolution.

Other leads went off in surprising directions. The anti-Castro Cartaya, it seemed, had worked with a suspected Cuban government spy. Even more perplexing, WFC had received a $2 million loan from the Narodny Bank, a KGB-connected Soviet financial institution that was responsible for scrounging up hard currency for Moscow. Police came to suspect that WFC was an intelligence front. Federal investigators found that about a dozen WFC officials had past associations with the CIA. [58]

"It was drugs, it was money laundering, it was everything," South Florida detective James Rider told me. "I know the CIA was in there somewhere."

The investigators also came to know the name of John Molina. He was not regarded as a powerful player though. He was just one of Cartaya's financial lieutenants carrying out orders. But the authorities recognized that UniBank was an important cog in Cartaya's money-laundering machine.

"All the money from Cartaya and his businesses would be funneled down there" to Panama, said one federal prosecutor who asked not to be identified by name. "Once it got into the Union de Bancos [UniBank], it just disappeared, just poof, up in a cloud of

---

[58] In *The Mafia, CIA & George Bush,* author Pete Brewton described an account from one federal prosecutor who was approached by a CIA officer who explained that "Cartaya had done a bunch of things that the government was indebted to him for, and he asked me to drop the charges against him."

smoke -- millions and millions of dollars just gone. It was impossible to trace any further."

By 1978, a joint federal-state task force had unearthed evidence of other crimes too, particularly drug money transfers. But both local police and federal prosecutors reported pressure from Washington and CIA headquarters to back off WFC. Too many of WFC's principals, it turned out, had cooperated with U.S. intelligence.[59]

Journalist Penny Lernoux investigated the WFC case for her book about financial crimes, entitled *In Banks We Trust*. As part of her reporting, Lernoux interviewed then-Florida State Attorney Janet Reno, who admitted that the government had bungled the case. "The bad guys really aren't very good at it," Reno said. "We're worse."

Beset with pressures and other problems, the two-year WFC investigation ended with only a minor tax case lodged against Cartaya. But Cartaya's scandal-plagued WFC empire did collapse in 1978. UniBank closed, too, costing depositors, primarily Colombians, about $18 million in losses. UniBank's president, John Molina, was out of a job and in a heap of political trouble.

In an interview with me, John Molina's brother, Pablo, confirmed UniBank's money-laundering role. Speaking from his cramped law office in Los Angeles, Pablo said John confided that UniBank "was set up as a front" for international arms smuggling and for making secret embargo-busting contacts inside Cuba, a reference that might explain the dealings with the Soviet bank and the suspected Cuban spy. What was less clear was whether Cartaya's bank was just out to make money or was collecting intelligence about Cuba's activities for the CIA -- or a combination of the two.

After the collapse of UniBank, Pablo said, John received personal protection from Gen. Noriega, who was involved in many of the same pursuits that had interested UniBank. With other friends in the right places, John Molina was soon back on his feet

---

[59] Detective Rider recalled a senior Treasury Department official assuring police investigators in the late 1970s that WFC was clean. A federal prosecutor in the case added that the CIA had intervened at the top levels of the FBI to protest the WFC probe.

financially, too. Because of his banking skills and contacts, Molina got a new job with Ron Martin who owned R&M Equipment Co. in Miami. Martin needed someone to handle banking transactions for R&M, an arms supply firm that was selling guns throughout Latin America and the Caribbean.

Pablo Molina said one of his brother's primary assignments for Martin was arranging letters of credit for the contras. "From 1980 to April 1987, my brother worked for the CIA arranging letters of credit to purchase arms for the contras and/or other U.S.-back[ed] governments in Centr[al] and South America," Pablo wrote in later letters to authorities in Washington.

Pablo Molina claimed, too, that one important money-laundering outpost for the arms operation was a jai-alai fronton, or stadium, located at the beach resort in Benidorm, Spain. "Benidorm was set up to launder money to help the contras," Pablo Molina said in the interview. "My impression is that it was CIA money that had to be laundered."

Pablo added that he thought Ron Martin was directly involved in the Benidorm operation because, in 1985, Pablo once overheard his brother telling Martin, "I sent the funds to Spain."[60] But Pablo said John's chief partner in the jai-alai operation was a Cuban-American named Joe Fernandez.

In a separate interview, Martin confirmed that John Molina and Joe Fernandez did work together on the Benidorm jai-alai fronton. Martin said, however, that the jai-alai operator was not the same Joe Fernandez who served as CIA station chief in Costa Rica and who worked closely with Oliver North's operation. But John Molina's activities likely would have crossed the path of the CIA's Joe Fernandez, too.

P**ablo Molina said his brother sank deeper into the Central American intrigue when he went to Costa Rica in late 1984 or early 1985. There, John Molina met Hugo Spadafora, the former Panamanian health minister who was fighting with the contras on the so-called Southern Front.

---

[60] In a 1987 divorce case in Miami, Martin's wife alleged that Martin owned a jai alai fronton in Benidorm, Spain. [Pete Brewton's *The Mafia, CIA & George Bush.*]

Spadafora had grown disillusioned with Eden Pastora's contra army because of its cocaine smuggling. Spadafora also planned to denounce Noriega for drug trafficking. John Molina tried to calm Spadafora down and offered Spadafora access to weapons to keep him in line. John Molina added a warning that Spadafora should not return to Panama, where Noriega was working with the CIA in its support of the contras.

But by mid-1985, Spadafora was furious with the drug corruption. He contacted the DEA's chief officer in Costa Rica, Robert Nieves, to complain about contra-drug trafficking. Spadafora declared that he intended to return to Panama where he would publicly denounce Noriega and the contras.

On Sept. 13, 1985, Spadafora boarded a bus for Panama City. At a check point inside Panama, soldiers stopped the bus and dragged Spadafora off. Spadafora's beheaded and tortured body was found a day later stuffed inside a U.S. mail bag on the Costa Rican side of the border.

The Spadafora murder touched off new suspicions about cocaine trafficking by the contras, their backers in Costa Rica and Noriega's Panamanian Defense Forces. In late 1989, Costa Rican prosecutors endorsed those suspicions and accused pro-contra Cuban-Americans along with other U.S. citizens of using Costa Rica as a drug transshipment point. As part of those findings, Costa Rica barred the CIA's Joe Fernandez and Oliver North from the Central American nation.[61]

In the 1980s, along the Honduran front, the contra-drug taint was spreading, too. Though Honduras had been a transit point for drugs since the late 1970s, the cocaine shipments swelled in the mid-1980s. The trafficking implicated senior Honduran military officers who had assisted the CIA and the contras. According to Kerry's 1989 report, "there is evidence that individuals in the

---

[61] Fernandez and North have denied any role in drug trafficking, but failed to return phone calls seeking comment about the Molina story. After retiring from the DEA, Nieves went to work with North and Fernandez at Guardian Technologies, a bulletproof vest company in Sterling, Va. When I reached Nieves there, he said he did not recall the name John Molina.

Honduran military, which controls the police, have protected the cocaine trade."

In one case, the FBI seized a $40 million shipment of cocaine in South Florida and arrested Honduran Gen. Jose Bueso-Rosa. He planned to use the cocaine to finance the assassination of the country's civilian president. Since Bueso-Rosa had collaborated with the CIA on the contra war, North and other administration officials intervened with the Justice Department, seeking leniency for the general.

To establish a foothold in this corrupt Honduran environment, Ron Martin opened the Arms Supermarket in partnership with key Honduran military officers. In particular, Martin relied on Cuban-American Mario Dellamico to befriend Honduran intelligence chief, Col. Hector Aplicano. Martin also built contacts inside the contras with top leaders, including Adolfo Calero and Enrique Bermudez.

When Congress cut off direct CIA support for the contras in 1984, the Arms Supermarket stepped forward as a source for continued contra military aid. For that operation, Martin explained that John Molina was the banker; a well-connected Panamanian, Enrique DelValle, supplied the money contacts; and Dellamico handled matters on the ground in Honduras.

"All the money ... came from Panamanian bankers who fronted the money with letters of credit" arranged by Molina, Martin told Iran-contra investigators. Martin said his operation succeeded in shipping about $1 million in weapons to the contras via the Honduran military. But millions of dollars more in weapons piled up at the warehouse in San Pedro Sula.

Rumors soon spread that the Arms Supermarket's money came from recycled drug profits. Martin, however, blamed those drug rumors on North's associates who wanted to corner the contra market. In the interview with me, Martin insisted again that the Supermarket had no drug ties. But he refused to specify where the millions of dollars originated.

"It came from other sources," Martin stated cryptically. Then, presumably referring to U.S. government officials, he added, "we explained it to them in detail, where everything came from."

Despite his broad denials, Martin did not rule out the possibility that John Molina was trafficking in drugs to support his own expensive life-style. "There was always the question of where John was getting his cash," Martin said. "We don't know where he was getting these wads of cash. ... John was living it up beyond his means."

For his part, Pablo Molina defended his brother against suggestions that John personally engaged in cocaine trafficking. Pablo was confident that John was no freelance drug smuggler. But Pablo remembered that John had his own suspicions about the Arms Supermarket's money.

"I'm not surprised that there is drug money involved in this," Pablo Molina told me. "John would say, 'There's too much money coming in. It's more than I can conceive is being brought in by the CIA. ... You can't imagine how much money is involved. Even Martin doesn't know how much is involved'."

In April 1987, John Molina began pulling out of Martin's weapons business and turning more attention to the Panamanian political scene. John Molina allied himself with Noriega's enemies and thus was a prime target for Noriega's henchmen, both because of Molina's CIA connections and his knowledge about the international arms trade. Meanwhile, exposed publicly as a drug trafficker in 1986-87 and no longer useful to the contras, Noriega had lost much of his backing in Washington.

Through the summer of 1987, John Molina worked on plans to start his own business, Pablo Molina said. But John still had to tidy up some loose ends for Martin. John Molina had to untangle the complex threads of contra corporate front companies. Those corporations were handled by the Panamanian law firm, Sucre y Sucre.

On Oct. 1, 1987, an earthquake rattled southern California. John Molina called from his car's cellular phone in Miami to check on Pablo's safety in Los Angeles. A Panamanian military officer was with John as they drove to the airport, Pablo recalled John telling him. John's presence suddenly was needed back in Panama City.

The next day, John Molina accompanied Enrique DelValle, a relative of Panama's president Eric DelValle, to the law offices of Sucre y Sucre in Panama City. By afternoon, Molina and DelValle had completed their contra-related business. They left the airy low-rise building together and walked toward Molina's red four-wheel-drive Mitsubishi.

As the two men climbed in, a Colombian gunman stepped up to the car and fired three shots into John Molina's head. The banker, who knew many of the secrets about the contras and cocaine, was dead.

The Terrorist

On Feb. 7, 1992, at 9 a.m., in Room 426 of the U.S. Embassy in Tegucigalpa, Honduras, two FBI agents sat down with a fugitive terrorist. For the next 6 1/2 hours, the agents debriefed the man who spoke with a faint slurping sound, the result of a bullet that had struck his face and nearly sliced off his tongue.

The fugitive, a sandy-haired man in his early 60s, labored through his story. He repeated his usual denial about committing the mass murder of 73 civilians with the bombing of a commercial airliner in 1976. But the agents were not interested in that long-ago act of terror. They wanted to know about the man's secret work for Ronald Reagan's White House.

In 1986, during a congressional ban on U.S. military assistance to the Nicaraguan contra rebels, the fugitive terrorist, Luis Posada Carriles, had been recruited into Oliver North's secret gunrunning operation. Though charged in Venezuela with blowing up a commercial airliner, the CIA-trained explosives expert had been made the contras' logistics chief. He oversaw caches of munitions stored at El Salvador's Ilopango airport. He paid North's crews with bags of cash delivered from Miami. In return for this contra help, Posada was rewarded with false government papers to conceal his identity.

After the 6 1/2-hour interview ended, Posada walked out of the U.S. Embassy to freedom. The 31-page summary of his interview was stamped "secret" and filed away in the records of the Iran-contra investigation conducted by Lawrence Walsh. In late 1996, I found a partially censored version of Posada's debriefing at the National Archives.

In some ways, the 1992 FBI interview was just one more strange chapter in Posada's long career as a shadow soldier in the Cold War. But the bizarre situation, in which an accused international terrorist could freely enter and leave a U.S. embassy, also spoke volumes about Washington's ambivalence about criminal activities by former CIA operatives. Many of these warriors have enjoyed virtual licenses to kill or to commit other crimes with what police agencies call "get-out-of-jail-free cards."

Like hundreds of other young Cuban exiles, Posada enlisted in the Cold War in 1960, after fleeing Castro's communist revolution. Posada received paramilitary training for the invasion of Cuba, but his battalion stayed behind in reserve in Nicaragua. So Posada missed out on the military debacle at the Bay of Pigs.

But Posada's war was only beginning. Back on the CIA payroll in the mid-1960s, he slipped arms into Cuba for possible future insurrections. He worked with anti-Castro extremist Orlando Bosch in sabotage attacks against Cuban targets, ranging from ships to embassies. "There was a time when I thought this was the way to liberate Cuba," Posada once told the *Miami Herald*. "Attack everything that served Fidel. Make him lose an embassy here, a consulate there."

When Castro didn't fall, however, some Cuban exiles volunteered as shock troops in the international war against communism. Felix Rodriguez, the future "Max Gomez," worked directly for the CIA in Southeast Asia killing Viet Cong and in South America hunting down Castro's comrade, Ernesto "Che" Guevara. Other exiles were farmed out to regimes elsewhere in South America to oversee anti-leftist "dirty wars." Posada landed a job with Venezuela's intelligence service, DISIP.

By the mid-1970s, violence was sweeping Latin America, with Cuban exiles often in the background. In 1973, the Chilean military staged a bloody coup to oust the elected government of Marxist president Salvador Allende, who died in the fighting. In 1976, the Argentine army invented a new meaning for the word, "disappeared," the fate of suspected leftists who were swept off the streets by the thousands and never seen again.

In 1976, too, Bosch and other Cuban exiles were itching to hit again at Castro. Bosch chaired a secret meeting in the Dominican Republic to plot strategy. Bosch has claimed that Posada was there, although Posada has publicly denied participating. Afterwards, Cuban exiles dramatically stepped up their terror campaign against Castro and his friends.

Cuban exiles also helped Chilean intelligence hunt down Allende's exiled foreign minister, Orlando Letelier, who was considered a Castro ally. As Letelier and an American co-worker, Ronni Moffitt, traveled down Embassy Row in Washington, D.C., on Sept. 21, 1976, assassins detonated a bomb taped to Letelier's car. Letelier and Moffitt died. The FBI discovered later that the murder occurred after the U.S. ambassador to Paraguay had alerted CIA director George Bush about a suspicious Chilean intelligence mission to the United States. But Bush and the CIA did nothing to thwart the attack.

Two weeks later, on Oct. 6, a Cubana airliner took off from Barbados. Nine minutes into the flight, a bomb exploded. All 73 people on board, including the Cuban national fencing team, died. Police arrested two men, both Posada employees who had gotten off the plane in Barbados. One of the men confessed to the bombing. But the police suspected that Posada was the mastermind. The men had called Posada immediately after the plane crashed. Then, when police searched Posada's residence, they found incriminating evidence, including Cubana flight schedules.

Venezuelan authorities charged Posada and Bosch with masterminding the bombing. The two Cuban exiles denied the charges, and the case became a political tug-of-war with Venezuela uncomfortable in prosecuting the pair -- who knew many of the government's intelligence secrets -- but unwilling to set them free.

Finally, in 1985, with the terror charges still pending, Posada bribed a guard and escaped from a Venezuelan jail.

Posada's first stop as a fugitive was the Caribbean island of Aruba. There, he got help from Felix Rodriguez, who arranged for Posada to fly to El Salvador. Rodriguez already was overseeing the secret resupply operation for the contras at Ilopango airport, where he had been placed by an old friend in the CIA, Donald Gregg. Rodriguez introduced Posada to Rafael "Chi Chi" Quintero, another Cuban with close ties to both the CIA and to retired Air Force Lt. Gen. Richard Secord who was overseeing the contra resupply mission for Oliver North.

Posada told the FBI agents that Quintero was the one who actually recruited him into the contra operation. Paid $3,000 a month, plus living expenses and given an ID in the name of "Ramon Medina," Posada arranged for safe houses and fuel for North's air crews. He also stored a top-secret U.S. encrypting device, known as a KL-43, at his house for secure communications to the CIA's Costa Rican station chief, Joe Fernandez, and to other U.S. officials covertly assisting the project.

In his FBI interview, Posada shed little new light on the old question of how much Vice President Bush knew about North's illegal activities. According to the FBI summary, "Posada ... recalls that Rodriguez was always calling Gregg. Posada knows this because he's the one who paid Rodriguez'[s] phone bill. ... Posada assumes that Rodriguez told Gregg and other friends about the resupply project." But Posada didn't know for sure.

On Oct. 5, 1986, when one of North's supply planes didn't return, Posada was the one who sounded the alarm. "Posada's first act was to call [Felix] Rodriguez, who was in Miami," the FBI summary read. "Rodriguez told him that Radio Havana had already announced the downing of an aircraft. ... Posada then went to the resupply houses and told everyone what had happened."

Posada, the fugitive terrorist, alerted Col. James Steele, the chief of the U.S. military group in El Salvador. Steele rushed over to meet with Posada and to review a map showing the flight plan of the lost plane. Another Posada call went to Luis Rodriguez, another Cuban exile with close ties to the contras.[62]

Soon after the Eugene Hasenfus disaster, Quintero and Robert Dutton, who also was working with North's operation, arrived in El Salvador. Dutton told Posada that the FBI had learned that he was managing the contra operation and agents wanted to interview him the next day. In effect, the FBI was reviving the moribund probe started by assistant U.S. attorney Jeffrey Feldman earlier in 1986.

But that interview of Posada never happened. With North's secrets finally spilling out, Attorney General Edwin Meese III intervened and suspended the probe of the resupply operation on national security grounds, supposedly because of SAT's dual role supplying missiles to Iran. The delay bought Posada and his associates precious time.

"Dutton and Quintero quickly left El Salvador," the Iran-contra summary read. "Posada was left all alone to clean up the mess during the post-Hasenfus period. Posada had to move all the equipment out of the houses and close them down. Posada had to get all the U.S. personnel out of the country, dispose of their personal weapons, communication gear, terminate the leases and utilities, pay off all of the outstanding bills and all other loose ends."

In another break for Posada, an earthquake hit El Salvador and diverted press attention from the contra questions. Seizing that opening, Posada slipped the American crew men out of the safe houses, took them to Ilopango and helped them depart in small numbers. With the help of the Salvadoran military, Posada then cleaned out the houses.

"During the course of cleaning up these houses, Posada collected papers, maps, house and fuel receipts, flight logs, photographs and other kind of miscellaneous items and put them in two boxes," the Iran-contra summary stated. "These boxes were stored at Ilopango and as far as Posada knows, they're still there."

Meese's investigative delay was important in another way. In a separate Iran-contra interview report that I found at the National

---

[62] A year later, the federal government would indict Luis Rodriguez as a drug trafficker.

Archives, DEA agent Celerino Castillo said that after the Oct. 5 shoot-down, Salvadoran drug agents planned to bust the safe houses over suspicions that North's pilots had doubled as narcotics traffickers. But Castillo added that the police arrived "too late and the houses had already been cleaned out."

After abandoning the safe houses, Posada hid out in Zanadu, a Salvadoran beach town. But by interrogating Eugene Hasenfus, the Sandinistas soon identified the mysterious "Ramon Medina" -- the contras' logistics chief -- as the fugitive terrorist, Luis Posada. The Cuban exile was once more a hunted man.

Still, Posada continued to find work. Salvadoran president Napoleon Duarte hired Posada as a special security adviser. Later, Posada moved to Guatemala where he worked for the state-owned phone company and gave informal security advice to Guatemala's president Vinicio Cerezo.

Then, on Feb. 26, 1990, two cars pulled up next to Posada's black Suzuki jeep as he was heading to work in Guatemala City. Gunmen opened fire, riddling Posada's car with more than 40 bullets. One penetrated Posada's chest and grazed his heart. Another cut through his jaw and nearly severed his tongue. Posada fired back and pulled into a gas station before collapsing. Cerezo's security men rushed Posada to a hospital where his life was saved, although his damaged tongue continued to slur his speech. After his recovery, Posada moved to Honduras and again went into hiding.

In 1992, Posada spoke with the FBI for those 6 1/2 hours. Then, he left the U.S. embassy and slipped back into obscurity. The Cuban government occasionally demands that the United Nations seek his return to Cuba to stand trial on terrorism charges. But the United States has taken no known steps to assist in Posada's apprehension.

As the Iran-contra probe ended in 1993, Posada's testimony slid into thick government's files and became "lost history."

Chapter 8
Contra-Coke

I n 1972, Alfred W. McCoy, a Yale academic and *Harper's* correspondent, was finishing a landmark book, *The Politics of Heroin in Southeast Asia*. His research had taken him on a harrowing tour through the war zones of Vietnam and Laos and into the equally risky apartments of well-armed drug lords in Europe.

But McCoy's findings were just as dangerous as his travels. Through numerous on-the-record interviews with participants in the heroin trade, he had discovered that U.S. intelligence had long collaborated with narcotics traffickers. He traced the alliance back to World War II when U.S. naval intelligence and the CIA's forerunner, the Office of Strategic Services, worked cozily with Mafia dons who helped the U.S. army pick its way through the hills of Sicily and up the spine of Italy.

After its creation in 1947, the CIA continued the relationships with crime syndicates. The Mafia out-muscled pro-communist unions in Italy, France and the United States in the early days of the Cold War. Meanwhile, the gangsters rebuilt their international routes for transporting narcotics.

In the 1950s, the ruthless French intelligence agency, the SDECE, allied itself with Indochinese warlords who trafficked in heroin. When Ho Chi Minh's Viet Minh forces defeated the French, the CIA inherited the SDECE's heroin-tainted Asian allies. By the 1960s, the alliance of convenience had gone operational. CIA-owned aircraft were transporting opium from Laotian poppy fields to market, as a favor to friendly Hmong tribesmen. McCoy had personally interviewed participants in the field who spoke with surprising frankness about a commodity that was seen as simply a valuable economic export from the Golden Triangle.

But McCoy's research was particularly unwelcome in Washington in 1972. President Nixon was trumpeting his "war on drugs" -- the first of many such wars declared by American presidents -- and the U.S. military was still reeling from negative publicity over the My Lai massacre and other atrocities in Vietnam. The CIA was coming under scrutiny, too, for running an assassination campaign called Phoenix.

So, in June 1972, with the book in galleys, the CIA took the offensive against McCoy's publisher, Harper & Row. The CIA dispatched a top official, Cord Meyer Jr., to visit old social friend, Cass Canfield Sr., Harper's owner. The CIA wanted to review the manuscript prior to publication and Harper's executives were amenable.

As the publication date neared, Harper & Row confronted McCoy with an ultimatum: for the book to be published, McCoy must acquiesce to the CIA's demand for prior review. Reluctantly, McCoy agreed. A week later, the CIA responded with a spate of denials to information in McCoy's book. The CIA also persuaded some witnesses who had been interviewed by McCoy to recant. It looked as if the book might be in trouble.

But investigative reporter Seymour Hersh picked up word of the CIA's maneuver and wrote a page-one story for *The New York Times*. *The Washington Post* weighed in, too, with an editorial lambasting the CIA's attempt at censorship. Harper & Row's spine stiffened and the book survived intact. Network news programs followed up McCoy's findings with investigations of their own, including a one-hour documentary on NBC's Chronolog program.[63]

---

[63] For details, see Alfred W. McCoy, *The Politics of Heroin*.

Though the CIA may have lost that round, its many friends in Washington had learned a valuable lesson: an American press corps that showed too much independence could be a threat to the kind of tough-minded *Realpolitik* crucial to the Cold War. So in the mid-to-late 1970s, conservative foundations, right-wing religious groups and pro-CIA foreign interests poured tens of millions of dollars into a strategy for influencing the national news media.

Part of that initiative groomed a "kept" conservative press. Another part of the strategy was housebreaking the mainstream news media. To that end, groups, such as Accuracy in Media, subjected working journalists to harsh criticism when they wrote critically of the national security establishment. In the 1980s, that outside effort merged with the Reagan administration's muscular "public diplomacy" strategy. By the mid-1980s, mainstream news outfits were falling into line.

The timing could not have been better for the Reagan administration. President Reagan's pet contra war was encountering some of the same negative attention that had beset the Vietnam War. The contras were facing accusations of massacres and witnesses were coming forward describing how drug traffickers had infiltrated the contra movement. Yet, despite McCoy's work in the 1970s and the disclosures of clumsy deceptions in the Iran-contra scandal, most of the national press was still ready to accept the administration's word that the stories of contra-drug trafficking were lies.

This time, instead of riding to the rescue of those who were piecing together the evidence, *The New York Times* and *The Washington Post* joined the administration's counterattacks. The *Times* proved especially influential in discrediting the allegations, but the *Post* joined in putting down or burying the stories about this disturbing scandal.

Only briefly did the *Post* have second thoughts. In 1991, when the Bush adminstration was prosecuting Panama's Manuel Noriega on drug-trafficking charges, the government called Medellin cartel kingpin Carlos Lehder to the witness stand. The imprisoned trafficker testified that the Medellin cartel had given $10 million to the Nicaraguan contras, a claim that one of Sen. John Kerry's witnesses had made years earlier and others had buttressed.

Cartel money launderer Ramon Milian Rodriguez had testified that he knew the cartel funneled millions of dollars to the contras in the 1980s as part of a $10 million pledge. Another major Colombian trafficker described supplying aircraft and money to contras based in Costa Rica. The Colombian cartel apparently was trying to ingratiate itself with President Reagan. Contra pilot Marcos Aguado testified that the smugglers "took advantage of the anti-communist sentiment ... and they undoubtedly used it for drug trafficking."

For once, after the Lehder testimony, the *Post* praised Kerry for his earlier investigation. "The Kerry hearings didn't get the attention they deserved at the time," a *Post* editorial admitted. "The Noriega trial brings this sordid aspect of the Nicaraguan engagement to fresh public attention." But the editorial did not explain that one of the principal reasons for that lack of attention was the *Post's* own neglect of the scandal.[64]

At the time of the Noriega trial, there also was no follow-up, no explanation of how the mainstream press had booted one of the biggest stories of the decade. There was no handwringing about how the media had failed to protect the public from government-connected cocaine smugglers. There was no renewed investigation of the evidence that might have implicated figures at the highest levels of Washington power, including possibly senior aides of the sitting president, George Bush.

In the years following the Noriega trial, historical amnesia again swept official Washington. The contra-cocaine tales became another chapter in the "lost history."

And that was where the contra-cocaine issue remained until August 1996. More than a decade after the contra-cocaine allegations had first surfaced, the *San Jose Mercury News* published a 20,000-word three-part series written by investigative reporter Gary Webb. The story received widespread international distribution through the newspaper's

---

[64] *The Washington Post*, Nov. 27, 1991.

sophisticated Internet site. Links to the main story allowed readers to examine and download many of the source documents upon which the story was based.

Webb's series tracked one West Coast network of contra-cocaine traffickers from the early-to-mid-1980s. Webb connected that cocaine to an early "crack" production network that supplied Los Angeles street gangs, the Crips and the Bloods. Webb concluded that the contra cocaine directly fueled the early crack epidemic that devastated Los Angeles and other U.S. cities.

In 1996, at a cocaine trafficking trial in San Diego, Danilo Blandon Reyes, a former contra supporter and drug dealer, testified that contra commander Enrique Bermudez gave the smuggling something of a green light. "There is a saying that the ends justify the means," Blandon said. "And that's what Mr. Bermudez told us in Honduras, OK. So we started raising money for the contra revolution."

At first, Webb's story caused hardly a ripple of official reaction, other than a not-too-surprising denial from the CIA. Director John Deutch cited a still-secret CIA study done in 1988 that supposedly found the CIA "neither participated in nor condoned drug trafficking by contra forces." Deutch, however, said he still would order another review "to dispel any lingering public doubts."

But the story touched a raw nerve in America's black communities that had been devastated by crack and related gang violence. Black leaders demanded a thorough investigation of the charges and punishment of U.S. government officials who might be implicated. The angriest reaction was from South-Central Los Angeles where crack had made the black neighborhood nearly synonymous with drive-by shootings. Scores of blacks -- many innocent bystanders -- had been killed in the violence, thousands of black youths had landed in prison and hundreds of "crack babies" had been born to mothers hooked on the powerful drug.

In Washington, Rep. Maxine Waters, D-Calif., led the Congressional Black Caucus in angry protests. On Sept. 11, 1996, veteran civil rights activist Dick Gregory drove to CIA headquarters with a roll of yellow "crime scene" tape. "We know where the criminals are," the aging Gregory told a news conference. "We're gonna rope them in." When he arrived at CIA headquarters in Langley, Va., Gregory and a black radio talk show host, Joe Madison, were arrested on charges of blocking an entrance. Gregory announced a hunger strike in protest of the CIA's alleged drug complicity.

The next day, a predominantly black crowd of up to 4,000 packed a conference hall at the Washington Convention Center to hear Waters denounce "the connection between the CIA and the crack cocaine introduced into our neighborhoods." Other speakers recounted how black families were shattered by crack violence and how black youths were jailed far longer for possessing crack -- an inexpensive concentrated rock-like form of cocaine -- than white users were for having powder cocaine. The crowd roared when the CIA was mocked as the "cocaine importation agency."

While the CIA issued denials and the black community seethed, the mainstream media continued its longstanding practice of either ignoring or dismissing the contra-drug allegations. Despite Gary Webb's story and the public fall-out, *The New York Times* showed no interest in the story. *The Washington Post* reported on Deutch's denial briefly in the news pages and then stuck Gregory's arrest in a gossip column.

The counterattack against Webb's series began in earnest in the conservative press, particularly *The Washington Times,* which had long backed the contras. On Sept. 12, reporter Andy Thibault penned an article that prominently quoted Vincent Cannistraro, who was described as "a retired CIA official." Cannistraro declared that "the testimony for things like this [contra drugs] originate with scam artists. ... This doesn't have any elements of authenticity."

Next, a former *Washington Times* reporter, Michael Hedges, used similar quotes from Cannistraro in another Webb-bashing article that Hedges wrote for his new employers, the *Scripps Howard News Service.* Calling Cannistraro a "retired CIA counter-terrorism and Latin America expert," Hedges quoted Cannistraro as declaring "these charges are completely illogical."

But neither Thibault nor Hedges identified the potential conflicts of interest in Cannistraro's comments. This "retired CIA official," in fact, was head of the Central American Task Force, which oversaw the contra operations in the early 1980s, exactly the time when Webb's article was alleging that the CIA was tolerating cocaine trafficking as a contra fund-raising device. In 1984, Cannistraro transferred to the National Security Council, where he was assigned to oversee covert assistance to the Afghan mujahedeen, another rebel force implicated in narcotics trafficking.

Thibault and Hedges also ignored the Iran-contra testimony of CIA officer Alan Fiers, Cannistraro's successor at the Central American Task Force. Fiers told the Iran-contra committees that "with respect to [drug trafficking by] the Resistance Forces [the contras] it is not a couple of people. It is a lot of people."

While leaving out Fiers's sworn testimony on the subject, Thibault found space to quote several anonymous Internet gossipers about Webb's stories. Thibault reported that one "Internet user reacted, 'while I'll certainly grant you that the CIA does some pretty slim[e]y stuff, I've never seen any evidence that this is going on'."

On Sept. 24, *The Washington Times* fired off another barrage, from one of its biggest guns, editor-at-large Arnaud deBorchgrave. In his first paragraph, deBorchgrave suggested that Webb's allegations were merely the result of "pro-Marxist CIA bashers" successfully planting the story and "snookering the *San Jose Mercury News*."

But Webb's article actually cited a wide variety of sources who had no connection to "pro-Marxist CIA bashers." Besides witnesses from the drug trade, including pro-contra Nicaraguans, Webb quoted a public defender, a prosecutor, a U.S. Senate subcommittee report, a chief of Nicaragua's anti-drug agency, a Los Angeles County sheriff, DEA agents, several DEA informants, and unnamed agents from U.S. Customs and the California Bureau of Narcotic Enforcement.

DeBorchgrave accused Webb of asserting that the objective of the CIA's involvement in drug trafficking was to "drug the blacks of our inner cities into submission and, presumably, relegate them to oblivion." There was no such claim in Webb's series.

DeBorchgrave also chided Webb for not realizing that the contras were swimming in $100 million a year in CIA money approved by Congress -- and thus had no motive for dealing drugs. "Maybe Mr. Webb is too young to remember that the CIA had no need for illicit contra funds in those days," deBorchgrave wrote. "It was all legal. Congress had voted $100 million in military assistance to the contras."

But it was deBorchgrave who was misstating history. Webb's series addressed the contras' financial needs in the early 1980s, when the contras never had enough money to fully fund their war. Congress did not approve the $100 million until summer 1986 and that money was not available to the contras until October 1986.[65]

Indeed, the contras' chronic money shortage was the principal reason why the Reagan administration chose to go to such extraordinary -- and politically dangerous -- lengths to raise funds from private individuals and third countries. Not only did Oliver North beg wealthy Americans for donations, but President Reagan and his top aides solicited funds from foreign potentates.

The contras' financial desperation got so bad in early 1986 that North admitted diverting millions of dollars in profits from secret Iranian arms sales to the contras. That reckless decision touched off the Iran-contra scandal. By no stretch of the imagination were the contras flush with cash before October 1986.

Still, *The Washington Times* had started a media juggernaut. *The Washington Post* joined the Webb bashing on Oct. 4, 1996, with a package of stories that started on page one and jumped inside to two full pages. The lead *Post* story by Roberto Suro and Walter Pincus acknowledged that contra-connected drug smugglers had brought tons of cocaine into the United States. "Even CIA personnel testified to Congress they knew that those covert operations involved drug traffickers," the *Post* story stated.

But the paper concluded that the contras had not "played a major role in the emergence of crack" cocaine. The *Post* argued that one of the Nicaraguan smugglers, Oscar Danilo Blandon, "handled

---

[65] DeBorchgrave's assertion about adequate funds for the contras in the early 1980s is particularly curious because he was editor of *The Washington Times* in 1984 when the newspaper organized a fund-raising drive on the contras' behalf.

only about five tons of cocaine." The *Post* conceded that another pro-contra Nicaraguan, Norwin Meneses, "who was Blandon's original supplier, may have handled more cocaine than Blandon." But the *Post* insisted that no single drug network could be blamed for touching off the crack explosion.

To complete the debunking, a second *Post* story supplied a rationale for why blacks could be easily misled by charges about U.S. government complicity in contra cocaine: African-Americans are easily duped by "conspiracy fears," the *Post* explained. The *Post* had thus neatly answered the growing public concern about the Reagan administration's blind eye toward contra-cocaine smuggling in the 1980s -- it wasn't "major" and blacks were paranoid.

On Oct. 9, 1996, a *Post* editorial reprised the newspaper's attacks and declared that the CIA-connected Nicaraguans had not "played a major role" in the crack epidemic. But the editorial did adjust the newspaper's position slightly by admitting that for any "CIA-connected characters to have played even a trivial role in introducing Americans to crack would indicate an unconscionable breach by the CIA."

Following the *Post's* front-page package, other major newspapers piled on. *The New York Times* accused Webb of exaggerating the significance of contra cocaine and of mistakenly identifying Meneses and Blandon as contra operatives. "While there are indications in American intelligence files and elsewhere that Mr. Meneses and Mr. Blandon may indeed have provided modest support for the rebels, including perhaps some weapons, there is no evidence that either man was a rebel official or had anything to do with the CIA," wrote correspondent Tim Golden.[66]

The *Los Angeles Times* took a similar tack, criticizing Webb for allegedly hyping his information and flogging an old story. The fact of contra-cocaine trafficking "has been well documented for years," the *Times* story noted.[67]

In the tag-team body-slamming of Webb's series, the major newspapers also made much of the CIA's exculpatory internal investigations in 1987 and again in 1988. But at an Oct. 24, 1996,

---

[66] *The New York Times,* Oct. 21, 1996.
[67] *Los Angeles Times,* Oct. 22, 1996.

hearing before the Senate Intelligence Committee, CIA inspector general Frederick Hitz conceded that the first CIA probe had lasted only 12 days. The second probe took only three days before concluding that "all allegations implying that the CIA condoned, abetted or participated in narcotics trafficking are absolutely false," he said.

Hitz acknowledged that in two months of his own investigation, he had been unable to collect the large volume of relevant documents that would allow him even to begin a credible examination of the issue. Hitz's admission undercut the reliability of the previous CIA probes, but the media didn't seem to be listening.

Still, for Webb and his work, the damage was done. Soon, Webb was the target for outright ridicule. When he included in a book proposal a suggestion that he would examine the possibility that the contra war was primarily a business to its participants, the Washington news media could barely contain its laughter. "Oliver Stone, check your voice mail," hooted the *Post's* media critic, Howard Kurtz.[68]

But Webb's suspicion wasn't so flaky. In fact, it had originated with the contras and their supporters. In one frank critique of the flailing contra war on March 17, 1986, Oliver North's emissary Robert Owen wrote, "The reality as I see it is there are few of the so-called leaders of the movement who really care about the boys in the field. THIS WAR HAS BECOME A BUSINESS TO MANY OF THEM." [Capitalization in the original.] Though the contra war had been a major story of the 1980s, the elite Washington journalists seemed to know very little about it.

By early December, Webb's "bogus" contra-cocaine allegations were ending up in round-ups of kooky conspiracies. The *Post's* chic Style section, which helps set the city's pecking order, included Webb's story as an example of "a time besotted with Bad Information." Writer Joel Achenbach chastised the *Mercury News* for implying "that the crack epidemic in urban America is a CIA plot."

---

[68] *The Washington Post,* Oct. 28, 1996.

Achenbach went on to poke fun at "defenders of the series
[who] are now, as we speak scouring the volcanic hills overlooking
Managua, seeking more evidence." But Achenbach saw a profound
responsibility for people like himself. "Bad Information is insidious
because it looks so much like Good Information," he explained. "It
takes an extremely practiced eye, a kind of controlled skepticism
that never quite slides into abject nihilism, to spear Good
Information from the thick bog of Bad."[69]

T he pounding and the ridicule had the predictable
effect on the executives at the *Mercury News* and its
corporate parent, Knight-Ridder. In the early months
of 1997, the newspaper began back-pedaling from its series. By
spring, the executive editor Jerry Ceppos was in retreat.

On May 11, Ceppos published a front-page column admitting
that the series "fell short of my standards" in the reporting and
editing of a complex story that contained many "gray areas."
Among the weaknesses, Ceppos said, were instances where the
paper included "only one interpretation of complicated, sometimes
conflicting pieces of evidence," such as assertions by Blandon
about when he stopped sharing profits with the contras and the
total amount of his assistance.

"We made our best estimate of how much money was
involved, but we failed to label it as an estimate, and instead it
appeared as fact," Ceppos said.

Further, Ceppos stated that the series "strongly implied CIA
knowledge" that a contra-connected cocaine ring was instrumental
in launching the crack epidemic in Los Angeles in the early 1980s.
"I feel that we did not have proof that top CIA officials knew of the
relationship," Ceppos said.

While noting these shortcomings, Ceppos still maintained that
"our series solidly documented disturbing information: A drug ring
associated with the contras sold large quantities of cocaine in
inner-city Los Angeles in the 1980s at the time of the crack
explosion there. Some of the drug profits from those sales went to
the contras."

---

[69] *The Washington Post*, Dec. 4, 1996.

Though nuanced, Ceppos's letter was hailed as vindication by *The Washington Post* and *The New York Times.* On May 13, 1997, both papers splashed stories about Ceppos's column on page one, highly unusual treatment for a case of press self-criticism. The *Post* story was written by media critic Kurtz, who obtained quotes from other media analysts who joined in bashing Webb and praising the *Mercury News'* retreat.

Rem Reider, editor of the conservative-leaning *American Journalism Review,* called Ceppos's column a "significant, major correction" and termed the Webb story "another dark day for journalism." Meanwhile, the big papers hailed Ceppos for publicly undercutting his own reporter. "I give him high marks for openness and candor, which is something newspapers don't have a very good record of doing," declared the *Los Angeles Times'* Washington bureau chief, Doyle McManus.

In an editorial entitled "The Mercury News Comes Clean," *The New York Times* declared that Ceppos's "candor and self-criticism set a high standard for cases in which journalists make egregious errors. ... Mr. Ceppos suggested that editors got too close to the story while it was being written and lost the ability to detect flaws that might have been obvious had they maintained a more skeptical distance."[70]

While praising the *Mercury News'* self-criticism, the major newspapers displayed none themselves. There were no critiques of their earlier false exonerations of the contras, conclusions that even the big papers were now abandoning. There was no suggestion that in 1980s, the newspapers had gullibly accepted the government's claims of contra innocence, including the provably false assertion that the contra-cocaine allegations were invented only after the Iran-contra scandal broke.

Nor was there a retraction of the 1984 stories promoting drug-trafficking accusations against the Sandinistas. *The New York Times* reported at the time that unidentified "senior administration officials" possessed U.S. intelligence information implicating top Sandinista officials, including Interior Minister Tomas Borge and

---

[70] *The New York Times,* May 14, 1997.

Defense Minister Humberto Ortega.[71] But the Sandinista drug story had plenty of what Ceppos might have called "gray areas."

When I questioned Drug Enforcement Administration officials, they acknowledged that they had no evidence against any Nicaraguan official other than the mysterious Federico Vaughn, whose true allegiance was in doubt. They also conceded that they had no knowledge of any cocaine shipment transiting Nicaragua, except for the load flown in and out by the U.S. sting operation. The State Department acknowledged, too, that it had "no evidence" of Sandinista drug connections since the Vaughn case.[72]

Indeed, the big media's contrasting handling of the Sandinista drug charges (which were bandied about carelessly) and the contra-cocaine allegations (which were handled with extraordinary defensiveness) highlighted what would appear to be a clear double-standard, an unprofessional bias. But the mainstream press critics avoided such a conclusion.

None of the reporters who gummed up important facts in denouncing the Sandinistas and defending the contras was known to have faced disciplinary action or public repudiation. There was no known case of any major news organization engaging in an internal review of these journalistic errors or apologizing to the readers for mistakes. *The New York Times* showed no eagerness to "come clean" itself.

That was not the case for Webb, however. His personal situation went from bad to worse. On June 5, 1997, Ceppos called Webb with the news that he was being yanked from the contra-drug story and that a follow-up series would not be published. Ceppos asserted that he had reservations about the credibility of a principal Webb source. Ceppos also said Webb had gotten too close to the story.

Ceppos's concern about an untrustworthy source apparently referred to convicted trafficker Carlos Cabezas who had claimed that a CIA agent, known as Ivan Gomez, oversaw the transfer of drug profits to the contras. The editor also ordered Webb, who was

---

[71] *The New York Times,* July 19, 1984.
[72] See *International Narcotics Control Strategy Report,* March 1988.

based at the newspaper's capital bureau in Sacramento, to report to San Jose the next day to learn about his future with the newspaper.

On June 6, Georg Hodel, a Swiss reporter based in Nicaragua who had helped Webb with the contra-cocaine investigation, called Ceppos to protest. For months, Hodel said he and other journalists in Central America had been facing professional and physical threats for their efforts to expose the history of contra-cocaine trafficking.

In a Feb. 2 article in *La Tribuna,* Hodel noted, former contra chief Adolfo Calero had explained what he thought should happen to these politically suspect Nicaraguan and foreign reporters. Calero used metaphorical language that referred to leftist Nicaraguan journalists as "deer" and fellow-traveling foreign reporters as "antelopes." "The deer are going to be finished off," Calero wrote. "In this case, the antelopes as well."

In calling Ceppos, Hodel explained, "I wanted him to understand the human as well as journalistic costs of what he was doing, not only to Webb but to other journalists associated with the story in Nicaragua. I thought he should know that his decision to distance himself from the 'Dark Alliance' series -- combined with earlier attacks from major American newspapers -- had increased the dangers to me and others who have been pursuing this story in the field."[73]

Ceppos ignored Hodel's appeal. Later that day, he informed Webb that the investigative reporter would be transferred to a suburban office in Cupertino, about 150 miles from Webb's house where he lives with his wife and three children. Webb understood the message as a not-so-subtle suggestion that he quit.

The Washington Post's Howard Kurtz heralded the news. "The *San Jose Mercury News* has apparently had enough of reporter Gary Webb and his efforts to prove that the CIA was involved in the sale of crack cocaine," Kurtz wrote. "Editors at the California newspaper have yanked Webb off the story and told him they will not publish his follow-up articles."[74]

---

[73] For details, see *iF Magazine,* Sept.-Oct. 1997.
[74] *The Washington Post,* June 11, 1997.

Webb took some time off to contemplate his future. Hodel, fearing for himself and his wife in Nicaragua, relocated back to Switzerland. Finally on Dec. 12, 1997, Webb agreed to resign from the *Mercury News,* effectively ending his career in daily journalism. He did continue work on a book about his experiences, with the same title as his newspaper series, *Dark Alliance.*

Back in Washington, the CIA and the Justice Department continued internal investigations that Webb's series had instigated.

Chapter 9
Crumbling Cover-up

The CIA's defensive line on contra-drug trafficking began to give way the month after Gary Webb resigned from the *San Jose Mercury News*. The first volume of the CIA inspector general's report was published on Jan. 29, 1998, and poked the first holes. But the national press corps, having already convinced itself of the investigative outcome and the craziness of the contra-cocaine suspicions, didn't notice.

The CIA also camouflaged the admissions behind a press release and an executive summary that stressed the positive and ignored the negative. In those summaries, CIA inspector general Frederick Hitz reasserted the CIA's contention that key figures from the Los Angeles crack ring did not have direct ties to the CIA and that their donations to the contra cause were relatively small. The summaries also denied that the CIA took any steps to protect contra-connected drug traffickers, Danilo Blandon and Norwin Meneses, key figures in Webb's series.

Drawing from those summaries, most major newspapers wrote fairly brief accounts of the CIA's report and led the stories with the agency's superficial claims of innocence. Only by reading deep into the 149-page report, entitled "The California Story," would journalists have found the real story, the CIA's grudging admission that not only were many of Webb's allegations true but actually understated the scandal. If the reporters had read the entire text of Volume One, they would have discovered that the CIA was acknowledging that cocaine smugglers played a significant early role in the Nicaraguan contra movement. The CIA also admitted that it intervened to block an image-threatening 1984 federal inquiry into a cocaine ring with suspected links to the contras.

The CIA conceded, too, that it received intelligence from a law-enforcement agency in 1982 that a U.S. religious group was collaborating with the contras in a guns-for-drugs operation. But the CIA turned a blind eye toward the allegations, claiming that to do otherwise would have violated the civil liberties of the religious group whose identity remained secret.

Toward the end of the Volume One, the CIA included a detailed account of its interviews with Blandon, Meneses and other figures in that drug gang. Blandon gave a surprising description of private meetings that he and Meneses had with contra military chief Enrique Bermudez.

Prior to the Sandinista revolution in 1979, Meneses had been notorious in Nicaragua as a drug kingpin. But Bermudez still welcomed Meneses and Blandon when they stopped in Honduras in 1982. The two drug smugglers were en route to Bolivia where they planned to arrange a shipment of cocaine to the United States.

During the stopover, Bermudez asked for their help "in raising funds and obtaining equipment" as well as procuring arms, the CIA report stated. As Webb reported in his "Dark Alliance" series, Blandon recalled that Bermudez advised the two drug dealers that when it came to raising money for the contras, "the ends justify the means."

In the CIA interview, Blandon said he was not sure exactly what Bermudez and the other contras knew about Meneses's cocaine operations. Nevertheless, Blandon added new details about how the contras helped him and Meneses continue on to Bolivia to complete the cocaine transaction.

After the meeting with Bermudez, contras escorted Blandon and Meneses to the airport in Tegucigalpa. The traffickers were carrying $100,000 in drug proceeds for their Bolivian drug deal, Blandon said. At the airport, however, Honduran authorities detained Blandon and confiscated his $100,000 on the correct suspicion that the money was illicit. The drug traffickers were in a serious fix.

But the contra escorts intervened to save the day. They told the Hondurans that Blandon and Meneses were contras -- and demanded that the $100,000 be returned. The Hondurans complied and the drug dealers went ahead with their trip.

In his CIA interview, Blandon did try to minimize the sums of Meneses's drug money that went into the contra coffers. He estimated the amounts in the tens of thousands of dollars, not millions. But he acknowledged that Meneses also was active in other contra support operations in California, serving as the contras' "personnel recruiter."

In a separate interview with the CIA, Meneses confirmed his recruiting role and added that he also served on an FDN fund-raising committee. But, like Blandon, Meneses played down the significance of drug trafficking as a contra-funding source. Meneses talked to the CIA officials at the prison in Nicaragua where he was incarcerated in November 1991 when Nicaraguan police arrested him on new charges of narcotics trafficking.

While at the prison, the CIA heard more damaging accounts from other members of the Meneses-Blandon drug ring. These other witnesses insisted that the drug smuggling was far more widespread inside the contra movement than Meneses and Blandon were letting on.

One Meneses lieutenant, Enrique Miranda, declared that Meneses had told him that Salvadoran military aircraft transported arms from the United States to the contras and then returned with drugs to an airfield near Fort Worth, Texas. Miranda said he witnessed one such shipment to the Fort Worth area, where maintenance workers handed the drugs to Meneses's people who then drove the contraband off in vans. Miranda recalled Meneses saying that he did not stop selling drugs for the contras until 1985.

The CIA received more corroboration about Meneses's contra-cocaine work from Renato Pena Cabrera, another convicted drug trafficker associated with Meneses. Pena claimed that he participated in contra-related activities in San Francisco from 1982-84 while serving simultaneously as Meneses's drug wholesaler in Los Angeles. "Pena says that a Colombian associate of Meneses's told Pena in 'general' terms that portions of the proceeds from the sale of the cocaine Pena brought to San Francisco were going to the contras," the CIA report stated.

Bermudez could not be questioned, because he was shot to death on Feb. 16, 1991, after the war ended and he returned to Managua. The murder was never solved.

The CIA report disclosed another case in which the U.S. intelligence agency discouraged a deeper probe into a contra-connected drug operation: the so-called Frogman Case. In that case, swimmers in wet suits were caught on Jan. 17, 1983, bringing 430 pounds of cocaine ashore near San Francisco. Eventually, 50 individuals, including many Nicaraguans, were arrested.

The case became a potential embarrassment to the CIA when a contra political operative in Costa Rica, named Francisco Aviles Saenz, wrote to the federal court in San Francisco and argued that $36,800 seized in the case belonged to the contras. Aviles wanted the money back.

The new CIA report indicated that CIA officials in Central America fretted about a follow-up plan by Frogman Case lawyers to depose Aviles and other Nicaraguans in Costa Rica. A July 30, 1984, cable from the CIA's Latin American Division expressed "concern that this kind of uncoordinated activity (i.e., the AUSA [assistant U.S. attorney] and FBI visit and depositions) could have serious implications for anti-Sandinista activities in Costa Rica and elsewhere."

The CIA's lawyers then contacted the Justice Department and arranged for the Costa Rican depositions to be canceled. "There are sufficient factual details which would cause certain damage to our image and program in Central America," CIA assistant general counsel Lee S. Strickland wrote on Aug. 22, 1984. Without further ado, the $36,800 was returned to the contras.

The CIA clearly feared that the Frogman Case could expose a deeper contra-cocaine connection. On Aug. 24, 1984, CIA headquarters explained to the Latin American Division that "in essence the United States Attorney could never disprove the defendant's allegation that his was (a contra support group) or

(CIA) money. ... We can only guess at what other testimony may have been forthcoming. As matter now stands, (CIA) equities are fully protected, but (CIA's Office of General Counsel) will continue to monitor the prosecution closely so that any further disclosures or allegations by defendant or his confidants can be deflected."[75]

But inside the CIA, General Counsel Stanley Sporkin still expressed concern about the case. In a weekly report to senior CIA officials, dated Oct. 26, 1984, Sporkin noted that "this matter raises obvious questions concerning the people we are supporting in Central America and we are continuing our inquiry into this matter internally in conjunction with all concerned components."

Six days later, however, Ernest Mayerfeld, counsel to the Directorate of Operations, challenged Sporkin's analysis. In a memo, Mayerfeld stated that he had contacted the CIA lawyer on the case and was assured "that he can avoid, with the excellent cooperation of the San Francisco prosecutor, any public disclosure of our involvement. I do not think this is a big flap and ought not to be made into one."

The story about the returned contra money surfaced in the *San Francisco Examiner* on March 16, 1986, as the Reagan administration was in the midst of a furious political battle to convince Congress to restore CIA funding for the contra war. The last thing the White House wanted was more evidence of contra-connected drug trafficking.

Within days of the newspaper story, San Francisco U.S. Attorney Joseph Russoniello stepped forward as point man for the counterattack, much as Mayerfeld had hoped. In a tough letter to the newspaper, Russoniello insisted that the return of the money was simply a budgetary decision and "had nothing to do with any claim that the funds came from the contras or belonged to the contras. ... No 'higher ups' were involved, as Congresswoman [Barbara] Boxer wrongfully surmises."

Volume One made clear that Russoniello's protest did not square with the documentary record. Volume One also revealed that not only was the top contra military commander, Bermudez, in close contact with a notorious drug lord but that the drug lord

---

[75] Parentheses were from the CIA report.

recruited other drug smugglers to work under the contra umbrella. Volume One demonstrated further that the contra connections gave the traffickers special protection from the U.S. government.

Another startling disclosure in the CIA report appeared in an Oct. 22, 1982, cable written by the office at the CIA's Directorate of Operations which receives information from U.S. law enforcement agencies. "There are indications of links between (a U.S. religious organization) and two Nicaraguan counter-revolutionary groups," the cable read. "These links involve an exchange in (the United States) of narcotics for arms." The cable added that the participants were planning a meeting in Costa Rica for such a deal.

Initially, when the cable arrived, senior CIA officials were interested and concerned. On Oct. 27, CIA headquarters asked for more information. The law enforcement agency expanded on its report by telling the CIA that representatives of the FDN and another contra force, the UDN, would be meeting with several unidentified U.S. citizens.

But then, the CIA reversed itself, deciding that it wanted no more information, on the grounds that U.S. citizens were involved. "In light of the apparent participation of U.S. persons throughout, agree you should not pursue the matter further," CIA headquarters wrote on Nov. 3, 1982.

Two weeks later, CIA headquarters mentioned the meeting again, however. CIA officials thought it might be necessary to knock down the allegations of a guns-for-drugs deal as "misinformation." The CIA's Latin American Division responded on Nov. 18, 1982, reporting that several contra officials had gone to San Francisco for meetings with supporters, presumably as part of the same guns-for-drugs scheme.

But no additional information about the scheme was found in CIA files. The CIA inspector general conducted one follow-up interview, with Pena. The drug trafficker stated that the U.S. religious organization was "an FDN political ally that provided only humanitarian aid to Nicaraguan refugees and logistical support for contra-related rallies, such as printing services and portable stages." The name of the religious organization and other identifying details were withheld in the publicly released version of the CIA report.

Though the identity of the religious group remained secret, suspicions naturally fell on the U.S.-based political organizations affiliated with Rev. Sun Myung Moon's Unification Church. For years, Moon's organization has emphatically denied ties to drug traffickers. But it has worked closely in the past with groups and individuals connected to organized crime and the drug trade.

Moon's Korea-based church got its first boost as an international organization when Kim Jong-Pil, the founder of the Korean Central Intelligence Agency, brokered a relationship between Moon and one of Japan's leading rightist financiers, Ryoichi Sasakawa. Sasakawa had been jailed after World War II as a war criminal, but was freed, along with Yoshio Kodama, by U.S. military intelligence officials eager to enlist their help in combatting leftist political forces in Japan.

Kodama and Sasakawa obliged by dispatching right-wing goon squads to break up anti-U.S. demonstrations. They also allegedly grew rich from their association with the *yakuza,* a powerful organized crime syndicate that profited off drug smuggling, gambling and prostitution in both Japan and Korea. Behind the scenes, Kodama and Sasakawa became powerbrokers in Japan's ruling Liberal Democratic Party.

In the early 1960s, Kim Jong-Pil's intelligence contacts with these right-wing leaders proved invaluable to Moon, who had made only a few converts in Japan. After Kim Jong-Pil opened the door to Kodama and Sasakawa in late 1962, 50 leaders of an ultra-nationalist Japanese Buddhist sect converted en masse to the Unification Church giving it a strong base in Japan that remains to this day.

According to David E. Kaplan and Alec Dubro in their authoritative book, *Yakuza,* "Sasakawa became an adviser to Reverand Sun Myung Moon's Japanese branch of the Unification Church" and collaborated with Moon in building far-right anti-communist organizations in Asia, including the Asian People's Anti-Communist League.

The church's sudden growth spurt did not escape the notice of U.S. intelligence officers in the field. One CIA report, dated Feb. 26,

1963, stated that "Kim Jong-Pil organized the Unification Church while he was director of the ROK [Republic of Korea] Central Intelligence Agency, and has been using the church, which had a membership of 27,000 as a political tool." Though Moon's church had existed since the mid-1950s, the report appeared correct in noting Kim Jong-Pil's key role in transforming the church from a minor Korean sect into a potent international organization supported by wealthy Japanese financiers.

In 1966, the Asian People's Anti-Communist League expanded into the World Anti-Communist League, an international alliance that pulled together traditional conservatives with former Nazis, overt racialists and Latin American "death squad" operatives. In an interview, retired U.S. Army Gen. John K. Singlaub, a former WACL president, said "the Japanese [WACL] chapter was taken over almost entirely by Moonies."

Through WACL and other political relationships, Moon built bridges to right-wing forces in South America during the 1970s. As DEA agent Michael Levine noted in his book *Deep Cover,* the DEA arrested Jose Roberto Gasser in May 1980 for allegedly smuggling 854 pounds of cocaine base. To Levine's amazement, Gasser, the son of a Bolivian WACL leader, "was almost immediately released" for what Levine suspected were geopolitical reasons. Gasser's father was a leading figure in the coup to overthrow Bolivia's left-of-center government. The putsch on July 17, 1980, became known as the Cocaine Coup because it gave the drug lords free rein of the country and allowed protected shipments of coca base to Colombia.

Among the first well-wishers arriving in La Paz to congratulate the new government was Moon's top lieutenant, Bo Hi Pak. The Moon organization was so proud of its new contacts that it published a photo of Pak meeting with Gen. Luis Garcia Meza, the new ruler. After the visit to the mountainous capital of Bolivia, Pak declared, "I have erected a throne for Father Moon in the world's highest city."

According to later Bolivian government and newspaper reports, a Moon representative invested about $4 million in preparations for the coup. CAUSA, one of Moon's anti-communist organizations, listed as members nearly all the leading Bolivian coup-makers.

Shortly after the putsch, the neo-fascist shock troops, recruited by fugitive Nazi Klaus Barbie, moved into the business of transporting cocaine for the drug lords. "The paramilitary units, conceived by Barbie as a new type of SS, sold themselves to the cocaine barons," wrote German investigative reporter Kai Hermann. "The attraction of fast money in the cocaine trade was stronger than the idea of a national socialist revolution in Latin America."[76]

As the drug lords consolidated their power in Bolivia, the Moon organization expanded its presence, too. Hermann reported that by early 1981, Thomas Ward, a leader of CAUSA, had arrived on the scene. Lt. Alfred Mario Mingolla, an Argentine intelligence officer dispatched to help the coup-makers, identified Ward as his paymaster, with Mingolla's $1,500 monthly salary allegedly coming from a CAUSA-connected office.

Moon's organization continued to flaunt its new-found influence in Bolivia. On May 31, 1981, Moon representatives sponsored a CAUSA reception at the Sheraton Hotel's Hall of Freedom in La Paz. Bo Hi Pak and Gen. Garcia Meza led a prayer for President Reagan's recovery from an assassination attempt.

"God has chosen the Bolivian people in the heart of South America as the ones to conquer communism," Bo Hi Pak declared in his speech. According to a later Bolivian intelligence report, the Moon organization sought to recruit an "armed church" of Bolivians, with about 7,000 Bolivians receiving some paramilitary training.

But by late 1981, the obvious cocaine taint was straining official U.S.-Bolivian relations. "The Moon sect disappeared overnight from Bolivia as clandestinely as they had arrived," Hermann reported. Only Ward and a couple of others stayed on with the Bolivian information agency as it worked on a transition back to civilian rule, Hermann wrote.

During the early 1980s, Moon's organization demonstrated unprecedented financial strength. In 1982, Moon launched *The*

---

[76] For details, see an English translation of Hermann's work published in *Covert Action Information Bulletin,* Winter 1986.

Washington Times, a right-wing daily that cost Moon an estimated $100 million a year in losses. In 1983, Moon established an important financial base in Uruguay with the purchase of the country's third largest bank, the Banco de Credito, which soon became the center of allegations about money-laundering.[77]

Moon's CAUSA also continued to organize pro-contra rallies in the United States and to coordinate contra activities with right-wing forces in Honduras and other Central American countries. Through the 1980s, Moon's *Washington Times* aggressively defended the contra operations and raised money for the contras after Congress cut off funding. In 1984, the *Times* also published the first reports about Sandinista drug suspicions, a story that helped the contra cause in Congress while killing a major DEA investigation of the Medellin cartel.

On May 7, 1998, another disclosure from the U.S. government's investigations of contra-cocaine trafficking shook the CIA's weakening defense lines. Rep. Maxine Waters, D-Calif., introduced into the *Congressional Record* a 1982 letter that she had received unceremoniously in the mail. The letter revealed that CIA director Casey secretly engineered an exemption sparing the CIA from a legal requirement to report on drug smuggling by agency assets.

The exemption was granted by Attorney General William French Smith on Feb. 11, 1982, only three months after President Reagan authorized covert CIA support for the Nicaraguan contra army. The exemption was an important clue to the contra-cocaine mystery. The letter suggested that the CIA's tolerance of illicit drug smuggling by its clients during the 1980s was official policy anticipated from the outset, not just an unintended consequence followed by an ad hoc cover-up.

Before the letter's release, the documentary evidence only supported the allegation that Reagan's CIA concealed drug trafficking by the contras and other intelligence assets in Latin America. The letter established that Casey foresaw the legal

---

[77] For details, see *iF Magazine,* Sept.-Oct. 1998.

dilemma that the CIA would encounter with federal laws requiring it to report illicit narcotics smuggling by foreign CIA agents.

The narcotics exemption was especially noteworthy in contrast to the laundry list of crimes which the CIA was required to disclose. Under Justice Department regulations, "reportable offenses" included assault, homicide, kidnapping, Neutrality Act violations, communication of classified data, illegal immigration, bribery, obstruction of justice, possession of explosives, election contributions, possession of firearms, illegal wiretapping, visa violations and perjury.

Yet, despite reporting requirements for many less serious offenses, Casey fought a bureaucratic battle in early 1982 to exempt the CIA from, as Smith wrote, "the need to add narcotics violations to the list of reportable non-employee crimes." In his letter, Smith noted that the law provides that "when requested by the Attorney General, it shall be the duty of any agency or instrumentality of the Federal Government to furnish assistance to him for carrying out his functions under" the Controlled Substances Act. But Smith agreed that "in view of the fine cooperation the Drug Enforcement Administration has received from CIA, no formal requirement regarding the reporting of narcotics violations has been included in these procedures."

On March 2, 1982, Casey thanked Smith for the exemption. "I am pleased that these procedures, which I believe strike the proper balance between enforcement of the law and protection of intelligence sources and methods, will now be forwarded to other agencies covered by them for signing by the heads of the agencies," Casey wrote.[78]

In the years that followed, "protection of intelligence sources and methods" apparently became the catch-all excuse for the CIA's tolerance of South American cocaine smugglers using the contra war as cover.

---

[78] At the time of Smith's letter, Kenneth Starr was a senior counselor in the attorney general's office, but it was not clear whether Starr had any input into the exemption. Starr's office did not respond to my written questions about his knowledge of the drug waiver.

Substantial evidence has surfaced revealing that many drug smugglers scurried under the contra umbrella in the early 1980s. They presumably understood that the Reagan administration would be loath to expose its pet covert action to negative publicity and possibly even to criminal prosecution.

According to the accumulated evidence, Bolivia's Cocaine Coup government of 1980-82 was only the first in line filling the contra-drug pipeline. Other contra-connected drug operations soon followed, including the Medellin cartel, the Panamanian government, the Honduran military, the Honduran-Mexican smuggling ring of Ramon Matta Ballesteros, and the Miami-based anti-Castro Cubans with their connections to Mafia operations throughout the United States. While it is impossible to estimate precise volumes of cocaine, clearly these operations represented a large portion of the illicit drug industry, far bigger than the Meneses-Blandon drug conduit that Webb had examined.

For her part, Rep. Waters stated that the Casey-Smith arrangement "allowed some of the biggest drug lords in the world to operate without fear that the CIA would be required to report their activities to the DEA and other law enforcement agencies. ... These damning memorandums ... are further evidence of a shocking official policy that allowed the drug cartels to operate through the CIA-led contra covert operations in Central America." The waiver also was evidence of premeditation.

The big media, finally and minimally, acknowledged the collapsing CIA defense in mid-summer 1998. After 12 years of dumping on the contra-cocaine allegations, *The New York Times* pulled what was called during Watergate a "modified limited hang-out," offering partial affirmation that the long-denigrated charges were true and would be supported by the long-awaited Volume Two.

On July 17, the *Times* reported that CIA inspector general Hitz had discovered that the CIA knew that about 50 Nicaraguan contras and their backers were implicated in cocaine smuggling. Then, without seriously examining the proof, the CIA kept working with about two dozen of the suspected smugglers in the 1980s, the *Times* wrote.

The article ran under a headline: "CIA Says It Used Nicaraguan Rebels Accused of Drug Tie." The one-column story was stuck in the lower left-hand corner of the front page -- the most obscure spot on the page. Citing unnamed government sources, it stated that "the new report [by Hitz] criticizes agency officials' actions at the time for the inconsistent and sometimes sloppy manner in which they investigated -- or chose not to investigate -- the allegations, which were never substantiated by the agency."

Though a reversal for the *Times*, the newspaper of record still let the CIA put its spin on the drug scandal. The *Times* quoted one U.S. intelligence official as saying, "the fundamental finding of the report is that there is no information that the CIA or CIA employees ever conspired with any contra organizations or individuals involved with the contras for the purposes of drug trafficking." The article also continued the attacks on Gary Webb.

According to what I was hearing from sources at the time, however, Volume Two was far more damning than presented in the *Times* story. Even the CIA's supposed innocence was very narrowly worded, I was told. The sources reported that Hitz's investigative document contained evidence that authorization for some cocaine trafficking tracked directly into President Reagan's National Security Council.

But in a larger sense, it was now clear, Hitz's Volume Two would confirm what had been alleged for more than a decade -- that the contra operation was riddled with drug trafficking and that the smugglers were protected by the Reagan administration for geopolitical reasons. Viewed in that context, the *Times* story looked more like a P.R. inoculation -- an attempt by the CIA to get out in front of the disclosures and neutralize any explosive impact -- rather than a hard-hitting expose of a serious crime of state.

Given the seriousness of the crimes, the *Times'* editorial writers also might have been expected to clamor for follow-ups and full disclosure of the evidence in Volume Two. Instead, there were no editorials, no follow-ups. Not surprisingly, there also was no self-criticism about how the *Times* had gotten the story so wrong for so long. The *Times* made no admission of journalistic errors.

Rep. Waters was one of the few public figures who demanded Volume Two's prompt release and immediate public hearings.

"There is no conceivable reason to keep this report classified," Waters said. "It is tantamount to protecting drug dealers. ... I cannot understand why a CIA report, which details the illegal efforts of Reagan-Bush administration officials to protect the involvement of top-level contras in drug trafficking, should continue to be protected."

Chapter 10
Justice Denied

The next official contra-cocaine report to surface was not Volume Two of the CIA's findings. It was a long-postponed report by the inspector general of the Justice Department. The report was ready for publicaion in December 1997, but was put on hold because of some ill-defined law-enforcement concerns.

The Justice report, written by inspector general Michael Bromwich, followed the pattern of the CIA's Volume One. Given the hostile Washington climate surrounding Gary Webb's series in late 1997, Bromwich opted for the safe approach, to denigrate Webb's work and declare no government wrongdoing.

But Bromwich did include deep in the body of the report the same kind of evidence of government malfeasance that could be found in the CIA's Volume One. The new evidence established that the Reagan administration knew from almost the outset of the Nicaraguan contra war that cocaine traffickers permeated the CIA-backed army, yet the administration did almost nothing to expose or to stop the contra-connected criminals. The report revealed example after example of leads not followed, corroborated witnesses disparaged, official law-enforcement investigations sabotaged, and even the CIA facilitating the work of drug traffickers.

Despite the evidence, Bromwich joined the long parade of investigators who shied away from obvious conclusions. In his report's press release on July 23, 1998, he stressed that "the Department of Justice's investigative efforts [in the 1980s] were not affected by anyone's suspected ties to the contras." The next day, *The Washington Post* trumpeted the findings with the headline, "Justice Dept. IG Rebuts CIA-Crack Allegations."[79]

Still, a close reading of Bromwich's investigative report showed that it uncovered powerful new evidence revealing how consistently the Reagan administration made the contras' image and need for money a priority over stopping the smuggling of cocaine into the United States.

Like Volume One, Bromwich's report focused on the West Coast contra-drug operations. But even from that limited review, the evidence indicated that the contras and their supporters ran several parallel drug-smuggling operations during the 1980s. The report also found that the CIA shared little of its information about contra drugs with law-enforcement agencies and on three occasions disrupted cocaine-trafficking investigations that threatened the contras.

The Justice report dated the first contra-drug links back to the start of the contra war in the early 1980s and then traced the pattern of crimes through the decade. As late as 1989, U.S. agents were still frustrating contra-cocaine investigations when they spirited drug-indicted contra backer John Hull out of Costa Rica so he could avoid trial there on narcotics and other charges.

According to Bromwich's report, one early contra-drug network centered on longtime Nicaraguan drug smuggler Norwin Meneses, a focus of Webb's series. From the early 1980s, U.S. law enforcement was hearing about the veteran drug smuggler, Meneses, and his contra ties from informants who were judged reliable.

One confidential informant, identified only as "DEA CI-1," said that at the start of the contra war, Meneses taught "American agents" how to penetrate Nicaragua. The informant added that Meneses and his cohorts, Oscar Danilo Blandon and Ivan Torres, also contributed drug profits to the contras.

---

[79] *The Washington Post,* July 24, 1998.

DEA CI-1 said, however, the trio distinguished between selling drugs for the contras (which they denied) and donating money "to help some of their contra friends and acquaintances, such as [contra leaders Eden] Pastora and [Adolfo] Calero," (which they acknowledged). In Bromwich's report, the informant's statement about drug money going into contra pockets received multiple corroboration.

Renato Pena, a money-and-drug courier for Meneses, said that in the early 1980s, the CIA was allowing the contras to fly drugs into the United States, sell them and keep the proceeds. Pena, who also was the northern California representative for the CIA-backed FDN contra army, said the drug trafficking was forced on the contras by the inadequate CIA assistance provided in the war's early years. That money, ranging from $19 million to $24 million annually, was "peanuts" and pushed the contras into the arms of cocaine traffickers, claimed Pena.

Pena added that the sums transferred by Meneses to the contras were large, far more than the thousands of dollars that some other witnesses said they observed. Pena said that a Colombian contact known as "Carlos" once told him: "We're helping your cause with this drug thing. ... We are helping your organization a lot."

Meneses also had a military supply role. Pena said he was present when Meneses called FDN commander Enrique Bermudez and took orders for contra military equipment. According to Pena, Meneses stayed close to Bermudez from 1981-82 through the middle of the decade. Pena also asserted that Bermudez knew about the drug dealing -- and Bermudez clearly had reason to know. Meneses had been a notorious drug trafficker in Nicaragua prior to the Sandinista revolution in 1979.

In the report, Bromwich finessed the question of Bermudez's knowledge. "Meneses's reputation had preceded him in the small Nicaraguan exile community and ... people who dealt with Meneses knew or should have known that money coming from him was likely from an illicit source," the inspector general wrote.

Much of the Meneses information from DEA CI-1 and Pena was corroborated further by Meneses's nephew, Jairo. After his arrest in 1984, Jairo Meneses told the DEA that he had asked Pena to help transport drug money to the contras. Jairo Meneses added that both Norwin Meneses and Danilo Blandon told him they were raising money for the contras. Jairo Meneses added that his uncle dealt directly with Bermudez.

R unning parallel to the Meneses operation was another contra-drug network headed by Julio Zavala and Carlos Cabezas, the convicted trafficker whom Gary Webb had interviewed for his unpublished follow-up series. Cabezas said he joined this "contra cocaine" enterprise in December 1981 when he traveled to Costa Rica for meetings with Julio Zavala and two other drug figures closely linked to the contra operations, Horacio Pereira and Troilo Sanchez. Troilo Sanchez was the brother of Aristedes Sanchez, a founder of the contra movement and one of the FDN's directors.

Cabezas said Horacio Pereira and Troilo Sanchez described themselves as contra operatives who were raising money through drug sales. According to the scheme, Cabezas said, cocaine from Peru was packed into hollow reeds which were woven into tourist baskets and then transported to Costa Rica or Honduras. From there, smugglers carried the baskets to the United States. Cabezas claimed that Fernando Sanchez, another of Troilo's brothers and the FDN representative in Guatemala, assisted in the deliveries.

Once the baskets arrived in San Francisco, they went to Zavala who arranged for the sale of the cocaine for the Pereira-Sanchez network, Cabezas said. But Zavala fell short as a businessman, and by spring 1982, Pereira had turned to Cabezas to manage the drug money. Cabezas estimated that between December 1981 and December 1982, he made more than 20 trips to Central America and carried between $1 million and $1.5 million to Pereira and Troilo Sanchez.

Carlos Cabezas said he personally witnessed some money paid to buy food for contra troops and their families near Danli, Honduras. Cabezas claimed that on two other occasions, he took $40,000 to $50,000 to Miami where he gave the money to Aristedes Sanchez, the FDN director.

Another U.S. informant, designated "FBI Source 1," backed up much of Cabezas's story. Source 1 said Cabezas and Zavala were helping the contras with proceeds from two drug-trafficking operations, one smuggling Colombian cocaine and the other shipping cocaine through Honduras.

To secure the cocaine franchise, Cabezas and Zavala had to agree to give 50 percent of their profits to the contras, said Source 1. He added that revenues from the cocaine sales then were taken to Honduras by Horacio Pereira and Fernando Sanchez to support the contras. The source also asserted that some of the cocaine was smuggled into the United States in the reeds of rattan chairs.

Seeking to discredit this batch of damning contra-cocaine allegations, Bromwich cited Source 1's reference to "rattan chairs" as a contradiction to Cabezas's claim about cocaine in "wicker baskets." Both rattan chairs and wicker baskets, however, use hollow reeds in their construction.

In 1983, the West Coast drug networks began to run afoul of the law. Fifty drug traffickers, many Nicaraguan exiles, including Cabezas and Zavala, were arrested in the so-called Frogman case, so named because some smugglers were caught in wet suits carrying cocaine ashore near San Francisco.

By summer 1984, the CIA had grown nervous that the Frogman case might expose other drug connections to the contras in Central America, Bromwich's investigation found. Contras in Costa Rica had claimed in a letter to the federal court that $36,800 seized from drug defendant Zavala actually belonged to them.

As word of the letter spread inside the Reagan administration, an alarmed CIA headquarters protested prosecution plans to depose contra figures in Costa Rica. Assistant U.S. attorney Mark Zanides said that in mid-1984, he was approached by CIA counsel Lee Strickland. In an "opaque conversation," Zanides recalled, Strickland said the CIA would be "immensely grateful" if the depositions were dropped -- and they were.

The investigative trip to Costa Rica was canceled, the money was returned to Zavala and the government explained the move publicly as a simple budgetary decision. But the secret of the CIA's intervention soon reached Central America. On Aug. 17, 1984, the CIA's station in Costa Rica messaged CIA headquarters with news that the U.S. consul was saying that the Frogman trip was "cancelled by 'the funny farm'," which the consul meant as "a reference to CIA."

On Aug. 22, CIA counsel Strickland wrote internally that "I believe the station must be made aware of the potential for disaster. While the [contra-drug] allegations might be entirely false, there are sufficient factual details which would cause certain damage to our image and program in Central America." Two days later, CIA headquarters sent a cable to the Costa Rica station acknowledging the CIA's role in derailing the depositions. "We can only guess as to what other testimony may have been forthcoming," the cable explained.

Recalling those maneuvers, a retired CIA official, identified only as "Ms. Jones," told Bromwich's investigators that in 1984, the "burning issue" in the Zavala case was the "explosive" potential for bad publicity if the drug case implicated the contras. "What would make better headlines?" she asked.

Though the evidence of CIA obstruction was clear, Bromwich only mildly objected in his report. He expressed "concern" that "the CIA considered the potential press coverage of a contra-drug link to be sufficient reason to attempt to influence the decision to return the money to Zavala."

In fall 1984, the CIA found other problems slithering out of the contra can of worms, Bromwich's report disclosed. On Oct. 25, 1984, the CIA discovered that Southern Front contra leader Adolfo "Popo" Chamorro was discussing a cooperation agreement with a major drug trafficker in Miami.

Under the deal, the FRS, a contra army run by Eden Pastora, would provide "operational facilities," meaning airstrips, in Costa Rica and Nicaragua. The FRS also would get documentation from the Costa Rican government to "facilitate the transportation of narcotics." The CIA, which had stormy relations with Pastora, did pass this intelligence to the Justice Department. On Nov. 9, 1984, the CIA identified the trafficker as Jorge Morales, a Colombian drug smuggler linked to the Medellin cartel.

According to the CIA: "On Oct. 16, 1984, Morales reportedly turned over to FRS two helicopters and a DC-3 aircraft. The agreement between Morales and FRS also includes training for two

FRS pilots in Miami, who in addition to their FRS military duties, will fly narcotics from Colombia to FRS-provided landing fields in Costa Rica and Nicaragua and then on to the United States."

On Nov. 5, the CIA reported that FRS pilot Gerardo Duran was to make a flight for Morales from Miami to the Bahamas. Later that month, the CIA learned that Eden Pastora was to meet with contras -- Adolfo "Popo" Chamorro and Roberto "Tito" Chamorro -- and the drug-trafficker Morales on Nov. 29 in Miami. The CIA added that the "presence of Duran in Miami indicates that a narcotics flight is scheduled and plans for the flight will probably be made during the meetings between the FRS officers and Morales."

However, the CIA passed on the information to the DEA on Dec. 5, a week after the scheduled meeting. As Bromwich noted, if the tip was received by Nov. 28, "the CIA should have notified the DEA immediately [so authorities] could have tried to coordinate the interception of that flight."

Whether the CIA was tardy or not, the DEA did not appear eager to pursue contra drug leads anyway. The DEA later complained that the CIA's source inside the Morales operation "had not furnished actionable information sufficient to predicate initiation of a criminal investigation." An internal CIA cable explained that the source was "frightened for his life and refused to cooperate with" the DEA.

Years later in prison, Morales agreed to cooperate with the DEA and told how his contra-drug conduit had developed. He said he first "associated with individuals alleged to have contra affiliations" in June 1983. Then, members of the Medellin cartel met at Opa Locka Airport in Florida with a contra group flown in by contra pilots Marcos Aguado and Gerardo Duran. Morales said CIA-connected rancher John Hull flew to Opa Locka with the group but did not participate in the meeting.

The next year, in May 1984, Morales said he was contacted by Marta Healy, ex-wife of Adolfo "Popo" Chamorro and the widow of a Morales pilot. She wanted money, pilots and aircraft for the contras and, in exchange, offered to help Morales with his then-pending drug indictment. Morales said she promised intervention from her "high-level CIA contacts, Octaviano Cesar and Popo Chamorro."

Subsequently, Morales said Octaviano Cesar, another prominent contra with CIA ties, made the request more specific: move weapons for the contras through Hull's ranch in northern Costa Rica, give specialized training to contra pilots and donate $100,000 to Chamorro's contra group. Morales said he countered with an offer of money, a safehouse in Miami, a boat, a helicopter, two airplanes and 10,000 gallons of fuel. In return for that help, Cesar was to supply pilots for marijuana smuggling and to "clear up" Morales's indictment.

With a deal in place, Morales said he arranged for weapons to be airlifted to Hull's ranch, with the first shipments in the summer of 1984. Cesar and Chamorro also let Morales transport cocaine from Hull's ranch to Colombians in Florida, Morales declared. Morales said the flights continued into 1986, when he was arrested.[80]

In the meantime, the CIA's contra war was running into other troubles along the Nicaraguan border. Reports filtered back from Central America of contras killing civilians, raping women and torturing captives. Yet, the contras failed to occupy any Nicaraguan territory and the CIA mounted its own operations to create the appearance of contra competence. When the CIA mined Nicaragua's harbors in 1984, an international furor erupted and Congress cut off all U.S. military support. During the two-year aid cut-off, the contras appeared to rely even more heavily on drug proceeds.

In 1986, the DEA developed evidence against Gerardo Duran, the contra pilot working with Morales. The DEA reported that "intelligence information received by the Costa Rica Country Office over the past several years indicates that [Duran] has been involved in facilitating the transshipment of hundred-kilogram quantities of cocaine [about 220 pounds] from South America to the United States through Costa Rica.

"Evidence gathered [by the Miami Field Division] shows that during the month of January, 1986, [Duran] was in charge of a crew

---

[80] Cesar and Chamorro denied knowing about Morales and drugs.

which loaded over 400 kilos of cocaine [880 pounds] into an aircraft in Costa Rica piloted by a DEA [confidential informant]. This cocaine was flown to the Bahamas and part of the load was subsequently smuggled into the United States."

The DEA, however, did not pursue the case very aggressively. It chose not to indict Duran in Miami "because he is Costa Rican and cannot be extradited from Costa Rica to the U.S.," Bromwich's report stated.[81]

The DEA also heard more corroboration of the West Coast allegations about Meneses and his contra links. One informant, "LA CI-1," told the DEA that after the Sandinistas took power, Meneses hosted early meetings of the contras and cultivated a relationship with Bermudez as a way to re-establish the drug network that Meneses had lost with the Sandinista victory.

In April 1986, another "reliable" informant, designated "SR3," told the DEA that Meneses was an FDN member who had trafficked in drugs both for his own profit and to raise money for the contras. SR3 himself had worked in the drug organization until Meneses fled to Costa Rica in 1985. SR3 confirmed, too, that Pena was a major contra fund-raiser in San Francisco and sent drug money to the contras.

According to SR3, Meneses used family members to smuggle drugs proceeds from San Francisco through New Orleans and into Central America for the contras. SR3 added that some of the money went to Colombia to buy weapons for the contras.[82]

The DEA also learned about other cocaine pipelines that directly implicated the CIA. On March 20, 1986, DEA's Costa Rica office quoted a source as saying that contra pilot Carlos Amador was planning a cocaine flight from Costa Rica through El Salvador to Miami. The source said Amador possibly was picking up the cocaine in Hangar No. 4 at Ilopango airport in El Salvador.

---

[81] Duran was arrested in Costa Rica in 1987 and convicted in 1992.

[82] The contras did maintain a major logistical base in New Orleans, which was the focus of corruption complaints, including allegations of drug smuggling. The base was run by Mario Calero, the brother of FDN political chief Adolfo Calero.

The cable requested that the DEA's Guatemala office, which covered El Salvador, should "ask Salvadoran police to investigate Amador, and any person(s) and/or companies associated with Hangar No. 4." The problem for the CIA was that it controlled Hangar No. 4. The CIA had allocated space there for Oliver North's contra resupply effort.

The DEA cable was followed by a cable, dated April 23, 1986, from the CIA station in Costa Rica to the station in El Salvador, asking about Amador and the drug-trafficking allegations. Two days later, the CIA's station in El Salvador urged the DEA to halt any inquiries about Hangar No. 4.

The CIA cable stated that Amador had stopped flying for the contras in early 1985, though it acknowledged that he went to work for the FDN afterwards in Honduras. While agreeing with the suspicions about Amador's drug trafficking, the CIA cable insisted that Amador only transported military supplies to Hangar No. 4.

"Based on that information, [El Salvador] Station would appreciate [Costa Rica] Station advising [DEA] not to make any inquiries to anyone re: hangar no. 4 at Ilopango since only legitimate [CIA] supported operations were conducted from this facility. FYI," the cable continued, "Station air operations moved from hangar no. 4 into hangar no. 5 which Station still occupies."

The CIA's request apparently did slow the investigation. But on June 10, 1986, the CIA's El Salvador station cabled the Costa Rica station with news that a U.S. embassy officer in San Salvador had requested more information about Amador. "The embassy officer said that if Amador is connected to [the CIA], [the DEA] will leave him alone, but if not they [the DEA] intend to go after him," the cable read. A week later, CIA headquarters denied any "association" with Amador. But the DEA's pursuit of drug trafficking in El Salvador would not prove easy.

Celerino Castillo was the DEA officer responsible for El Salvador. On June 23, 1986, Castillo reported debriefing an informant known as "STG6," who knew Amador and other alleged traffickers. STG6 said Amador used Salvadoran military credentials to land at Ilopango without the normal Customs search. STG6 added that Amador smuggled arms to the contras and cocaine from El Salvador to Miami. By fall, Castillo learned that a U.S.

government agency, later identified as the CIA, had "obtained a U.S. visa" for Amador, a contradiction of the CIA's claim that it had no association with the alleged drug trafficker.

Yet, while the DEA slowly pieced together the contra-drug puzzle in Central America, the Reagan administration kept the lid on the new evidence back in Washington. The public diplomacy teams planted stories in major newspapers dismissing the contra-drug allegations as fiction. The Justice Department assisted in the cover-up, too, by stonewalling requests from the Senate Foreign Relations Committee for evidence on contra-cocaine trafficking.

The strategy worked. By containing the contra-drug scandal in mid-1986, President Reagan won congressional approval for renewed CIA contra funding, the $100 million annual amount that contra backers had always claimed was needed to fund the war properly.

A t all levels, the Reagan administration preferred not to have confirmation of the contra-cocaine crimes, Bromwich's report revealed. The chief of the Salvadoran Air Force responded to the DEA's growing suspicions about Ilopango drug trafficking by asking U.S. Ambassador Edwin Corr to place drug-sniffing dogs at the airfield. Corr rebuffed the request on the grounds that the initial evidence did not justify the expense. But the allegations continued.

In fall 1986, DEA agent Castillo began looking into the mysterious activities of a former U.S. military official, Walter Grasheim, who operated out of San Salvador. Informant STG6 had identified Grasheim as "head of smuggling operations" at Ilopango. "Grasheim owns and operates Hangar #4," alleged the informant who worked at the airport. "Said hangar is utilized by international cocaine and arms traffickers. Hangar #4 is also utilized by the Contra Movement in El Salvador."

On Oct. 27, Castillo opened a file on Grasheim as part of a larger investigation of drug trafficking at hangars four and five. Castillo's investigative report identified 13 other "documented narcotics traffickers" who used the hangars. The suspicions led to a search of Grasheim's house, which uncovered plastic explosives, grenades, sniper equipment, silencers, anti-tank rockets, automatic rifles and night-vision gear, but only small amounts of marijuana. Grasheim denied any drug role and said he had been hired by Salvadoran authorities as a military adviser.

On Oct. 30, Castillo briefed Corr, who knew Grasheim when he worked in the U.S. embassy's Military Group. Officially, Corr "welcomed any investigation on Grasheim but ... asked ... that the investigation be conducted in a very discreet manner," Castillo reported in a memo.

Unknown to Castillo, however, Corr went behind the agent's back. The ambassador sent a "back-channel" cable to the State Department asking DEA headquarters to review Castillo's investigation. DEA headquarters responded by judging the evidence inadequate and closing down the Grasheim file only days after the inquiry had started.

Suddenly, Castillo was under the embassy's watchful eye. In an interview with Bromwich's investigators, Corr said Castillo resisted the orders to drop the case and continued "to snoop around the airport and make allegations." Corr warned Castillo that unless he had more evidence, he should stop this "witch hunt."

T he fall of 1986 brought more bad news for the contra operations. The Iran-contra scandal broke wide open, after a Beirut magazine disclosed secret U.S. arms sales to Iran, a project that generated profits which North diverted into contra accounts.

Despite this evidence of other illicit contra fund-raising, the official Iran-contra investigations steered clear of any comprehensive examination of contra-drug trafficking. Most Democrats seemed as leery about the serious charges as were the Republicans. According to an internal CIA memo, the agency's Central American Task Force chief Alan Fiers told congressional intelligence committees that the CIA would brief the DEA on the CIA's information about contra-drug trafficking. But that meeting apparently never happened and was never demanded.

Bromwich's report stated that "neither the DEA nor the CIA [Office of the Inspector General] could locate any record of any such discussions. Alan Fiers refused to be interviewed by the [Justice inspector general]. In response to our letter to him, he called us and said in a short conversation that he recalled only one instance when the CIA passed contra and narcotics-related information to the DEA" -- regarding Jorge Morales and Pastora's renegade contra group.

In 1989, with the Iran-contra scandal provoking new congressional restrictions on contra aid, the DEA soon got wind of more contra-cocaine shipments. DEA supervisor Thomas deTriquet recalled that a reliable informant had passed on information about drug dealers using contra pilots to transport cocaine through Hangar No. 5, the one controlled by the CIA.

When Castillo and deTriquet went to Ilopango to investigate, however, a CIA officer turned them away, the report said. The DEA agents then went to the U.S. embassy where the CIA chief of station assured them that there was no drug activity at Hangar No. 5. Robert Stia, DEA country attache in Guatemala, complained to headquarters that "DEA cannot develop the most important information, that relating to those allegations and intelligence in regards to Ilopango Air Force Base."

Stia also reported that in March 1989 a confidential source relayed information from a Salvadoran Air Force officer that the Salvadoran government and the CIA were running large shipments of cocaine through air bases at La Union and San Miguel in El Salvador. The goal again was to raise money for the contras, the source claimed.

Stia noted, too, that the U.S. Embassy objected to Castillo's involvement because he was always "digging up things." Stia said the deputy ambassador had put "stringent controls" on handling Castillo's "country clearance" for entering El Salvador. Castillo was soon hounded out of the DEA.

Summing up this recurring contra-drug defensiveness, Bromwich grasped the obvious:

> We have no doubt that the CIA and the U.S. Embassy were not anxious for the DEA to pursue its investigation at the airport. The DEA's [first] investigation of drug trafficking activities at Ilopango was closed in 1986, perhaps with the intervention of the U.S. Embassy. Moreover, as reflected in the CIA's

cables in the Amador case, the CIA requested that the
DEA not investigate its operations at Ilopango, and the
CIA vouched that they were legitimate CIA-supported
operations. It is also clear that there was intelligence,
although not hard evidence, that some contra resupply
pilots were trafficking in drugs.

At the end of the 1980s, the contras still were failing
militarily. But Nicaragua's economy was in shambles and the
Sandinistas lost at the polls in 1990. Contrary to the predictions of
The New Republic and other contra enthusiasts, the Sandinistas did
relinquish power and the war ended. Some contra-connected drug
traffickers, such as Norwin Meneses, returned to Nicaragua and
reestablished their drug networks. But Meneses finally got caught
and was sent to prison.

Some contra-cocaine witnesses, such as Jorge Morales, were
deemed credible in later DEA investigations of non-contra drug
trafficking, though dismissed as not credible when they implicated
the contras. Morales's non-contra DEA cooperation won him early
release from prison. He returned to Colombia, where he died in a
car crash in 1991.

No official from the Reagan administration was ever held
legally accountable for contra-drug trafficking or for obstructing
justice. Although recognizing the obvious obstructions, Bromwich
proposed no punishment for those involved.

B romwich adopted a similarly tolerant view of the
evidence that U.S. officials in Costa Rica frustrated
that country's effort to try a key contra backer on
drug-trafficking and other criminal charges. John Hull, the
American farmer in Costa Rica whose land became a base for
contra raids into Nicaragua, averted prosecution by fleeing Costa
Rica in 1989 with the help of U.S. government operatives.

Bromwich's report disclosed that Hull escaped from Costa
Rica in a plane flown by a pilot who worked for the DEA. The
report, however, could not reconcile conflicting accounts about the
direct involvement of a DEA officer and concluded, improbably,
with a finding of no wrongdoing. The finding made Bromwich's

report the latest chapter in a long saga of U.S. government protection of Hull, a fervent anti-communist who became a favorite of the Reagan-Bush administrations.

For years, contra-connected witnesses had cited Hull's ranch as a cocaine transshipment point for drugs heading to the United States. According to Bromwich's report, the DEA even prepared a research report on the evidence in November 1986. In it, one informant described Colombian cocaine off-loaded at an airstrip on Hull's ranch. The drugs were then concealed in a shipment of frozen shrimp and transported to the United States. The alleged Costa Rican shipper was Frigorificos de Puntarenas, a firm controlled by Cuban-American Luis Rodriguez while employing central figures from the contra network, Moises Nunez and Felipe Vidal.

But Hull remained untouchable, even though five witnesses implicated him during Sen. John Kerry's investigation of contra-drug trafficking. The drug suspicions just glanced off the pugnacious farmer, who had cultivated close relationships with the U.S. Embassy and conservative Costa Rican politicians.

In January 1989, however, Costa Rican authorities finally acted. They indicted Hull for drug trafficking, arms smuggling and other crimes. Hull was jailed, a move that outraged some U.S. congressmen. A letter, signed by senior Democrat Lee Hamilton and others, issued a veiled threat to cut off U.S. economic aid if Hull were not released.

Costa Rica complied, freeing Hull pending trial. But Hull didn't wait for his day in court. In July 1989, he hopped a plane, flew to Haiti and then to the United States.

Hull got another break when one of his conservative friends, Roberto Calderon, won the Costa Rican presidency. On Oct. 10, 1990, Calderon informed the U.S. embassy that he could not stop an extradition request for Hull's return, but signaled that he would prefer that the request be rejected. The embassy officials got the message. A cable noted that the new president was "clearly hoping that Hull will not be extradited." The Bush administration fulfilled Calderon's hope by rebuffing Costa Rican extradition requests, effectively killing the case against Hull.

B ut Bromwich's report revealed that behind the scenes, another drama was playing out: an internal investigation into whether DEA personnel had conspired to thwart Hull's drug prosecution.

That phase of the story began on May 17, 1991, when a Costa Rican journalist told a DEA official in Costa Rica that Hull was boasting that a DEA special agent had assisted in Hull's 1989 flight to Haiti. The DEA launched an internal inquiry headed by senior inspector Anthony Ricevuto.

The suspected DEA agent, whose name was withheld in Bromwich's report, admitted knowing Hull but denied helping him escape. [The agent was identified as Juan Perez in press accounts. See *San Francisco Chronicle*, Aug. 14, 1991.]

According to Bromwich's report, Ricevuto learned that one of the agent's informants, a pilot named Harold Wires, had flown the plane carrying Hull. When interviewed on July 23, 1991, Wires said the DEA agent [Perez] had paid him between $500 and $700 to fly Hull to Haiti aboard a Cessna. In Haiti, Wires said, they met another DEA pilot Jorge Melendez and Ron Lippert, a friend of the DEA agent [Perez]. Melendez accompanied Wires back to Costa Rica, and Lippert flew with Hull to the United States.

From DEA records, investigator Ricevuto confirmed that Melendez had been a DEA informant and freelance pilot. But when questioned, Melendez denied seeing Hull in Haiti. Then, 20 days later, Ricevuto got a call from Wires who reversed his initial story. Wires suddenly was claiming that the DEA agent [Perez] did not know that Hull was on the Cessna as he flew out of Costa Rica.

Later, Wires amended his story again, saying that the agent [Perez] gave him $700 to pay for the Cessna's fuel but only for the return flight. Wires also claimed it was the agent's friend, Lippert, who asked Wires to fly Hull out of Costa Rica, not the agent. Wires added that he took the assignment because he felt the CIA had abandoned Hull. As for his shifting stories, Wires acknowledged that during the DEA investigation, he received an angry call from Hull who wanted to make sure that the DEA agent was cleared of suspicion.

Though Hull's overheard comments about the DEA agent's role had started the investigation, Hull weighed in on Oct. 7, 1991, with a letter. "I have no idea if [the accused agent] knew how and when I was leaving Costa Rica," Hull wrote. He then added, cryptically, "I assumed the ambassador was fully aware of my intentions."

For his part, Lippert, who flew with Hull from Haiti to the United States, told Ricevuto that the DEA agent [Perez] indeed had helped plan Hull's escape. But a DEA polygrapher was brought in to test Lippert and judged him "deceptive." No polygraphs apparently were ever administered to Wires, Hull or Perez.

So, despite the evidence that DEA personnel conspired in the flight of an accused drug trafficker, the DEA cleared the agent of any wrongdoing. Bromwich endorsed that finding as "reasonable."

Chapter 11
CIA Confession

In fall 1998, when the CIA's Volume Two finally was cleared for release, the Washington news media was deep into its Monica Lewinsky obsession. Special prosecutor Kenneth Starr had recommended President Clinton's impeachment and the Republicans felt they were on the verge of major electoral gains that would spur the ouster of Clinton over the sex-and-lies scandal.

Even if the Clinton administration had highlighted the report's release, it likely would have received only minor press notice. But the administration did nothing to draw attention to what amounted to a CIA confession that the long-denied charges of contra-cocaine trafficking protected by the spy agency were true.

On the afternoon of Oct. 8, with no public announcement, the CIA uploaded inspector general Frederick Hitz's Volume Two onto the agency's official Web site. The report made clear that cocaine traffickers and money launderers had swarmed through the Nicaraguan contra movement in the 1980s to a far greater extent than was ever known. The criminal allegations reached directly into Ronald Reagan's White House, according to the 361-page declassified report.

Despite the unceremonious delivery, I thought that finally the major newspapers would have no choice but to deal seriously with the contra-cocaine story. Eager not to be beaten on a story that I had covered for many years, I downloaded the entire report through my computer and eagerly began reading the findings. The report had some of the same disjointed quality of the other reports, but it contained stunning admissions. I was wrong, however, about the competitiveness from other news outlets.

Two days later, *The New York Times* published on an inside page a tepid re-write of its earlier sourced story, pegged now on the finished report. The new article missed the greater significance of the inspector general's findings. There was again no sense that the *Times* reporter had fully read or comprehended the report's contents.[83] But the *Times* at least wrote something the same month. *The Washington Post* waited 25 days -- until the morning of the Nov. 3 elections -- before it published anything, a watered-down version of the report's contents, omitting the most serious charges and again buried on an inside page. The *Los Angeles Times* published no news story at all after Volume Two was released.

Yet, Hitz's report came as close to a confession of a serious crime of state as any U.S. government agency has ever made. Beyond identifying more than 50 contras and contra-related entities implicated in the drug trade, Hitz detailed how the Reagan administration protected these drug operations and frustrated federal investigations which threatened to expose the crimes in the mid-1980s. In perhaps the most stunning disclosure, Hitz published evidence that drug trafficking and money laundering tracked into Reagan's National Security Council where Oliver North oversaw contra operations.

Hitz also revealed that the CIA placed an admitted drug money launderer in charge of the Southern Front contras in Costa Rica. Hitz disclosed, too, that the second-in-command of contra forces on the Northern Front in Honduras had escaped from a Colombian prison where he was serving time for drug trafficking.

Hitz did continue to defend the CIA on one point: that the CIA did not conspire with the contras to raise money through cocaine trafficking. But Hitz made clear that the contra war took precedence over law enforcement and that the CIA withheld evidence of contra crimes from the Justice Department, the Congress and even the CIA's own analytical division.

---

[83] *The New York Times*, Oct. 10, 1998.

Among Hitz's new disclosures:

The CIA knew the criminal nature of its contra clients from the start of the war against Nicaragua's leftist Sandinista government. The earliest contra force, called ADREN or the 15th of September Legion, had chosen "to stoop to criminal activities in order to feed and clothe their cadre," according to a draft CIA field report in June 1981. ADREN employed terrorist methods, including the bombing of Nicaraguan civilian planes and hijackings, to disrupt the Sandinista government, the CIA knew. [Graf 180][84]

Cocaine smuggling was also in the picture. According to a September 1981 cable to CIA headquarters, ADREN decided to use drug trafficking as another financing mechanism. Two ADREN members made the first delivery of drugs to Miami in July 1981, the CIA cable reported. [Graf 181]

ADREN's leaders included Enrique Bermudez and other early contras who would later direct the major contra army, the CIA-organized FDN. The CIA later corroborated the allegations about ADREN's cocaine trafficking, but insisted that Bermudez had opposed the drug shipments to the United States which went ahead nonetheless. [Graf 542]

The truth about Bermudez's claimed opposition to drug trafficking, however, was less clear. According to Volume One of Hitz's report, Bermudez enlisted Norwin Meneses, a large-scale Nicaraguan cocaine smuggler, to raise money and buy supplies for the contras. Bermudez told Meneses that in raising money for the contras, "the ends justify the means."

There were other indications of Bermudez's drug-smuggling tolerance in Hitz's findings. In February 1988, another Nicaraguan exile linked to the drug trade accused Bermudez of narcotics trafficking, according to Hitz's report. Continuing its long defense of Bermudez, however, the CIA dismissed the source as "unstable." [Graf 545]

---

[84] The graf markings correspond to the declassified version of Volume Two.

On the Southern Front, in Costa Rica, the drug evidence centered on the forces of Eden Pastora, another leading contra commander. But Hitz discovered that the U.S. government may have contributed to the drug problem, too. Hitz revealed that the CIA put a now-admitted drug operative -- known by his CIA pseudonym "Ivan Gomez" -- in a supervisory position over Pastora.

Hitz reported that the CIA discovered Gomez's drug history in 1987 when Gomez failed a security review on drug-trafficking questions. The CIA then hushed up the discovery.

In internal CIA interviews, Gomez admitted that in March or April 1982, he helped family members who were engaged in drug trafficking and money laundering. In one case, Gomez said he assisted his brother and brother-in-law transporting cash from New York City to Miami. He admitted that he "knew this act was illegal." [Grafs 672-73]

Later, Gomez expanded on his admission, describing how his family members had fallen $2 million into debt and went to Miami to run a money-laundering center for drug traffickers. Gomez said "his brother had many visitors whom [Gomez] assumed to be in the drug trafficking business." Gomez's brother was arrested on drug charges in June 1982.

Three months later, in September 1982, Gomez started his CIA assignment in Costa Rica. [Graf 678] In November 1985, the FBI learned from an informant that Gomez's two brothers had been large-scale cocaine importers, with one brother arranging shipments from Bolivia's infamous drug kingpin Roberto Suarez. [Graf 695]

Despite all this suspicious drug activity, the CIA insisted that it did not unmask Ivan Gomez until 1987, when he failed a security check and confessed his role in his family's drug business. The CIA official who interviewed Gomez concluded that "Gomez directly participated in illegal drug transactions, concealed participation in illegal drug transactions, and concealed information about involvement in illegal drug activity," Hitz wrote. [Graf 674-75]

But senior CIA officials still chose to protect Ivan Gomez. They rejected a proposal that the Gomez case be referred to the Justice Department. Their rationale was the 1982 CIA-DOJ agreement that spared the CIA from a legal obligation to report narcotics crimes by non-employees. [Graf 714] Instead, the CIA eased Gomez, an independent contractor, out of the agency in February 1988, without alerting law enforcement or the congressional oversight committees. [Graf 728]

Later, convicted drug trafficker Carlos Cabezas charged that in the early 1980s, Ivan Gomez was the CIA agent in Costa Rica who was overseeing drug-money donations to the contras. Gomez "was to make sure the money was given to the right people [the contras] and nobody was taking ... profit they weren't supposed to," Cabezas declared publicly.

At the time of Cabezas's declarations, the CIA continued to withhold the information about Ivan Gomez's drug ties, but sought to discredit Cabezas as a fabricator. Cabazes did have trouble identifying Gomez's photo and put Gomez at one meeting in early 1982 -- before Gomez officially started his CIA assignment. Still, Hitz's report offered the first hard evidence that Gomez did engage in drug-money laundering, as Cabezas alleged.

Questioned by Hitz's investigators, one senior CIA official who had supported the gentle treatment of Gomez had second thoughts. "It is a striking commentary on me and everyone that this guy's involvement in narcotics didn't weigh more heavily on me or the system," the official acknowledged. [Graf 711] As for the decision not to make a criminal referral, the official added: "That view that Gomez is not technically an employee and therefore reporting may not be required is slicing it pretty thin." [Graf 713]

Also on the Southern Front, Hitz discovered evidence connecting the contras and President Reagan's NSC staff to the Medellin cartel. The protagonist for this part of the contra-drug mystery was Moises Nunez, a Cuban-American veteran of the Bay of Pigs fiasco who moved to Costa Rica in 1977. Nunez, also known as "Dagoberto," called himself an anti-communist businessman who simply gave the contras some food.[85]

---

[85] See Martha Honey's *Hostile Acts*.

But Nunez had a more direct tie-in to the contra operation. He worked for two drug-connected seafood importers, Ocean Hunter in Miami and Frigorificos de Puntarenas in Costa Rica -- as well as for Oliver North's NSC operation. Frigorificos de Puntarenas was created in the early 1980s as a cover for drug-money laundering, according to sworn testimony by two of the firm's principals -- Carlos Soto and Medellin cartel accountant Ramon Milian Rodriguez.[86] According to Hitz's report, Nunez was the general manager of Frigorificos de Puntarenas. [Graf 806]

In the mid-1980s, media accounts began citing Nunez as an important contra-cocaine link. On March 25, 1987, the CIA questioned Nunez about these cocaine-trafficking suspicions. According to Hitz's report, Nunez fingered his superiors at the NSC.

"Nunez revealed that since 1985, he had engaged in a clandestine relationship with the National Security Council," Hitz reported. "Nunez refused to elaborate on the nature of these actions, but indicated it was difficult to answer questions relating to his involvement in narcotics trafficking because of the specific tasks he had performed at the direction of the NSC. Nunez refused to identify the NSC officials with whom he had been involved." [Graf 490]

After this first round of questioning, CIA headquarters authorized an additional session to press Nunez for more details about the NSC-drug connection. But then senior CIA officials reversed the decision and ordered no further efforts at "debriefing Nunez." Hitz noted that "the cable [from headquarters] offered no explanation for the decision" to stop the Nunez interrogation. [Graf 491]

When asked about that decision, former Central American Task Force planning chief Louis Dupart said he did not recall the reason for halting the Nunez debriefing. But Dupart added, "the Agency position was not to get involved in this matter, and to turn it over to others because 'it had nothing to do with the Agency, but with the National Security Council. We ... told Congress and [Iran-

---

[86] See *Senate Foreign Relations report: Drugs, Law Enforcement and Foreign Policy*, Dec. 1988.

contra special prosecutor Lawrence] Walsh. That's all we had to do. It was someone else's problem'." [Graf 492]

Task force chief Alan Fiers added that the Nunez-NSC drug lead was not pursued "because of the NSC connection and the possibility that this could be somehow connected to the Private Benefactor program [the contra money handled by North]. A decision was made not to pursue this matter." [Graf 494]

According to CIA records, the CIA briefed Sens. Warren Rudman and William Cohen, two Republicans on the Senate Intelligence Committee, about the Nunez case. Dupart offered to arrange a committee interview with Nunez but that apparently never happened. [Graf 493] The CIA did interview Nunez again in September 1987 -- five months after his admission and in the midst of the Iran-contra scandal. Nunez began insisting that he had no relationship with the NSC. [Graf 495]

By then, however, Joe Fernandez, former CIA station chief in Costa Rica, had confirmed to congressional Iran-contra investigators that Nunez "was involved in a very sensitive operation" for North's "Enterprise." The exact nature of that NSC-authorized activity has never been divulged.

The CIA gave Walsh the material about Nunez's claim of NSC authorization, but not until February 1988 -- nearly a year after the admission and then only as part of a large batch of documents delivered at the end of Walsh's investigation of North's activities. If supplied in a timelier fashion, the Nunez statement and the other evidence of money laundering might have put into focus a part of the North case that always remained fuzzy: his personal handling of cash transfers arranged through an officer at Republic National Bank and through Southern Air Transport.[87]

During the Iran-contra investigation, Walsh never zeroed in on the money laundering or the drug trafficking. In March 1988, a month after the CIA's belated delivery of the Nunez material, Walsh indicted North for crimes related to false statements, document destruction and other relatively minor offenses.

---

[87] For details, see Chapter 7.

W hile Moises Nunez worked for the NSC, Hitz found that other drug-connected Cuban-Americans worked directly for the CIA on the contra project.

One of Nunez's Cuban-American associates, both in the Frigorificos-Ocean Hunter companies and with the contras, was Felipe Vidal, another veteran of anti-Castro operations. Known for a friendly style and a reputation as a lady's man, Vidal also had a criminal record as a narcotics trafficker in the 1970s. The CIA still hired him to serve as a logistics coordinator for the contras, Hitz reported. [Grafs 508-511]

Before long, the CIA learned that its employee still had drug connections. A December 1984 cable to CIA headquarters revealed Vidal's ties to Rene Corvo, another Cuban-American suspected of drug trafficking who was working with Vidal raising money for the contras. [Graf 512] There were drug problems, too, with Ocean Hunter where Vidal worked. In January 1986, the DEA in Miami seized 414 pounds of cocaine concealed in a shipment of yucca that was going from a contra in Costa Rica to Ocean Hunter. [Graf 526]

Despite the evidence and the suspicions, the CIA kept Vidal on its payroll and protected his secrets. By fall 1986, Sen. John Kerry had heard enough rumors about Vidal to demand information about him as part of Kerry's congressional contra-cocaine inquiry. On Oct. 15, 1986, Kerry received a briefing from Alan Fiers who didn't mention either Vidal's drug arrests or conviction from the 1970s. [Graf 527] The omissions hampered Kerry's investigation.

Vidal was not yet in the clear, however. In 1987, the U.S. attorney in Miami began investigating Vidal, Ocean Hunter and other contra-connected entities. This prosecutorial attention worried the CIA. The CIA's Latin American division felt it was time for a security review of Vidal. But on Aug. 5, 1987, the CIA's security office blocked the review for fear that the Vidal drug information "could be exposed during any future litigation." [Grafs 520-22]

The U.S. Attorney in Miami did request documents about "contra-related activities" by Vidal, Ocean Hunter and 16 other entities. But the CIA advised the prosecutor that "no information had been found regarding Ocean Hunter," a statement that was clearly false. [Graf 528] The CIA continued Vidal's employment as an adviser to the contra movement until 1990, virtually the end of the contra war. [Graf 510]

C onnected to Vidal and his associate Rene Corvo was another suspicious character, Cuban exile Frank Castro. According to Hitz's report, the CIA knew that Frank Castro, an anti-communist veteran of the CIA's Cuba operations, was implicated in terrorism and drug trafficking by the time he began assisting the contras in the early 1980s. But the CIA withheld information about Frank Castro from Congress in 1986, a decision that further undercut Sen. Kerry's investigation into the contra-drug secrets -- especially into links between the contras and the Medellin cartel.

Kerry did receive an FBI interview report done with Frank Castro on Aug. 10, 1987. According to the interview, Castro acknowledged traveling to John Hull's farm and assisting Corvo and the other Cuban-Americans operating in Costa Rica. "CASTRO advised that 'PACO' CHANES [Francisco Chanes] and 'DAGO' NUNEZ [Moises Nunez] also helped RENE CORVO and the Cubans," the FBI report read.

But without the CIA's information -- revealing the Castro-Corvo ties to the Medellin cartel and Nunez's work for the NSC -- Kerry's final report in 1989 mentioned Frank Castro only in passing. Lacking corroboration, the Kerry report also left out -- or downplayed -- several other promising leads that suggested a cartel tie-in to the contra war, particularly the testimony from money launderer Ramon Milian Rodriguez and Wanda Palacio's eyewitness accounts of cocaine loaded onto Southern Air Transport planes.

In *Cocaine Politics,* published in 1991, authors Peter Dale Scott and Jonathan Marshall offered a more complete picture of Frank Castro. They described him as the man who "brought together the intelligence, terrorist and criminal forces in the contra movement." Scott and Marshall wrote, "Castro's career intersects many of the historical intrigues that fostered the narco-terrorist apparatus in the contra movement. ... These strands, unexplored by Congress and largely ignored by the media, suggest that the contra-drug connection was not merely an isolated incident but rather part of an ongoing history of illegal activities that enjoyed at least some official protection from U.S. intelligence agencies."

According to a government biography, cited in the Hitz report, Frank Castro was born in Cuba on June 4, 1942, as Eulalio Francisco Castro. After Fidel Castro's revolution, Frank Castro fled to the United States and sought asylum in 1961. He received military training from the U.S. Army in 1962-63 at Forts Knox, Jackson and Carson. [Appendix B]

Scott and Marshall filled in some other gaps. They wrote that Castro joined a paramilitary training camp in Central America for the CIA's war against Fidel Castro. That force, commanded by Bay of Pigs political leader Manuel Artime, launched attacks on Cuban economic targets. By the early 1970s, Castro had changed his first name to Frank and had become a U.S. citizen, but was still active in the anti-Castro underground. He took part in more violent attacks -- bombings and attempted bombings -- against Cuban and Soviet facilities.

Cocaine Politics reported that Castro emerged as "one of the most militant of the exile terrorists. In 1976, he helped found a new terrorist front uniting the most extreme organizations. Known as CORU, it unleashed a wave of bombings, kidnappings and assassinations throughout the Americas in the late 1970s."

The Hitz report noted that the CIA was aware of another unsavory aspect of Frank Castro's Miami-based activities: his participation in major drug-trafficking operations. By 1979, he had developed a reputation as a south Florida drug dealer, though U.S. law enforcement never seemed to put him away.

In 1981, Frank Castro was the main subject of the so-called Tick-Talks drug case. Miami police arrested him on four counts of narcotics trafficking, but the charges eventually were dismissed in a plea bargain in which Castro pled guilty to a weapons charge and was fined $500.

Federal records show that in 1983, Frank Castro was the subject of another drug case -- a plot to smuggle 425,000 pounds of marijuana through Beaumont, Texas. But federal authorities were hesitant to move because of Castro's CIA ties.

On Nov. 22, 1983, the CIA's Directorate of Operations wrote a memo which stated that the CIA's general counsel wanted a search of records on Castro because the Justice Department was prosecuting him for drug trafficking in Texas. DOJ was checking out Castro's claims of affiliation with the CIA. Hitz said an unsigned, handwritten note was attached. It read: "DOJ is willing to drop [the charges] if he [Frank Castro] was in fact associated [with] Agency."

At that time, Frank Castro was assisting the contras, a top CIA project that faced congressional opposition and money problems. To help out, Castro financed a training base in the Everglades and pulled together Cuban-Americans and Nicaraguans into an outfit called the Saturnino Beltran Commandos. Though the armed group trained openly and announced plans to fight in Nicaragua, the Reagan administration did nothing to interfere.

Frank Castro also walked on the marijuana smuggling case. In June 1984, the Texas drug charges were dropped, though the precise reasons were not clear. Soon, Frank Castro's money was flowing to contra leader Eden Pastora, who was struggling to build a Southern Front in Costa Rica. The CIA took note. In a cable, dated July 12, 1984, the CIA reported its belief that Pastora's deputy, Adolfo "Popo" Chamorro, had picked up money from Frank Castro in the Dominican Republic.

In another cable, dated Oct. 12, 1984, the CIA identified Frank Castro as the man who controlled Rene Corvo, a Cuban-American who was leading an armed force of 30-40 contras in northern Costa Rica. Seven of Corvo's Cuban-Americans had been based at a Costa Rican landing zone controlled by American farmer John Hull.

The CIA recognized that Frank Castro, the alleged narco-terrorist, was the moneyman behind these contra operations. According to an Oct. 25, 1984, cable, Hull told the CIA that Castro donated money as well as two helicopters, two light aircraft and one C-47 transport plane to Pastora's army.

The C-47 was believed located at Ilopango airport in El Salvador where it was used by contra pilot Marcos Aguado. The plane participated in suspected drug flights for Colombian cartel figure Jorge Morales, who also was contributing money to the contras.

In November 1984, Oliver North's emissary Robert Owen reported his own suspicions to Washington. "Several sources are now saying Pastora is going to be bankrolled by former Bay of Pigs veteran Frank Castro, who is heavily into drugs," Owen wrote. "The word has it Pastora is going to be given $200,000 a month by Castro."

Later in November or possibly in early December, Corvo traveled to Colombia on a suspected drug mission, according to Hitz's report. On Dec. 12, 1984, the CIA reported internally that Frank Castro was installing a cocaine-processing lab in northern Costa Rica and using the contra war as a cover.

CIA cables stated that in early 1985, Frank Castro was presenting himself as a representative of Colombian drug trafficker Jorge Ochoa, a top figure in the Medellin cartel. Castro allegedly passed on Ochoa's offer to pay $1 million for someone to assassinate U.S. Ambassador Lewis Tambs, who had moved from Colombia to Costa Rica.

As reports about contra-drug trafficking surfaced in late 1985 and early 1986, the CIA fretted that Frank Castro could become a public-relations embarrassment. According to a March 7, 1986, cable, the CIA identified Castro as the main liaison between Colombian drug dealers and Miami-based Cubans. A CIA cable on April 15, 1986, called Castro and Corvo "dangerous and counterproductive" for the contras. In another report, dated Feb. 13, 1987, the FBI echoed that conclusion, saying "Castro has very good connections with [the] Medellin cartel" and, particularly, with the Ochoa brothers.

But in 1986-87, the Frank Castro-Medellin-contra connection was a dark secret that the Reagan administration wanted to keep. In August 1986, the Senate Foreign Relations Committee requested information about Castro, Corvo and other Cuban-Americans who were linked to drug lords. The Reagan administration stonewalled the Senate's inquiry. The Justice Department announced finally that it could provide no data because of an ongoing investigation. "Rambling through open investigations gravely risks compromising those efforts," Justice announced.

Hitz noted, "no records have been found to indicate that CIA shared the information it collected concerning Castro with Congress." The withheld evidence limited Kerry's ability to verify allegations linking the the contras and the Colombian cartels.

In 1988, near the end of the contra war, the federal government did indict Castro and several other Cuban-Americans and contra backers for Neutrality Act violations. But the case made no reference to drug trafficking. In 1989, a federal judge dismissed the charges, ruling that the United States effectively had been at war with Nicaragua.

Hitz revealed that drugs also tainted the highest levels of the Honduran-based FDN, the largest contra army and the one most closely associated with the CIA. Beyond the longstanding suspicions about FDN military chief Bermudez, Hitz discovered that Bermudez's top deputy had a drug-trafficking history as well.

Juan Rivas, a contra commander who rose to be chief of staff, admitted that he had been a cocaine trafficker in Colombia before the war. The CIA asked Rivas, known as "El Quiche," about his background after the DEA began suspecting that Rivas was an escaped convict from a Colombian prison. [Graf 562]

In interviews with CIA officers, Rivas acknowledged that he had been arrested and convicted for packaging and transporting cocaine for the drug trade in Barranquilla, Colombia. After several months in prison, Rivas said, he escaped and moved to Central America where he joined the contras. [Graf 563]

Defending Rivas, CIA officials insisted that there was no evidence that Rivas engaged in trafficking while with the contras. But one CIA cable noted that he lived an expensive lifestyle, even keeping a $100,000 thoroughbred horse at the contra camp. [Graf 566] Contra military commander Bermudez later attributed Rivas's wealth to his ex-girlfriend's rich family. But a CIA cable in March 1989 said, "some in the FDN may have suspected at the time that the father-in-law was engaged in drug trafficking." [Graf 567]

Still, the CIA moved quickly to protect Rivas from exposure and possible extradition to Colombia. Again, politics and P.R. were paramount. In February 1989, CIA headquarters asked that the DEA take no action "in view of the serious political damage to the U.S. Government that could occur should the information about Rivas become public." [Graf 569]

In a Feb. 22, 1989, note, the CIA's director of operations, Richard Stoltz, argued that "what we have here is a single, relatively petty transgression in a foreign country that occurred a decade ago and that is apparently of no current interest to DEA." [Graf 573] Rivas was phased out of the contra leadership with an explanation of poor health. With U.S. government help, he was allowed to resettle in Miami. Colombia was not informed about his fugitive status. [Graf 581]

Another senior FDN official implicated in the drug trade was its chief spokesman in Honduras, Arnoldo Jose "Frank" Arana, a huge man known as "Fat Frank" to reporters.

The drug allegations against Arana dated back to 1983 when a federal narcotics task force put him under criminal investigation because of plans "to smuggle 100 kilograms of cocaine [220 pounds] into the United States from South America." On Jan. 23, 1986, the FBI reported that Arana and his brothers were involved in a drug-smuggling enterprise, although Arana was not charged.

Arana sought to clear up another set of drug suspicions in 1989 by visiting the DEA in Honduras with a business associate, Jose Perez. Arana's association with Perez, however, only raised new alarms. If "Arana is mixed up with the Perez brothers, he is probably dirty," the DEA responded.

Through their ownership of an air-services company called SETCO, the Perez brothers were associated with Juan Matta Ballesteros, a major cocaine kingpin implicated in the 1985 kidnap-murder of DEA agent Enrique Camarena.[88] Hitz reported that someone at the CIA scribbled a note on the DEA cable about Arana stating: "Arnold Arana ... still active and working, we [CIA] may have a problem." [Grafs 608-15]

Despite its drug ties to Matta Ballesteros, SETCO emerged as the principal company for ferrying supplies to the contras in Honduras. During congressional Iran-contra hearings, FDN political leader Adolfo Calero testified that SETCO was paid from bank

---

[88] In 1990, Matta Ballesteros was found guilty in Los Angeles of conspiracy to kidnap Camarena. In a separate trial, Matta Ballesteros was convicted of drug trafficking. Considered one of the biggest drug lords ever convicted in the United States, he is serving a life sentence in federal prison.

accounts controlled by Oliver North. SETCO also received $185,924 from the State Department for ferrying supplies to the contras in 1986.

Hitz found other air transport companies used by the contras implicated in the cocaine trade, too. According to the report, even FDN leaders suspected that they were shipping supplies to Central America aboard planes that might be returning with drugs. Mario Calero, Adolfo Calero's brother and chief of contra logistics, grew so uneasy about one air-freight company that he told U.S. law enforcement that the FDN only chartered the planes for the flights south, not the return flights north. [Graf 550]

Hitz found that some drug pilots who came under suspicion simply rotated from one part of the contra operation to another. Donaldo Frixone, who had a drug record in the Dominican Republic, flew contra missions for the CIA from 1983-85. Frixone then was implicated in September 1986 smuggling 19,000 pounds of marijuana into the United States. In late 1986 or early 1987, he popped up working for Vortex, another U.S.-paid contra supply company linked to the drug trade. [Grafs 996-1000]

One of Hitz's most dramatic findings was new evidence implicating Southern Air Transport, the principal airline of North's Iran-contra operations and formerly owned by the CIA.

In the mid-1980s, Southern Air was one of the few direct links between North's contra resupply program and his secret shipments of missiles to Iran. SAT was flying both routes -- to Central America and to Iran -- and was handling money for North.

SAT crewmen were involved in the most famous North resupply flight, the one shot down over Nicaragua on Oct. 5, 1986, with Eugene Hasenfus the only survivor. After the crash, Attorney General Edwin Meese III briefly suspended a federal investigation into Southern Air Transport on national security grounds. Wanda Palacio, who had ties to the Medellin cartel, also told Senate investigators that she witnessed Ochoa operatives loading cocaine aboard SAT planes in both 1983 and 1985. Walsh's Iran-contra probe connected SAT to money laundering, moving $467,000 in bags from SAT's petty cash fund in Miami to Ilopango airport in El Salvador.

The CIA possessed other troubling information about SAT, according to the Hitz report. On Jan. 21, 1987, deputy CIA director Robert Gates wrote in a memo that U.S. Customs was investigating a new allegation of drug trafficking by SAT crew members. Gates said that tip about SAT came from Mario Calero. [Grafs 906 & 1090]

A Feb. 28, 1991, cable from DEA to CIA also linked SAT to drug smuggling and money laundering. The DEA reported that SAT was "of record" in DEA's database from 1985-90 for alleged involvement in cocaine trafficking. One entry in August 1990 alleged that $2 million had been delivered to SAT's business sites and several SAT officials were suspected of smuggling "narcotics currency." [Grafs 906-07]

Still, no government action was taken against Southern Air Transport, whose executives denied any involvement in drug trafficking.

T he drug stain spread to the Miskito Indian contras as well, according to other internal CIA cables contained in Hitz's report. In 1987-88, one contra from the KISAN organization alleged that Miskito contra leader Steadman Fagoth had participated in at least two cocaine operations to raise money.

One scheme involved killing Colombian traffickers in the Yucatan and stealing their cocaine for sale in the United States. The source "believed that Fagoth and other associates probably had consummated the scheme [and] that Fagoth -- along with two Honduran military officers -- had sold marijuana and other drugs." [Grafs 587-589] The CIA received other information alleging that a KISAN leader, named Roger Herman Hernandez, was involved with cocaine smuggling through Roatan Island in Honduras.

Even after the Iran-contra scandal broke, the CIA continued to work with reputed drug traffickers in supplying the contras, Hitz discovered. In 1987, the CIA turned to a wealthy Honduran businessman, Alan Hyde, despite U.S. government reports identifying Hyde as a major cocaine trafficker. [Grafs 914-25]

The CIA used Hyde for contra logistical support through late 1988 or early 1989, the Hitz report said. [Graf 927] The concerns about drug trafficking apparently were overridden because some U.S. officials in Honduras grew personally friendly with Hyde, who threw lavish parties and socialized with influential Americans.

Ultimately, the CIA criticized Hyde more for allegedly stealing contra equipment than for smuggling drugs. When asked why guns topped drugs on the CIA's complaint list, a senior CIA officer said "it was an issue of relative order of priorities. ... The issue of stealing our guns had a higher priority than verifying whether Hyde was smuggling cocaine into the U.S." [Graf 944]

Hitz's report added another new piece to the contra-Bolivian cocaine puzzle. One contra fund-raiser, Jose Orlando Bolanos, boasted that the Argentine government was supporting his anti-Sandinista activities, according to a May 1982 cable to CIA headquarters. Bolanos made the statement to undercover DEA agents in Florida as he offered to introduce them to his Bolivian cocaine supplier. [Graf 465] Bolanos's comment fit with the testimony of Leonardo Sanchez-Reisse, the Argentine intelligence officer who testified in 1987 about the Argentines laundering Bolivian drug profits for the contras.[89]

The Bolivian-contra connection apparently continued through most of the decade. Hitz cited a Sept. 29, 1988, cable from the U.S. Embassy in La Paz reporting that the son of drug kingpin Roberto Suarez claimed that the U.S. government was protecting drug traffickers in Huanchaca, Bolivia, and that the traffickers were kicking in profits to the contras. [Last graf, Appendix D.]

Hitz learned that a chief reason for the CIA's protective handling of contra-drug information was Langley's "one overriding priority: to oust the Sandinista Government. ... [CIA officers] were determined that the various difficulties they encountered not be allowed to prevent effective implementation of the contra program." [Graf 121]

One CIA field officer explained, "The focus was to get the job done, get the support and win the war." [Graf 147] A chief of

---

[89] For details, see Chapter 1.

station added, "There is derogatory stuff [about the contras], but we were going to play with these guys. That was made clear by [CIA director] Casey and [Latin American Division chief Duane] Clarridge." [Graf 150]

CIA analysts explained that they prepared few finished intelligence reports about contra-drug trafficking, in part, because of political pressures. "The policymakers, one analyst asserts, really wanted to 'get' the Sandinistas on this subject [drugs]," Hitz wrote. The Directorate of Operations [DO] "assigned a low priority to collecting intelligence concerning the contras alleged involvement in narcotics trafficking." [Grafs 1071-72]

Some analysts complained that the DO went further, actually withholding contra-cocaine evidence from the Directorate of Intelligence. One senior analyst said he "felt that Fiers was not showing the analysts any reporting that would cause problems for the Contra program." [Graf 1077]

In the mid-1980s, because of a lack of available information, the CIA analysts incorrectly concluded that "only a handful of contras might have been involved in drug trafficking." [Graf 1091] That assessment was passed on to Congress and the major news media, which largely accepted the false account as true.

Hitz also found that CIA officials, including Fiers's deputy Dupart, fed information to congressional Republicans to discredit Kerry's investigation in 1986. Dupart told GOP aide Rick Messick that the FBI had "extensive information on people who had been interviewed by Kerry's staff." [Graf 1102]

As disturbing as the declassified version of Volume Two was, government sources told me the classified version was even worse. One of the still-secret findings from the CIA's investigation implicated a CIA veteran of the contra operation directly in a conspiracy to smuggle cocaine into Los Angeles in the late 1980s, the sources said. The suspect was a CIA employee from the Los Angeles "station" who allegedly participated in the drug conspiracy from 1988-90.

The smuggling operation reportedly shipped cocaine into predominately black neighborhoods of South Central Los Angeles. But the alleged trafficking was distinct from the smuggling reported by the *San Jose Mercury News.* The *Mercury News* described a contra-connected drug pipeline that pumped cheap cocaine into South Central during the early 1980s.

The new Los Angeles allegations reportedly were kept out of the public report because the case remained under active investigation. One U.S. government source indicated that the allegations were included as a classified appendix to Hitz's report. The sources did not identify the CIA employee by name.

Hitz stated that the new L.A. allegations were not directly part of his contra-cocaine study, though he added they were under review. "It does not come within the rubric of our [contra-cocaine] study," Hitz said. But he added: "We are working on it."

When asked about the purported secret appendix on the L.A.-CIA drug connection, the CIA's public affairs office researched the question and then responded with a refusal to either confirm or deny the allegations. "The information from the classified version that was removed [for the publicly released version] was removed to protect sources and methods," a CIA spokesman said. "There were also law enforcement concerns" related to informant relationships.

The CIA press office also faxed over a copy of the press release issued on Oct. 8 when the second volume of Hitz's report was posted on the CIA's Internet site. The spokesman underlined the sentence reading: "No information has been found to indicate that CIA as an organization or its employees conspired with, or assisted, contra-related organizations or individuals in drug trafficking to raise funds for the contras or for any other purpose."

The press statement -- and the comments by Hitz -- could be seen as technically accurate if the Los Angeles-based CIA employee was no longer assigned to the contra war at the time of the alleged trafficking. Still, the CIA's reluctance to make criminal drug referrals against its officers and allies fits with a long history of CIA defensiveness about drug-trafficking charges. In the half century of the CIA's existence, there has not been one known criminal case against a CIA officer for engaging in drug trafficking.

The CIA's spotless record has raised the eyebrows of some in Congress as well as in the general public. By the absence of any known public prosecutions, some critics have suggested that either the CIA has recruited only angels or that it may not be policing itself very well.

I n the aftermath of the Hitz report, I published the following editorial in *iF Magazine* and at *The Consortium* Internet site. Entitled "A Media Disgrace," it read:

Nothing could better explain why this publication exists than the shocking neglect that the big media has shown toward the CIA's new contra-cocaine report. The report by the CIA's inspector general described how the Reagan administration tolerated cocaine trafficking into the United States under the umbrella of the contra war in Nicaragua during the 1980s. The report established that cocaine smugglers penetrated the contra operation at all levels -- and that the CIA hid the evidence.

Rarely, if ever, has a U.S. agency made such a devastating set of admissions about its own activities. The CIA's inspector general effectively confirmed the contra-cocaine allegations which the Reagan-Bush administrations had denied for more than a decade. Yet, the readers of America's major dailies will know little of this history. The document was released onto the CIA's Internet site on the afternoon of Oct. 8. But the admission of a serious crime of state drew barely a yawn from the national press.

The Washington Post and the *Los Angeles Times* -- two papers which had long pooh-poohed the contra-cocaine charges -- ignored the inspector general's findings altogether. Two days later, *The New York Times* kissed off the CIA's findings in a brief story on page A5, below the fold. It noted, accurately, that the report was "blunt and often critical" and that the CIA "repeatedly ignored or failed to investigate allegations of drug trafficking by" the contras.[90] But the reality detailed in the report was much worse. The CIA had confirmed many of the allegations and withheld the evidence from both law enforcement and Congress.

The nation's dominant newspapers seemed to have reached an absurd juncture where the CIA can admit guilt and the major news outlets will still protect the CIA's image. In one strange way, however, the editorial decisions made sense. Today, more senior journalists have a career interest in downplaying contra crimes than do the senior officials at the CIA. Many of the CIA top brass responsible for the contra operation are long gone, but many of today's star reporters rose to prominence by going along with the propaganda fed to them by the Reagan-Bush administrations.

Since the contra-cocaine charges were first raised in the mid-1980s, the major newspapers have been consistent in dismissing the allegations. When Sen. John Kerry confirmed many of the charges in a 1989 Senate report, his findings were buried deep inside the big papers -- and he was ridiculed as a "randy conspiracy buff." When Gary Webb's "Dark Alliance" series revived the scandal in 1996, the major media lashed out at him and the black community for not accepting the long-standing conventional wisdom.

Since then, the big papers have grudgingly admitted some substance to the charges, but the admissions are quickly forgotten -- or even reversed. When the outlines of the new CIA report became known over the summer, *The New York Times* admitted that the CIA had found evidence of widespread contra-drug

---

[90] *The New York Times,* Oct 10, 1998.

smuggling, with about 50 contras and allied entities implicated in the cocaine trade.[91]

But it was a fleeting admission. On Sept. 27, when the *Times* published a combined review of Gary Webb's *Dark Alliance* book and a second book, *Whiteout*, by Alexander Cockburn and Jeffrey St. Clair, the old conventional wisdom was back in place. Reviewer James Adams termed the two books "unsatisfactory" and mocked their suggestions of a CIA cover-up of contra-cocaine crimes as "laughable."

Adams's review then misstated what was already known about the upcoming CIA report. "It matters little," Adams wrote, "that the CIA's own inspector general said he found no evidence to support allegations of agency involvement in or knowledge of the drug trafficking in the United States." Even based on the *Times'* own mild admissions in July, the summary wasn't true. But the *Times* published it, discrediting the work of other journalists who had taken on a tough story.

When the CIA report was released on Oct. 8, it became even clearer how wrong Adams's review had been. As for the "laughable" cover-up, a CIA station chief explained it: "There was derogatory stuff [about the contras], but we were going to play with these guys," that message had been delivered from CIA director William J. Casey and other senior officials.

But why won't the *Times* and other big newspapers just "come clean" now that the facts are so clear? The reason seems to be that they don't have to. The editors know that no one can or will hold them accountable, as long as they stick together. If the public doesn't know

---

[91] *The New York Times*, July 17, 1998.

how devastating the CIA's admissions were, then no one will know how poorly the major newspapers performed.

The *Times*, which likes to call itself "the newspaper of record," apparently believes that it controls -- and can manipulate -- that record. If anything, the behavior of the *Post* and the *Los Angeles Times* has been worse. The big media's betrayal of the public trust is one of the reasons this publication exists. Our goal is simple: to write an honest first draft of our nation's recent history. [*iF Magazine*, Nov.-Dec. 1998]

By the late 1990s, the Watergate press corps of the 1970s was a distant memory. Rather than digging for the facts about important crimes of state, the Washington news media now saw its job as burying the truth, even when the government confessed. President Reagan's public diplomacy teams had achieved a lasting legacy. Even government admissions were now part of the "lost history."

Part Two
Before, After & During

Chapter 12
How Others See It

The Hunted

Tyranny, like cowardice, often comes in small pieces, compromises that seemed reasonable at the time, "the best we could get," but in totality can doom a noble ideal. That was the worthwhile truth that Angus Mackenzie recalled to our attention in his posthumously published book, *Secrets: The CIA's War at Home.*

The book is very much Mackenzie's story as he charted the course of his short life -- from legends that he heard during boyhood days about American Minute Men who stood their ground at Compo Hill in his native Westport, Conn., in 1777, to a different reality two centuries later when the CIA rode roughshod over timid politicians and other supposed protectors of U.S. civil liberties.

Secrets also is the story of a democratic ideal smothered by a government that came to see an informed electorate as an obstacle to the prosecution of a long Cold War. Yet, this was a slow strangulation, a garotte closing around the victim's neck so no single twist would be recognized as life-threatening.

Mackenzie's personal conflict with this national security state came from his practice of what he thought were enshrined constitutional rights: freedom of the press and the right to dissent. To his amazement, his Vietnam-era underground newspaper, *The*

People's Dreadnaught, made him a target of his own government. "One of the fundamental lessons passed on from generation to generation is that Americans have the greatest of all freedoms, the freedom to express ourselves in open and public debate," Mackenzie wrote. "Imagine my surprise ... when I found myself in trouble with the law for publishing a newspaper."

Mackenzie then challenged the secrecy-holders through lawsuits brought under the Freedom of Information Act. Over time, he broke through some -- but not all -- of the stonewalls. Mackenzie kept up that struggle until May 13, 1994, when he died of brain cancer at the age of 43. For the next two-and-a-half years, his family pulled together the final pieces of his manuscript.

The resulting work was an important road map for Americans who wonder how their country lost its way, from the era of Thomas Paine and the Minute Men, to an era when citizens were denied an honest accounting of 50 years of history, even after the end of the Cold War threat that was used to justify the secrets in the first place.

Mackenzie's *People's Dreadnaught* was one of hundreds of independent publications that sprang up in the 1960s and early 1970s as young Americans grew bitterly disillusioned by U.S. policies in Vietnam. Mackenzie's first encounter with angry law enforcement came with local authorities who arrested him on obscenity charges for selling an issue that contained an account of the My Lai massacre.

But Mackenzie and his friends also found themselves approached by long-haired strangers who encouraged the commission of crimes, from drug sales to vandalism. Only years later, as a result of his lawsuits, did Mackenzie discover that those approaches were entrapments set by undercover police and were part of a nationwide pattern.

"I learned that editors at scores of other underground newspapers had experienced similar treatment at the hands of local and state authorities," Mackenzie wrote. "I learned that local cops who proved themselves effective tormentors of underground editors were rewarded by federal authorities. ... I learned that [an IRS intelligence unit] was specifically assigned to target the dissident antiwar press and furthermore that the IRS was connected to two larger surreptitious operations, one run out of the Central Intelligence Agency (code-named MHCHAOS) and the other out of the Federal Bureau of Investigation (code-named COINTELPRO)."

Mackenzie's initial suit earned a jury award of only $2,500 but he added: "Our lawsuit was most valuable for what I learned about the cynical contempt in which some agents of the government hold the First Amendment." His investigation then pressed onward into other areas of secrecy, that of censorship and the punishment of government officials who broke the code of silence.

The book's narrative starts with the doubts that some members of Congress had about the proposed National Security Act of 1947. Rep. Clare E. Hoffman, a conservative Michigan Republican, had agreed to introduce the bill but later was stunned at the open-ended language. The CIA would get the authority to perform "functions and duties related to intelligence affecting the national security as the National Security Council may from time to time direct."

Hoffman and others feared that the CIA might evolve into an American Gestapo, which "could secretly manipulate elections or could undermine political opponents," Mackenzie wrote. "The greatest danger was that, once created, the CIA would be hard to contain."

The Truman administration agreed to add some language barring the CIA from domestic police and national security functions, but little notice was taken of a simple phrase granting the CIA director powers "for protecting sources and methods from unauthorized disclosure." After some modest compromise, nearly all congressional opposition faded away, but Hoffman rued his initial support for the CIA. He concluded that the agency would become a threat to American democracy. Over the next five decades, some of Hoffman's fears would become reality.

But as the CIA's powers grew, so too did intermittent challenges by American citizens who experienced the agency's abuses. One of the most significant abuses began with the CIA's demand in 1966 for a "run down" on *Ramparts* magazine which was preparing a story about the CIA's penetration of U.S.

universities and student organizations. The order led to dossiers on 22 of *Ramparts* writers and editors. An important line had been crossed. The war against the underground press was under way.

The chief of that CIA operation, Richard Ober, soon was collecting IRS records on the magazine and its publisher. The justification for the investigation was the purported suspicion that foreign communist agents were inspiring the articles. Stories suggesting those ties were planted in U.S. newspapers, although the CIA knew from its investigation that the money was coming from a wealthy American philanthropist.

The *Ramparts* case also led the CIA to tighten government-wide procedures for preventing future leaks and to undertake a much broader domestic spying operation, known as MIICHAOS. Soon, the CIA was sneaking informants and troublemakers inside underground newspapers and other antiwar activities. One government informant, Salvatore John Ferrara, proved doubly effective because his pose as an underground journalist let him glean defense strategies on criminal cases involving antiwar dissidents, including the notorious Chicago Seven trial.

Despite the crackdowns, a devastating leak of government secrets still occurred in 1971 with Daniel Ellsberg's release of the Pentagon Papers. The documents detailed the deceptions that had led the nation into the Vietnam War. Furious at the leak, President Nixon struck back with creation of his illegal Plumbers operation. But even more significant was the imposition of ever-stricter regulations on government employees who had access to secrets.

By 1972, the CIA had gotten into the business of censoring books, including one by former senior CIA officer Victor Marchetti. CIA officials insisted that Marchetti's account of CIA misconduct would jeopardize national security and would violate his secrecy agreement with the government. Through the courts, the CIA won important new victories, making Marchetti's book the first ever in America to be published with deletions from government censors. The case also convinced the CIA to compel more and more government officials to sign secrecy pledges that would forever prevent them from telling the American people the truth.

The mid-1970s saw the CIA's bid for wider secrecy suffer other setbacks, however. Published disclosures of CIA abuses and congressional investigations into the secret agency exposed secret after embarrassing secret from the CIA's most sensitive files. For the first time with hard facts, Americans were alerted to the danger of clandestine CIA missions at home.

In 1976, however, a new director, George Bush, rode to the CIA's rescue. With his own impressive array of contacts and his noblesse-oblige style, Bush spearheaded a clever counter-offensive that falsely pinned the murder of the CIA's Athens station chief, Richard Welch, on anti-CIA disclosures in a magazine called *CounterSpy*. Internally, the CIA concluded that Welch's identity already was blown and that the magazine was not at fault. But Bush and other CIA defenders pushed hard for new laws criminalizing national security disclosures.

These initiatives continued to gain ground under President Jimmy Carter and reached a fever pitch during the early years of Ronald Reagan's presidency. Though the Soviet Union was in demonstrable decline, the White House ratcheted up the secrecy. Reagan signed a new presidential order demanding that information be classified if officials believed its release might endanger national security.

Mackenzie's book detailed how the Reagan administration succeeded in maneuvering secrecy critics into a series of crippling compromises that expanded secrecy laws. Some of the sacrifices were promoted by "bipartisan" Democrats, such as Rep. Lee Hamilton of Indiana. Others were tolerated by ACLU officials, such as Morton Halperin. The rationale often was that the compromise was better than what the Reagan administration might do otherwise. But the Executive Branch gained crucial ground in its demand to punish officials who divulged secrets.

Ex-CIA officer Ralph McGehee was shocked when he read Reagan's new secrecy order. "People in government who become disillusioned and quit at an earlier age than me will virtually lose their freedom of expression," he said. "The people most able to give informed views will be unable to comment."

With the CIA again on the rise, director William J. Casey began bullying even mainstream news organizations into withholding stories on national security grounds. "Casey's threats of prosecution against the [*Washington*] *Post* and other major periodicals also demonstrated the increase in the CIA's power since 1966, when the agency had 'run down' the left-wing *Ramparts*," Mackenzie observed.

By the mid-1980s, Vice President Bush was promoting terrorism as the new rationale for domestic security. Some of these "terrorists" were Americans critical of U.S. policies in Central America. Bush also sought curtailment of the Freedom of Information Act because "terrorists groups may have used" it to gain information about FBI surveillance.

Ironically, the end of the Cold War did not appreciably lessen the government's hunger for secrecy. After his election in 1992, President Clinton vowed that a new era of candor was at hand. But by and large, Clinton failed to follow through. As Mackenzie observed, "at the beginning of his presidency, Clinton did not boldly challenge the bureaucracy and relied on others -- often the bureaucrats themselves -- to carry out reforms. In the case of the CIA, he relied on [his CIA director James] Woolsey, a Yale lawyer whose background and sensibilities were similar to those of many career officers under him."

Mackenzie concluded his account by remembering those Minute Men from 1777. "The issue," he wrote "is freedom, as it was for the Minute Men at Compo Hill. ... Until the citizens of this land aggressively defend their First Amendment rights of free speech, there is little hope that the march to censorship will be reversed. The survival of the cornerstone of the Bill of Rights is at stake."

The Hunter

Perhaps more than any U.S. politician, Richard Nixon influenced the course and tone of the Cold War, from the earliest stirring of the McCarthy era through the divisive war in Vietnam to Watergate and, less visibly, through the two decades afterwards as a secret adviser to presidents. Few leaders have cast as long and as dark a shadow on their times, as did Richard Nixon.

Yet, in the years after his 1974 resignation over the Watergate scandal, Nixon underwent a stunning image make-over. He built for himself a reputation as a thoughtful elder statesman, a mellower "new Nixon," one who had made mistakes but was himself a victim of unreasonable political enemies. However, release of more White House tapes, the bane of his Watergate defense in 1974, betrayed him again after his death in 1994.

While Nixon's estate continued to battle to keep many of the conversations secret and get $213 million in compensation for the rest of them, bits and pieces of the record continued to slip out into the public domain. In late December 1998, the legal fight pushed more of Nixon's crude remarks out from behind government secrecy.

In federal court, Justice Department lawyers introduced a sample of those comments to challenge the money demands of Nixon's estate. Department lawyers argued that Nixon never would have released the tapes except in a heavily deleted form, so they would not have been worth what the estate was claiming. But the tapes' contents were far more interesting than the legal arguments.

In one White House discussion about a personnel plan to recruit women and minorities, Nixon voiced doubt that women were "worth the effort." As for blacks, "you can usually settle for an incompetent, because there are just not enough competent ones, and so you put incompetents in and get along with them, because the symbolism is vitally important. You have to show you care." Regarding other American ethnic groups, the president opined that "the problem [was] finding a Mexican that is honest. And Italians have somewhat the same problem."

Another embarrassing case was Nixon's angry diatribe against House Majority Leader Hale Boggs, D-La., who gave a critical floor speech on April 5, 1971. Boggs had denounced FBI director J. Edgar Hoover for allowing the FBI to tap the telephones of members of Congress and to put agents on college campuses to spy on anti-war students and teachers. Boggs demanded Hoover's resignation and deplored the actions as "the tactics of the Soviet Union and Hitler's Gestapo."

In retaliation for his outspokenness, Boggs soon found his reputation disparaged by leaks that he suspected came from the FBI. But a White House tape of a phone call between Nixon and House Minority Leader Gerald Ford, R-Mich., revealed that Nixon also had a strong interest in denigrating Boggs. On April 6 -- one day after Boggs's House speech -- Nixon asked Ford, "what's the matter with your opposite number?" Ford responded, "He's nuts." Nixon continued, "He's on the sauce, isn't that it? ... Or is he crazy? ... You cannot have a nut. I think he's off his rocker."

Less than a week later, columnist Jack Anderson traced a leaked report about Boggs as a "heavy drinker" back to the FBI. Years later, the FBI released a clipping of that story with Hoover's notations, "This shows what comes from over dissemination of our memos and reports. H."[92] The implication was that the White House, not the FBI, leaked the smear.

The Nixon tapes released in late 1998 followed the National Archives' release of other Nixon tapes in 1997. They, too, eroded Nixon's carefully constructed image of a misunderstood victim. The tapes revealed again the cynical and criminal nature of Nixon's presidency. The tape transcripts, published in Stanley I. Kutler's book, *Abuse of Power,* covered more than 200 hours of Nixon's Oval Office discussions about Watergate and other political crimes.

Most mainstream press accounts expressed shock at the contents of the tapes, but missed the larger import of the disclosures. The big papers focused on Nixon's psychological state. *The Washington Post* wondered why he didn't destroy the tapes. [Oct. 30, 1997] *The New York Times* mused over whether the president was paranoid about enemies who were "after me." [Oct. 31, 1997]

But there was widespread agreement that the tape recordings destroyed any doubt about Nixon's guilt over both setting up the criminal "Plumbers" operation and obstructing justice after five burglars from that operation were arrested inside the Democratic National Committee headquarters in the Watergate complex in Washington, D.C., on June 17, 1972.

---

[92] *The Washington Post,* Dec. 27, 1998.

On the tapes, Nixon was caught commissioning the Plumbers as retaliation for the 1971 publication of the secret Pentagon Papers history of the Vietnam War. He also discussed hush money for the Watergate burglars; monitored a White House political slush fund; oversaw day-to-day cover-up strategies; thanked a Greek-American businessman for secret cash; and agreed to keep a friendly U.S. ambassador in Athens.

But the tapes offered unexamined insights, as well, into two controversial gambits from Nixon's earlier political life, events that were the past to Nixon's Watergate prologue: the Alger Hiss case in 1948 and a Republican scheme to derail Vietnam peace talks in 1968. Both events contributed to Nixon's pugnacious political style that finally came a cropper in the Watergate scandal.

According to the tapes, Nixon flashed back to the Alger Hiss case on July 1, 1971, while venting anger over the publication of the Pentagon Papers. In a lecture to chief of staff H.R. Haldeman and national security adviser Henry Kissinger, Nixon criticized Attorney General John Mitchell for worrying about what "is technically correct" in punishing those who leaked the secret history of the Vietnam War. Nixon wanted a more ruthless attack that would include counter-leaks to discredit former Pentagon official Daniel Ellsberg and others connected to the publication. Nixon set few limits.

"Thank God I leaked to the press [during the Hiss controversy]," Nixon declared. "[In the Pentagon Papers release,] we're up against an enemy, a conspiracy. They're using any means. We are going to use any means. Is that clear? Did they get the Brookings Institute raided last night? No. Get it done. I want it done. I want the Brookings Institute safe cleaned out and have it cleaned out in a way that makes somebody else [responsible]."

Nixon then reminisced about how he used unchecked documents -- the so-called Pumpkin Papers -- to stampede a federal grand jury in New York into indicting Hiss, a former State Department official from Franklin Roosevelt's New Deal years. At the time, in fall 1948, the Cold War was in its infancy, the McCarthy era of anti-communist black lists was just beginning and Nixon's young political career hung in the balance.

As a member of the House Un-American Activities Committee (HUAC), Nixon had championed charges by an ex-communist named Whitaker Chambers that Hiss had been a secret Communist Party member. Hiss had denied the charge under oath, and Chambers's shifting accounts had put Nixon's ally in hot water. Indeed, a federal grand jury in New York appeared headed toward a perjury indictment of Chambers. Hiss was on the verge of exoneration. Nixon faced a political calamity that could have driven the young congressman from the national stage. For Nixon, the prospective clearing of Hiss was a personal crisis.

Then, in November 1948, Chambers reversed prior assertions that he had never received classified papers from Hiss. Chambers began claiming that he had secret State Department documents that Hiss allegedly had handed over as part of a Soviet spy ring. On Dec. 2, 1948, Chambers led HUAC investigators to a hollowed-out pumpkin on his farm in Maryland where he had stashed several rolls of microfilm. Nixon, who was on a Caribbean vacation, dramatically returned to Washington to examine the microfilm and to star in committee hearings. Nixon made direct appeals to the grand jury to indict Hiss, not Chambers.

With the grand jury's term scheduled to expire and without time for a careful analysis of the newly discovered documents, the grand jury voted narrowly to do as Nixon proposed. Hiss was indicted for perjury and Chambers was spared. After one hung jury and with much of the evidence against him classified, Hiss was convicted of perjury and was sent to jail still professing his innocence. Years later, after the collapse of the Soviet Union, extensive searches of Moscow's archives failed to produce evidence that Hiss was a Soviet agent. But in the late 1940s, the Hiss case made Nixon a Cold War hero.

In 1971, Nixon referred to the Hiss crisis in explaining to Haldeman and Kissinger how one played to win. "If I were called before a grand jury in New York [in 1948] and told to give up the fucking [Pumpkin] papers to the grand jury, I [would have] refused," Nixon declared in 1971. "I said I will not give up [Chambers's] papers to the Department of Justice because they're out to clear Hiss. I played it in the press like a mask. I leaked out the papers. I leaked everything, I mean, everything that I could. I leaked out the testimony. I had Hiss convicted before he ever got to the grand jury.

"And then when the grand jury got there, the Justice Department trying desperately to clear him and couldn't do it. The grand jury indicted him. ... Now, why would I do that? I did that because I knew I was fighting people who had power. ... Now, how do you fight this [Ellsberg case]? You can't fight this with gentlemanly gloves. ... We'll kill these sons of bitches."

Nixon then referred to an obscure White House official named Cooke who had given Ellsberg some papers when Ellsberg worked at the Rand Corp. "I want to get him [Cooke] killed," Nixon said. "Let him get in the papers and deny it. ... Get a story out and get one to a reporter who will use it. Give them the facts and we will kill him in the press. Isn't that clear? And I play it gloves off. Now, Goddammit, get going on it."

One of Nixon's schemes for discrediting the Pentagon Papers was to transform it into another spy scandal, like the Hiss case, to be promoted by HUAC's successor, a House subcommittee on internal security. Part of the plan was to feed the panel a Jewish suspect. "Don't you see what a marvelous opportunity for the committee," Nixon said on July 2, 1971. "They can really take this and go. And make speeches about the spy ring. ... But you know what's going to charge up an audience. Jesus Christ, they'll be hanging from the rafters ... Going after all these Jews. Just find one that is a Jew, will you."

In the months that followed, Nixon's men did "play it gloves off." Under Nixon's direct supervision, a Plumbers unit was recruited to dig up dirt on Ellsberg and others. White House burglars broke into the office of Ellsberg's psychiatrist. Then, expanding the operation, Nixon's intelligence team began scouring for intelligence about leading Democrats, with bugs placed on phones at DNC headquarters at the Watergate.

The operation blew up on June 17, 1972, with the arrest of five White House burglars inside the DNC offices. As the tapes make clear, Nixon immediately took charge of the cover-up: issuing orders, brainstorming P.R. strategies and trying to blackmail Democrats with threats of embarrassing disclosures.

One of Nixon's recurring threats was to reveal that President Johnson supposedly had ordered the bugging of the Nixon campaign in 1968. The threat was dropped only after Nixon's subordinates concluded that Nixon did not have his facts straight and that the disclosure could be a deadly two-edged sword.

The 1968 bugging issue revolved around a Republican initiative to undermine Johnson's Paris peace talks that could have ended the Vietnam War and brought home 500,000 American soldiers then fighting in Indochina. The Nixon-Agnew campaign, however, feared that this "October Surprise" would catapult Vice President Hubert Humphrey to victory and again deny Nixon the White House.

According to Seymour Hersh's *The Price of Power,* Kissinger learned of Johnson's peace plans and warned the Nixon-Agnew campaign. "It is certain," Hersh wrote, "that the Nixon campaign, alerted by Kissinger to the impending success of the peace talks, was able to get a series of messages to the Thieu government making it clear that a Nixon presidency would have different views on the peace negotiations."

The chief emissary was Anna Chennault, an anti-communist Chinese leader who was working with the Nixon-Agnew campaign. Hersh quoted one former Johnson Cabinet official as stating that the U.S. intelligence "agencies had caught on that Chennault was the go-between between Nixon and his people and President [Nguyen van] Thieu in Saigon. ... The idea was to bring things to a stop in Paris and prevent any show of progress."

In her autobiography, *The Education of Anna,* Chennault acknowledged that she was the courier. She quoted Nixon aide John Mitchell as calling her a few days before the 1968 election and telling her: "I'm speaking on behalf of Mr. Nixon. It's very important that our Vietnamese friends understand our Republican position and I hope you have made that clear to them."

Reporter Daniel Schorr added fresh details in *The Washington Post*'s Outlook section [May 28, 1995]. Schorr cited decoded cables which U.S. intelligence had intercepted from the South Vietnamese embassy in Washington. On Oct. 23, 1968, Ambassador Bui Dhien cabled Saigon with the message that "many Republican friends have contacted me and encouraged me to stand firm." On Oct. 27, he wrote, "The longer the present situation continues, the more favorable for us. ... I am regularly in touch with the Nixon entourage."

On Nov. 2, Thieu withdrew from his tentative agreement to sit down with the Viet Cong at the Paris peace talks, killing Johnson's last hope for a settlement of the war. A late Humphrey surge fell short and Nixon won a narrow election victory.

In *The Price of Power,* Hersh quoted Chennault as saying that in 1969, Mitchell and Nixon urged her to keep quiet about her mission, which could have implicated them in an act close to treason. As the war dragged on for another four years, tens of thousands of U.S. soldiers died, as did hundreds of thousands of Indochinese.

But in 1972, obsessed with justifying the Watergate bugging, Nixon referred back to the Paris peace talk gambit. He claimed that he was told by FBI director Hoover that Johnson had ordered the bugging of a Nixon campaign plane to ascertain who was undermining the Paris peace talks. On July 1, 1972, White House aide Charles Colson touched off Nixon's musings by noting that a newspaper column claimed that the Democrats had bugged Chennault's telephones in 1968. Nixon pounced on Colson's remark, indicating that he was aware that those alleged wiretaps targeted the GOP sabotage of the peace talks.

"Oh," Nixon responded, "in '68, they bugged our phones too."

Colson: "And that this was ordered by Johnson."

Nixon: "That's right"

Colson: "And done through the FBI. My God, if we ever did anything like that you'd have the ..."

Nixon: "Yes. For example, why didn't we bug [Democratic presidential candidate George] McGovern, because after all he's affecting the peace negotiations?"

Colson: "Sure."

Nixon: "That would be exactly the same thing."

Nixon's complaint about Johnson bugging "our phones" in 1968 became a refrain as the Watergate scandal unfolded. Nixon wanted to use that information to pressure Johnson and Humphrey into twisting Democratic arms so the Watergate investigations would be stopped. On Jan. 8, 1973, Nixon urged Haldeman to plant a story about the 1968 bugging in the *Washington Star*. "You don't really have to have hard evidence, Bob," Nixon told Haldeman. "You're not trying to take this to court. All you have to do is to have it out, just put it out as authority, and the press will write the Goddamn story, and the *Star* will run it now."

Haldeman, however, insisted on checking the facts. In *The Haldeman Diaries*, published in 1994, Haldeman included an entry dated Jan. 12, 1973, which contains his book's only deletion for national security. "I talked to Mitchell on the phone," Haldeman wrote, "and he said [FBI official Cartha] DeLoach had told him he was up to date on the thing. ... A *Star* reporter was making an inquiry in the last week or so, and LBJ got very hot and called Deke [DeLoach's nickname], and said to him that if the Nixon people are going to play with this, that he would release [deleted material -- national security], saying that our side was asking that certain things be done. ... DeLoach took this as a direct threat from Johnson. ... As he [DeLoach] recalls it, bugging was requested on the planes, but was turned down, and all they did was check the phone calls, and put a tap on the Dragon Lady [Anna Chennault]."

Ten days after that entry, on Jan. 22, 1973, Johnson died of a heart attack. Haldeman apparently shelved the 1968 bugging ruse as a non-starter. After 18 more months of writhing and wriggling, Nixon was forced by the courts to relinquish a few of the incriminating tapes. They contained enough damning evidence to force Nixon to resign on Aug. 9, 1974.

I n disgrace, Nixon retreated to his estate at San Clemente, where he began a long campaign to rebuild his reputation. But Nixon never did stop scheming, nor did his allies. As Nixon battled to keep the rest of his White House tapes secret, his allies accused the "liberal press" and other enemies of unfairly hounding Nixon from office over Watergate.

By the late 1970s, conservatives were mounting a determined counter-offensive, with millions of dollars pouring in from conservative U.S. foundations and right-wing organizations abroad. The right argued that the Soviet Union was rapidly expanding its power, while the United States was in decline. The holding of 52 American hostages in Iran in 1979-80 became a case in point.

In spring 1980, with another presidential campaign in full swing, Nixon was active again. He was in touch with ex-CIA officers who were plotting an independent strategy for dealing with the Iran crisis. One of those ex-officers, Miles Copeland, told me that Nixon and Kissinger received copies of a hostage rescue plan drafted by CIA "old boys," including legendary CIA spies Kermit and Archibald Roosevelt.

"Now I'm not at liberty to say what reaction, if any, ex-President Nixon took, but he certainly had a copy of this," Copeland said in a videotaped interview in 1990. "We [also] sent one to Henry Kissinger. ... So we had these informal relationships where the little closed circle of people who were a, looking forward to a Republican president within a short while, and b, who were absolutely trustworthy and who understood all these inner workings of the international game board."[93]

By summer 1980, upset over President Carter's failed Iranian rescue operation, Nixon reportedly was itching for a more direct role. According to a 1989 article in the London *Sunday Telegraph*, Nixon met in late July 1980 in Great Britain with Alan Bristow, a helicopter specialist with close ties to the British Special Air Services, SAS, a clandestine military arm of British intelligence. *Sunday Telegraph* reporter Simon O'Dwyer-Russell had interviewed Bristow who described Nixon's detailed interest in a possible second rescue attempt. When I contacted O'Dwyer-Russell, he added that Bristow said an angry Nixon paced the floor and fumed about Carter's ineptness.

When I asked Copeland about this possible second rescue, he said Nixon concluded that there was no need for such an operation because the hostages would be released after the November election. "Nixon ... knew that all we had to do was wait until the election came, and they were going to get them out," Copeland said. "The intelligence community certainly had some understanding with somebody in Iran in authority. ... We had word [from Iran] that

---

[93] For details on the October Surprise case, see Robert Parry's *Trick or Treason* and *The October Surprise X-Files*.

'don't worry. As long as Carter wouldn't get credit for getting these people out, as soon as Reagan came in, the Iranians would be happy enough to wash their hands of this'."

Carter did fail to free the hostages who were released immediately after Reagan's inauguration on Jan. 20, 1981. However, precisely what happened with the so-called 1980 "October Surprise" story would become another chapter of "lost history."

By the late 1980s, when those "October Surprise" allegations began to surface, conservatives possessed a powerful political/media machine that could shut down any more Watergate-style inquiries that threatened Republicans. Indeed, this conservative machine outlasted the Reagan-Bush era and turned offensive once President Clinton took office.

Ironically, in early 1993, Clinton extended an olive branch to Richard Nixon, the godfather of the Republican dirty tricks machine. Clinton invited the aging Nixon to a public meeting at the White House, an honor that neither Ronald Reagan nor George Bush had extended. "Clinton added impetus not only to the reexamination of Nixon's career but to his relevance as a historical dramatist," wrote Nixon aide Monica Crowley who chronicled the last years of Nixon's life in a 1996 book, *Nixon Off the Record*. "He [Nixon] wielded the most influence when he advised his successors, and of those successors, he advised Bill Clinton the most extensively."

Still, Nixon remained a Republican partisan. Even as Clinton was welcoming Nixon into the White House, Nixon was scheming with Sen. Bob Dole and others how to destroy the Democratic president. Nixon hoped that the Whitewater controversy could bring down Clinton to balance the scales for Watergate.

On April 13, 1994, four days before the stroke that would kill him, Nixon told Crowley, "Our people must not be afraid to grab this thing and shake all of the evidence loose. Watergate was wrong; Whitewater is wrong. I paid the price; Clinton should pay the price. Our people shouldn't let this issue go down. They mustn't let it sink."

Two weeks later at Nixon's funeral, Clinton praised the ex-president and glossed over the crimes that had forced Nixon from office. "May the day of judging President Nixon on anything less than his entire life and career come to a close," Clinton stated.

By 1994, however, the Nixon-inspired GOP attack machine had altered the political landscape in ways that Nixon barely could have imagined during the dark days of Vietnam and Watergate. The sophisicated apparatus had married the vast powers of the national security state with the modern techniques of propaganda and political warfare. This coupling was the nightmare that Angus Mackenzie foresaw. But its success was so total that the very existence of this fearsome machine would go almost unreported.

Chapter 13
Lying First

C entral America was not the only front in the Reagan administration's propaganda wars. The principal enemy, after all, was the Soviet Union, the "Evil Empire." In President Reagan's view, Sandinista-ruled Nicaragua was just one of Moscow's distant outposts, a beachhead on the American continent. The Reagan administration was always eager to strike propaganda blows against the Soviet Union.

One dramatic opportunity presented itself on the night of Aug. 31, 1983, when Korean Air Lines flight 007, a 747 jumbo jet strayed hundreds of miles off-course and penetrated some of the Soviet Union's most sensitive air space. The airliner flew over military facilities in Kamchatka and Sakhalin Island.

Over Sakhalin, KAL-007 was finally intercepted by a Soviet Sukhoi-15 fighter. The Soviet pilot tried to signal the plane to land, but the KAL pilots did not heed the repeated warnings. Amid confusion about the plane's identity -- a U.S. spy plane had been in the vicinity hours earlier -- Soviet ground control ordered the pilot to fire. He did, blasting the plane out of the sky and killing all 269 people on board.

The Soviets soon realized they had made a horrible mistake. U.S. intelligence also knew from sensitive intercepts that the tragedy had resulted from a blunder, not from a willful act of murder.[94]

But in 1983, the truth about KAL-007 didn't fit Washington's propaganda needs. The Reagan administration wanted to portray the Soviets as wanton murderers, so it brushed aside the judgment of the intelligence analysts. The administration then chose to release only snippets of the taped intercepts and packaged them in a way to suggest that the slaughter was intentional.

"The Reagan administration's spin machine began cranking up," wrote Alvin A. Snyder, then-director of the U.S. Information Agency's television and film division, in his book, *Warriors of Disinformation*. USIA director Charles Z. Wick "ordered his top agency aides to form a special task force to devise ways of playing the story overseas. The objective, quite simply, was to heap as much abuse on the Soviet Union as possible."

In a boastful but frank description of this successful disinformation campaign, Snyder noted that "the American media swallowed the U.S. government line without reservation. Said the venerable Ted Koppel on the ABC News 'Nightline' program: 'This has been one of those occasions when there is very little difference between what is churned out by the U.S. government propaganda organs and by the commercial broadcasting networks'."

Of course, if the journalists hadn't gone along, they could have expected to be flogged for disloyalty by the public diplomacy team. So, most Washington reporters ran with the pack. *Newsweek* published a cover line: "Murder in the Sky," exactly the "theme" that the White House wanted conveyed to the public.

I was at the AP at the time and made a small contribution to questioning the official story. I felt the released intercepts of the Russian air-to-ground communications were suspicious. So I took the English language translation, as well as the original Russian, to Russian language experts, including one

---

[94] Much as on July 3, 1988, the USS Vincennes fired a missile that brought down an Iranian civilian airliner in the Persian Gulf, killing 290 people, an act that Reagan explained as an "understandable accident."

who taught Pentagon personnel how to translate Russian military transmissions.

The Russian language experts noted one important error in the English translation as released by the State Department. In the context of the Soviet pilot trying to communicate with the KAL plane, the administration translated the Russian word "*zapros*," or inquiry, as "IFF" for "identify: friend or foe." The experts, whom I interviewed, said "*zapros*" could mean any kind of inquiry, including open radio transmissions or physical warnings.

The significance of the mistranslation was central to the administration's case. Since an IFF transmission can only be received by Soviet military aircraft, that was cited as proof that the Russians made no attempt to warn the civilian airliner. U.S. officials had extrapolated from "IFF" to advance the "murder in the sky" argument. In reality, the letters "IFF" -- or the Russian equivalent -- were never spoken.

Still, as Snyder revealed years later, the mistranslation was only one of the ways the Soviet transmissions were doctored. Snyder first suspected alterations when the intercepts were delivered to his office for adaptation into a video that was to be shown at the United Nations.

"The tape was supposed to run 50 minutes," Snyder observed. "But the tape segment we [at USIA] had ran only eight minutes and 32 seconds. ... 'Do I detect the fine hand of [President Nixon's secretary] Rosemary Woods here?' I asked sarcastically'." But Snyder had a job to do: producing the video that his superiors wanted. "The perception we wanted to convey was that the Soviet Union had cold-bloodedly carried out a barbaric act," Snyder noted.

Only a decade later, when Snyder saw the complete transcripts -- including the portions that the Reagan administration had hidden -- would he fully realize how many of the central elements of the U.S. presentation were false. The Soviet pilot apparently did believe he was pursuing a U.S. spy plane, according to the complete intercepts. He also was having trouble in the dark identifying the plane. At the instructions of Soviet ground controllers, the pilot had circled the KAL airliner and tilted his wings to force the aircraft down. The pilot said he fired warning shots, too. "This comment was also not on the tape we were provided," Snyder stated.

It was clear to Snyder that in the pursuit of its Cold War aims, the Reagan administration had presented false accusations to the United Nations, as well as to the people of the United States and the world. The ends of smearing the Soviets had justified the means of falsifying the historical record. In his book, Snyder acknowledged his role in the deception and drew an ironic lesson from the incident. The senior USIA official wrote, "The moral of the story is that all governments, including our own, lie when it suits their purposes. The key is to lie first."

The idea of lying as a routine practice of statecraft spilled over into the Reagan administration's military activities. For political ends, the White House even denied the truth about American soldiers who fought and died in Central America. During the 1980s, the Reagan administration insisted that U.S. soldiers were not in combat in El Salvador and other hot spots when they were.

In 1981, fearing comparisons to Vietnam, President Reagan limited the number of Green Beret trainers in El Salvador to 55 and ordered them to avoid combat zones. They were to train only in safe barracks. They were not to advise the Salvadorans in the field. The U.S. trainers also were forbidden to carry M-16s. They were to have only side arms for self-defense. Throughout the decade, the White House and the Pentagon repeatedly asserted that these rules were followed. Few reporters challenged the story.

On Sunday, May 5, 1996, however, a solemn ceremony took place in an open grassy space at Arlington National Cemetery. A small memorial stone was unveiled to honor 21 American soldiers who died in combat against leftist guerrillas in El Salvador. As family members wiped tears from their eyes, Salvadoran children placed tiny American flags next to the soldiers' names, casualties from the secret wars of the 1980s.

"For too long, we have failed to recognize the contributions, the sacrifices, of those who served with distinction under the most dangerous conditions," said former U.S. Ambassador to El Salvador, William G. Walker. The next day, *The Washington Post* focused on the human interest side of the story in a front-page piece entitled "Public Honors for Secret Combat."

But what received little attention amid the honors and the tears was the confirmation that for much of a decade, the Reagan-Bush administrations had conducted a secret war in which American soldiers engaged in not-infrequent combat. The 21 dead surpassed the number who died in the 1989 invasion of Panama and some Americans who were close to the Central American conflicts contended that the actual number of U.S. dead was higher.

The *Post* story made only a passing attempt to explain why so little was known about these years of classified combat and why the government cover-ups had been so successful. "Reports of firefights involving U.S. troops were closely held, and field commanders were told in no uncertain terms not to nominate soldiers for combat awards," the *Post* reported.

The newspaper then quoted Joseph Stringham, a retired one-star Army general who commanded U.S. military forces in El Salvador in 1983-84. "It had been determined this was not a combat zone, and they were going to hold the line on that," Stringham said. "I've puzzled over why. It may be something as fundamental as the bureaucracy not wanting to reverse itself."

The Reagan administration also might have been surprised how easy it was to distract the Washington press corps and the Congress. The lies did not go completely unchallenged, however.

As early as 1981-82, a few American reporters in Central America were stumbling over the reality of secret U.S. combat operations. One top U.S. military adviser told me about an incident in which he was on patrol with a Salvadoran army unit and thought he was spotted by *New York Times* correspondent Raymond Bonner. Renowned for his tough reporting on the early years of the war, Bonner was not easily intimidated into doubting his own perceptions. To head off a possibly embarrassing disclosure, the Green Beret told me that U.S. officials quickly lined up the Salvadoran soldiers and gave them false affidavits to sign, declaring that there was no American with them.

Another case of gutsy reporting was a long investigative article by Frank Greve and Ellen Warren of the Knight-Ridder newspaper chain on Dec. 16, 1984. The piece brought to light the term "bodywashing," the practice of reporting false details about the circumstances surrounding the deaths of U.S. soldiers involved in secret operations.

The Knight-Ridder story focused on an elite Army helicopter unit, the 160th Task Force of the 101st Airborne Division stationed at Fort Campbell, Ky. The article quoted family members who suspected that their loved ones had died in combat in Central America and that cover stories had then been concocted about the pilots' fate. "If downed or captured, the soldiers, who wore civilian clothes and flew at night, were told to expect no U.S. government acknowledgement or intervention, the relatives said," according to the Knight-Ridder article.

In 1984, the Reagan administration insisted that it had no knowledge of casualties from secret fighting in Central America. But the Knight-Ridder story ended with a chilling quote from a former covert military specialist who explained the practice of "bodywashing."

"If a guy is killed on a mission," the former officer said, "and if it was sensitive politically, we'd ship the body back home and have a jeep roll over on him at Fort Huachuca," a remote Army intelligence base in Arizona. "Or we'd arrange a chopper crash, or wait until one happened and insert a body or two into the wreckage later. It's not that difficult."

Also in December 1984, I wrote an article for *The Associated Press* describing how American helicopter crews assigned to the CIA had fired on Nicaraguan troops earlier that year. The first incident occurred on Jan. 6, 1984, during a raid on the Nicaraguan port of Potosi. The second clash occurred on March 7, 1984, at the southern port of San Juan del Sur in support of CIA operations to mine Nicaraguan harbors. The administration did not even bother to deny the AP story. White House spokesman Larry Speakes simply declared that "I think the CIA is probably checking to see what the facts are."

The two stories shone a glimmer of light on the secret Central American conflicts, but neither the AP nor the Knight-Ridder article generated much follow-up by other Washington journalists. The administration continued to insist publicly that U.S. soldiers in the region were avoiding combat situations -- and the national media accepted the White House word.

Even after the 12-year Reagan-Bush reign ended, there was little interest in Washington to right the historical record. Ironically, conservatives were the ones who led the belated fight to gain recognition for the U.S. soldiers who fought and died in El Salvador. Andy Messing, a former Special Forces major who worked closely with Oliver North on Central America in the 1980s, was one of those who insisted on the historical correction.

After a CBS "60 Minutes" broadcast on the issue in 1995, conservative Rep. Robert K. Dornan, R-Calif., pushed through legislation mandating that the Pentagon give Armed Forces Expeditionary Medals to soldiers who served in El Salvador from January 1981 until February 1992. "The U.S. government was going to allow a clever blurring of the history of the civil war to go unchallenged," commented former Special Forces Sgt. Greg Walker. "We wanted to correct the history. ... We wanted to honor our dead and bring closure to their families."

The little monument to the secret warriors sits next to a sapling in an otherwise vacant sector of Arlington National Cemetery. Like the war it commemorates, it is barely noticeable to passers-by visiting the rows of white headstones that cover the cemetery's rolling hills.

Normally helpful cemetery employees were nonplussed when asked about the location of the marker several days after the ceremony. One cemetery employee had no idea where it was and another directed a questioner to Section 59, the wrong place.

The small shiny stone actually lies across Eisenhower Avenue from Section 59, in Section 12. There were no flowers or flags. The names of the 21 dead soldiers were not engraved on the stone, just the words: "El Salvador 1981-1992. Blessed are the peacemakers. In sacred memory of those who died to bring hope and peace."

Chapter 15
The CIA Analysts

A nother threat to the Reagan administration's propaganda successes came from an unlikely source, from the analytical division of the CIA. Some employees actually believed the Biblical quotation near the entrance: "And ye shall know the truth and the truth shall make you free."

At CIA headquarters in Langley, Va., CIA intelligence analysts have long prided themselves on the intellectual integrity of their assessments about world events. The analysts held to a tradition of delivering to the White House data that often conflicted with what presidents wanted to hear. President Eisenhower was challenged on the Soviet bomber gap and President Kennedy on the missile gap. Presidents Johnson and Nixon didn't like the discouraging words on the Vietnam War.

The CIA's "operations" branch may have stumbled into many bloody controversies. But the CIA's "analytical" division maintained a relatively good -- though by no means perfect -- reputation for supplying straightforward intelligence to policymakers. Some well-educated analysts viewed themselves as superior to the crass politicians who came and went.

Like so much else at the CIA, however, that tradition changed in the early 1980s, with Ronald Reagan's determination to enforce his "Evil Empire" vision of the Soviet Union. Even before taking office, Reagan conservatives made clear their displeasure with the

CIA's analytical product that detected weaknesses in a crumbling Soviet empire.

The Reagan transition team on intelligence publicly denounced CIA career analysts for allegedly underestimating the Soviet commitment to world domination. "These failures are of such enormity," the transition report claimed, "that they cannot help but suggest to any objective observer that the agency itself is compromised to an unprecedented extent and that its paralysis is attributable to causes more sinister than incompetence."[95]

Those lurking suspicions that CIA professionals were soft on communism pervaded the early months of the administration. The analysts resisted a wide range of accusations that Reagan wished to level against the Soviet Union. These charges included blaming Moscow for the world's terrorism, Yellow Rain chemical warfare in Indochina, the Pope assassination attempt and virtually all revolutionary movements in the Third World.

To make Reagan's apocalyptic world view stick, CIA director William J. Casey set out to purge the CIA's analytical division of those who wouldn't toe the party line. There was little tolerance for those who saw the Soviet Union as a declining power eager for detente with the West.

The CIA purge helped in another way, too. If the only acceptable analysis was of a powerful Soviet Union expanding its military superiority over the United States, then a massive U.S. arms build-up made sense. A compliant CIA analytical division also would cut off the potential for critical information reaching Congress and the public about the administration's overt-covert paramilitary operations in Nicaragua and elsewhere.

So, out of view in the closed community of the CIA, Casey elevated Robert Gates, one of the hardest of anti-Soviet hardliners, to head the Directorate of Intelligence [DI], the analytical side. In *Foreign Policy* magazine [summer 1997], former CIA senior analyst Melvyn Goodman described the effect: "The CIA's objectivity on the Soviet Union ended abruptly in 1981, when Casey became the DCI [director of central intelligence] -- and the first one to be a member of the president's Cabinet. Gates became Casey's deputy director

---

[95] For more details, see Mark Perry's *Eclipse*.

for intelligence [DDI] in 1982 and chaired the National Intelligence Council."

The change came largely through a bureaucratic reshuffling. Gates restructured the DI from a subject-matter framework with specialists at, say, nuclear proliferation looking at the world as a whole, to a geographical one. That allowed Gates to move his allies, who became known as "Gates clones," into key positions. Some of those who rose were David Cohen, David Carey, George Kolt, John McLaughlin,[96] Jim Lynch, Winston Wiley and John Gannon.

With the Gates regime in place, career analysts in sensitive positions soon found themselves the victims of bureaucratic pummelings. According to several former CIA analysts whom I interviewed, some were verbally berated into changing their analyses; some faced job threats and allegations of psychiatric unfitness; others experienced confrontations with supervisors who literally threw papers in the analysts' faces.

The new CIA leadership asserted itself with special verve on sensitive ideological issues. Early on, the Reagan administration pressed the CIA to adopt an analysis that accepted right-wing press reports pinning European terrorism on the Soviets. The CIA analysts knew that these charges were false, in part because they were based on "black" or false propaganda that the CIA itself had been planting in the European media. But the "politicization" tide was strong.

In 1985, Gates closeted a special team to push through another administration-desired paper arguing that the KGB was behind the 1981 wounding of Pope John Paul II. CIA analysts again knew that the charge was bogus -- because of penetration of East Bloc intelligence services -- but could not stop the paper from leaving CIA and being circulated around Washington.

On another ideologically sensitive front, analysts said they faced pressure to back off an assessment that Pakistan was violating nuclear proliferation safeguards. That was politically touchy because Pakistan's military government was aiding the CIA-backed Afghan rebels fighting Soviet troops, a major covert war run by the CIA's operations directorate.

---

[96] Not the pundit.

Reagan always wanted the threat from the Soviet Union painted as darkly as possible, whether the facts were there or not. Analysts grew so fearful of submitting reports on Soviet weakness that the CIA fell way behind the curve in recognizing the coming Soviet collapse. The political pressures opened other intelligence "black holes," including the misleading CIA assessments about "moderates" in Iran that justified the Iran-contra arms sales. A compliant CIA analytical division -- like the browbeaten press – quietly gave up the fight.

But the plight of the CIA analysts has received little attention in Washington. The story surfaced only briefly in 1991 during Robert Gates's confirmation hearings to become President Bush's CIA director. Then, a handful of analysts braved the administration's displeasure by protesting the "politicization of intelligence."

Led by analyst Melvyn Goodman, these dissidents fingered Gates as a key "politicization" culprit. Their testimony added more doubts about Gates, who already was under fire for his dubious testimony on the Iran-contra scandal. But President Bush lined up solid Republican backing and enough accommodating Democrats, particularly Sen. David Boren, the Senate Intelligence Committee chairman, to push Gates through as CIA director.

The Gates confirmation marked what some saw as the final victory for those who put politics over accurate analysis. John A. Gentry, a CIA economic analyst and a former Army Special Forces officer, resigned with a blunt resignation letter. It read: "I can no longer work in an organization in which satisfaction of bureaucratic superiors is more important than superior analysis."

Gentry compiled his criticisms in a book entitled, *Lost Promise: How CIA Analysis Misserves the Nation.* Gentry minced no words. One recommendation in the book stated that "the destructiveness of some managers' meanness, dishonesty and lack of intellectual integrity is so great that significant numbers -- including many senior officers -- should be fired from the Agency."

There was a brief window for possible CIA analytical reform with Bill Clinton's election in 1992. The "politicization" issue was put squarely before Clinton's incoming national security team by former CIA analyst Peter W. Dickson who wrote a two-page memo on Dec. 10, 1992, to Samuel "Sandy" Berger, a top Clinton national security aide.

Dickson was an analyst who suffered retaliation after refusing to rewrite a 1983 assessment that noted Soviet restraint on nuclear proliferation. His CIA superiors did not want to give the Soviets any credit for demonstrating caution on the nuclear technology front. But Dickson stood by his evidence and soon found himself facing accusations about his psychological fitness.

Dickson urged Clinton to appoint a CIA director who understood "the deeper internal problems relating to the politicization of intelligence and the festering morale problem within the CIA." Dickson saw a housecleaning at the top as crucial:

> This problem of intellectual corruption will not disappear overnight, even with vigorous remedial action. However, the new CIA director will be wise if he realizes from the start the dangers in relying on the advice of senior CIA office managers who during the past 12 years advanced and prospered in their careers precisely because they had no qualms about suppressing intelligence or slanting analysis to suit the interest of Casey and Gates. This is a deep systemic problem. ...
>
> The lack of accountability also became a systemic problem in the 1980s. ... A recent CIA inspector general investigation confirms the near total breakdown in confidence among employee[s] that management is willing to deal honestly and objectively with their complaints. Many of them concern the lack of professional ethics and in some cases personal abuse at the hands of senior officer managers -- a group of individuals beholden and therefore loyal to Gates.

Dickson, a creative thinker who also investigates historical mysteries such as the real backgrounds of Columbus and Shakespeare, recommended that Clinton focus on "intellectual integrity and accountability" in selecting a new CIA director. But Clinton instead was focusing "like a laser beam" on the economy and other domestic issues, as he promised during the campaign. With Clinton's sensitivity over his Vietnam draft avoidance, he may have feared, too, that restructuring the CIA would lead to a reprise of his alleged lack of patriotism and create a distraction from his domestic agenda.

Clinton did oust Gates but avoided confronting the problem head-on by installing James Woolsey, a neo-conservative Democrat who had worked closely with the Reagan-Bush administrations. Under Woolsey, the Gates team, *sans* Gates, consolidated its bureaucratic power.

Woolsey's tenure was marred by the discovery that CIA counter-intelligence officer Aldrich Ames sold secrets to Moscow for almost a decade, mostly during the Reagan-Bush administration. But Congress turned on Woolsey for not acting decisively enough in disciplining senior officers who had supervised Ames.

Clinton replaced Woolsey with John Deutch, a brilliant but prickly scientist from the Massachusetts Institute of Technology. Deutch made few significant changes at the CIA and soon was headed back to academia. After the GOP-controlled Senate blocked Clinton's nomination of his national security adviser Anthony Lake to be CIA director, the president settled on George Tenet, a former Senate Intelligence Committee staffer who had served as Deutch's deputy. It was Tenet who oversaw Boren's half-hearted confirmation inquiry into Gates in 1991.

Like the others, Tenet chose to surround himself with many of Gates's former allies. Tenet did oust David Cohen, whom the analysts considered one of Gates's most aggressive enforcers. But other Gates-connected officials remained in key positions inside the CIA. John McLaughlin was deputy director for intelligence; David Carey was the CIA's executive director; Winston Wiley was assistant deputy director for intelligence; and Gannon was director of the National Intelligence Council.

Seeing the Casey-Gates team still dominating the senior levels of the CIA discouraged many of the analysts who went public to protest the "politicization." In interviews, these former CIA analysts complained that Clinton allowed the CIA to continue drifting into a backwater of shoddy scholarship.

"Clinton missed an opportunity to get the CIA on the right track," said Goodman. "The CIA's in a hell of a lot of trouble."

"He blew it," declared Dickson. "He threw it away. It's too late now." Dickson predicted that the CIA, having passed its 50th anniversary, will continue on a path of gradual decline and growing irrelevance.

"I don't see any improvement," added Gentry. "You're 15 years into decay" and Clinton's CIA appointees have "fussed around at the margins, but they haven't made the cultural, leadership and even moral changes that are needed. ... I see no indication anywhere that Clinton has taken any interest in anything that has occurred. ... Clinton is quite content to have a weak intelligence community."

Chapter 16
Sins of the Father

T he night of Sept. 21, 1976, was a grim one in Washington. That morning, one of the worst terrorist incidents in the capital's history had shaken the stately buildings along Embassy Row.

A bomb had ripped apart the car carrying Chile's former foreign minister Orlando Letelier and two American co-workers. Letelier and a woman, Ronni Moffitt, died from the blast. Moffitt's husband was wounded.

That evening at a dinner at the Jordanian Embassy, Sen. James Abourezk was distraught. Letelier had been a personal friend, and his violent death in the heart of Washington was weighing heavily on Abourezk's mind. During the meal, Abourezk found himself seated with the gangly, preppy figure of George Bush, director of the Central Intelligence Agency. Abourezk thought he might enlist Bush's help in solving the murder.

Given Letelier's status as an ascerbic critic of Chile's military dictatorship, there already were suspicions that agents of Gen. Augusto Pinochet had planted the bomb. Abourezk raised the issue with the CIA director. He asked Bush to commit the CIA to the search "to find the bastards who killed" Letelier. Abourezk recalled that Bush looked concerned and responded, "I'll see what I can do. We are not without assets in Chile."

The problem with Bush's promise, however, was that some of the CIA's top "assets" in Chile were implicated in the murder.

According to U.S. intelligence sources, one of those CIA assets was Gen. Manuel Contreras, the head of the intelligence agency, DINA. Contreras was the architect of the Letelier assassination.

The other trouble with Bush's pledge was that the assassination had been carried out almost literally under the CIA's nose -- and Bush had little interest in exposing his own failings. At best, Bush could be accused of gross negligence as a CIA director. He had missed a clear warning and allowed a major terrorist operation to unfold in the U.S. capital. There was also the darker possibility that Bush's CIA had granted DINA license to hunt down and neutralize a Chilean dissident on American soil.

This 23-year-old story of international intrigue and murder -- like other unsolved mysteries involving the 41st president -- has fresh relevance in 1999 with Bush's oldest son, Texas Gov. George W. Bush, touted as the Republican frontrunner for the 2000 presidential campaign and an early favorite to capture the White House.

With George W.'s experience limited to state government in Texas, sources close to the Bush entourage expect that the governor will look to his father's network for foreign policy expertise. In other words, if elected president, George W. will likely make his foreign policy an extention of his father's. So, the lingering suspicions about President Bush's involvement in a variety of questionable and illegal acts are reasonable issues to weigh when considering George W. Bush's candidacy for the Republican nomination.

These mysteries include:

--Bush's connection to the Letelier assassination and to other Latin American human rights catastrophes, such as the launching of the Argentine "dirty war" in 1976, also on Bush's CIA watch.

--Bush's precise role in the now-corroborated accounts of Republican secret contacts with Iranian radicals holding 52 U.S. hostages in 1980, while President Carter was trying to negotiate their release.

--Bush's knowledge about the involvement of his Cuban-American allies in cocaine trafficking under the umbrella of President Reagan's Nicaraguan contra war in the 1980s.

--Bush's participation in supplying secret military assistance to the armies of Iraqi dictator Saddam Hussein in the 1980s, including weaponry and technology through Pinochet's Chile.

--Bush's close financial and political relationship with Rev. Sun Myung Moon, a major conservative funder but also a controversial religious-business figure who advocates the subjugation of the American people under a totalitarian theocracy. Moon also controls what appears to be a major money-laundering operation and has ties to organized-crime figures from Asia and South America.

None of these issues was settled during Bush's one-term presidency. By the late 1980s and early 1990s, national news outlets were unwilling to take on those kinds of tough investigative stories and simply accepted the guidance of Bush's well-connected advisers who dismissed the stories as unfounded. Bush was never questioned in detail and under oath about any of these issues. He was able to escape with cursory denials, often made in fleeting news conference comments.

After leaving office in 1993, Bush also refused to submit to a final interview with Iran-contra special prosecutor Lawrence Walsh. Walsh believed he had an understanding with Bush that the president would undergo the interview after the 1992 election. Instead, Bush pardoned six Iran-contra figures, effectively killing Walsh's investigation. Bush then rebuffed the requested interview that was to explore the new evidence revealing Bush's deeper role in the scandal.

Though there were questions about Bush's possible intelligence ties early in his business and political careers, his CIA relationship became official in January 1976 when President Ford named him director of central intelligence.

Bush took over the spy agency at a crucial juncture. The CIA had struggled through a series of congressional and other investigations that pried loose some of the CIA's most embarrassing secrets, from assassination plots to drug experiments on unsuspecting subjects. The proud CIA had become a national laughingstock.

Bush moved quickly to reassure the badly shaken agency that its mission was still appreciated. He gave pep talks at Langley and trooped up to Capitol Hill where he vigorously defended the CIA and its personnel. Bush got high marks cooperating with congressional leaders to set up the first permanent oversight committees.

"For that period, Bush did a remarkable job," senior clandestine services official Theodore Shackley told me. "He was very warm, very human, very interested. You could get in to see him without difficulty."

But Bush's year at CIA was not all hand-holding and back-slapping. It was a violent time when CIA-trained Cuban exiles launched another bloody round of terrorism that included attacks on Cuban diplomats and the fatal bombing of a civilian Cubana airliner.

Bush's CIA also failed to stop DINA's efforts to extend its Operation Condor assassination program to the United States. That failure occurred even though clues were in the hands of top CIA officials, apparently including Bush, two months before the Letelier bombing.

The first clue that a terrorist operation was under way came from Paraguay. There, two Chilean DINA agents went to the U.S. embassy to obtain U.S. visas to attach to phony Paraguayan passports. A senior Paraguayan official told U.S. Ambassador George Landau that the two agents were on a mission to the United States to investigate front companies being used by Chilean dissidents. The agents were supposed to rendezvous with Bush's deputy, Gen. Vernon Walters.

Landau smelled something fishy. Normally, he knew, operations of this sort were coordinated through the CIA station in the host country and were cleared with CIA headquarters in Langley. To check on the curious visa request, Landau fired off an urgent cable to Walters. Landau also copied the fake passports and sent the photostats to Langley.

The urgent return cable came from CIA director Bush. He informed Landau that Walters was in the process of retiring and was out of town. When Walters returned, he reported that he had "nothing to do with this" mission. Landau immediately canceled the visas. The next step should have been for Bush's CIA to query DINA about what was afoot. Normal procedure -- as well as common sense -- would mandate a call from Langley to Santiago asking whether some mistake had been made, a message missed.

To this day, Bush has never responded to this question and the CIA has not released the communications between Langley and Santiago over the Paraguay mission. One troubling possibility is that the CIA had sanctioned the attack, which originally was conceived as a discreet poisoning of Letelier, not his death by car bomb.

According to intelligence sources, the CIA did contact DINA after the bombing. Santiago station chief Wiley Gilstrap questioned Contreras. Gilstrap then reportedly cabled Langley with Contreras's assurance that the Pinochet government was not involved. Contreras pointed the finger at communists supposedly trying to turn Letelier into a martyr.

Bush's CIA promptly adopted Contreras's false denial as its own analysis and leaked it. Typical was *Newsweek*'s report that "the Chilean secret police were not involved. .... The [Central Intelligence] agency reached its decision because the bomb was too crude to be the work of experts and because the murder, coming while Chile's rulers were wooing U.S. support, could only damage the Santiago regime."[97]

Rather than fulfilling his pledge to Abourezk, Bush did little during his remaining months at CIA to shed light on the murder. "Nothing the agency gave us helped us break this case," said federal prosecutor Eugene Propper. The CIA never volunteered Landau's cable about DINA's suspicious mission or copies of the fake passports that included a photo of the chief assassin, Michael Townley. Nor did Bush's CIA divulge its knowledge of the existence of Operation Condor, the cross-border assassination program run by South American military dictatorships hunting down dissidents abroad.

---

[97] *Newsweek*, Oct. 11, 1976.

FBI agents in Washington and Latin America broke the Letelier case two years later. They discovered Operation Condor and tracked the assassination to Townley and his accomplices in the United States, right-wing Cubans. The CIA's analysis clearing the Chilean government had sent investigators in the wrong direction. But it was unclear if Bush authorized the leaking of the false assessment or was aware at the time that it was disinformation.

B ush's career as CIA director ended in January 1977 with the inauguration of Jimmy Carter. The Democratic president appointed Navy Adm. Stansfield Turner, who pushed through unpopular reforms at the CIA, including downsizing the agency's powerful operations directorate. The CIA's "old boys" fumed.

By 1980, with Bush running for president, senior CIA officers were openly pining for the election of their former boss. "The seventh floor of Langley was plastered with 'Bush for President' signs'," recalled George Carver, a senior CIA analyst. A host of former CIA officers signed up for the campaign.

Bush failed to win the GOP nomination in 1980, but he was picked as Ronald Reagan's running mate. That choice swept the ex-CIA officers into the Reagan-Bush campaign. Many of the former spies manned a 24-hours-a-day Operations Center at Reagan-Bush headquarters in Arlington, Va. A chief concern of those intelligence agents was President Carter's delicate negotiations aimed at bringing 52 American hostages out of Iran before the November election, the so-called "October Surprise."

According to an unpublished chapter of a later congressional review of the October Surprise case, "many of the [Operations Center's] staff members were former CIA employees who had previously worked on the Bush campaign or were otherwise loyal to George Bush."

The center was run by Stefan Halper, son-in-law of former CIA official Ray Cline, the "secret" chapter read. "Halper often wrote memoranda on the hostage issue addressed to senior campaign officials urging them to attack Carter more aggressively on his handling of the crisis," stated the chapter, which I uncovered in

1994 while digging through the records of the congressional inquiry.[98]

One question raised by the advice from Halper and others was why Republicans felt confident enough to highlight the hostage issue. Such a strategy could have backfired if Carter did secure the hostages' freedom in late October. One possible answer was the existence of back-channel contacts between the Reagan-Bush campaign and the Iranian government that offered assurances that a release would not come until after the election.

Over the years, more than a score of witnesses -- including senior Iranian officials, top French intelligence officers, Israeli intelligence operatives and even PLO chief Yasir Arafat -- have confirmed the GOP-Iranian contacts.[99]

In 1996, during a meeting in Gaza, Arafat personally told Carter that senior Republican emissaries approached the Palestine Liberation Organization in 1980 with a request that Arafat help broker a delay in the hostage release. "You should know that in 1980 the Republicans approached me with an arms deal if I could arrange to keep the hostages in Iran until after the [U.S. presidential] election," Arafat told Carter. Arafat claimed he rebuffed offer.[100]

But Arafat's spokesman Bassam Abu Sharif said the GOP gambit pursued other channels as well. In an interview with me in Tunis in 1990, Bassam indicated that Arafat learned upon reaching Iran that the Iranians and the Republicans had made other arrangments.

"The offer [to Arafat] was, 'if you block the release of hostages, then the White House would be open for the PLO'," Bassam said. "I guess the same offer was given to others, and I believe that some accepted to do it and managed to block the release of hostages."

Beyond the question of GOP contacts, however, is the issue of Bush's alleged role. Two October Surprise witnesses have stated

---

[98] For details, see Robert Parry's *The October Surprise X-Files*.

[99] See Robert Parry's *Trick or Treason* and *iF Magazine*, Nov.-Dec. 1997.

[100] See *Diplomatic History*, Fall 1996.

that Bush personally participated in the 1980 contacts with Iran. Israeli intelligence official Ari Ben-Menashe and pilot Heinrich Rupp placed Bush in Paris for meetings with Iranians on Oct. 19, 1980.

Two other witnesses -- a diplomat and a journalist -- supplied important corroboration that senior Republicans were discussing Bush's direct involvement contemporaneously. After the October Surprise issue received some national attention in 1991, a former Foreign Service officer named David Henderson recalled a conversation he had with a journalist in mid-October 1980. During an interview in Washington while he still worked for the State Department, Henderson said *Chicago Tribune* reporter John Maclean mentioned hearing that Bush was on his way to Paris to talk with Iranians about the American hostages. Henderson dated his talk with Maclean as Oct. 18, 1980.

Questioned about Henderson's memory, Maclean confirmed that a well-placed Republican had told him about the Bush trip to Paris in mid-October 1980. But Maclean would not divulge his source's identity. Though the source's name remained a secret, I was able to confirm that Maclean did have high-level contacts in the 1980 Reagan campaign. Among the congressional October Surprise documents, I found a handwritten calendar belonging to Ronald Reagan's foreign policy adviser, Richard Allen. The calendar showed that Allen met with Maclean the week before the alleged Paris meetings.

To make a secret trip to Paris, however, Bush would have had to slip away from official Secret Service protection, and Secret Service logs indicated Bush was at his Washington home that day. The Secret Service records were always the strongest evidence undercutting the October Surprise allegations. Many investigators accepted them as conclusive proof that the allegations were a hoax. But there remained some doubt because the Bush administration denied both federal prosecutors and Congress unfettered access to the relevant logs.

According to the parts of the logs that were released, Bush was taking time off at home in Washington during the hours in question. The logs cited two side trips, one in the morning to the Chevy Chase Country Club and one to a private residence in the afternoon. However, key details that would have allowed the written record to be corroborated, such as whom Bush saw and what exactly he was doing, were deleted.

In 1992, congressional investigators were allowed to interview about nine Bush-assigned agents informally, but none under oath and none could supply any credible details about Bush's activities. Most had no memory of the recorded trips. Only one supervisor, Leonard Tanis, asserted that he recalled Bush attending a morning brunch at the Chevy Chase Country Club with Barbara Bush and Supreme Court Justice Potter Stewart and his wife.

Tanis's account collapsed, however, when Mrs. Bush's Secret Service records showed her jogging at the C&O Canal that morning. Mrs. Stewart, Justice Stewart's widow, also denied having brunch with the Bushes that day. Confronted with the contradictory information, Tanis acknowledged that he might have been thinking of another event.

The Secret Service was even more unhelpful about the afternoon trip. Those records showed both Mr. and Mrs. Bush traveling to a private residence, but the Secret Service would not divulge the address or the identity of the person visited. Some Democratic investigators suspected that the trip might have involved only Barbara Bush and that the logs had been falsified to give Bush an alibi.

In spring 1992, however, President Bush demanded publicly at two news conferences that he be cleared of any suspicion about a secret trip to Paris. With Bush running for re-election, Republicans on the task force threatened to obstruct further funding if Bush's demands were not met.

Finally, the congressional task force, headed by Rep. Lee Hamilton, agreed to accept a Secret Service compromise in which the task force was given the name of the person visited in the afternoon but prohibited from ever interviewing the witness or divulging the person's identity. After accepting the strange compromise and never questioning the alibi witness, Hamilton's task force agreed to clear Bush in an interim report issued on July 1, 1992.

In large part, the acceptance of the Bush alibi determined the remaining course of the October Surprise investigation. Ben-Menashe, a prominent witness, was judged unreliable because he had claimed to see Bush in Paris. Even when additional evidence surfaced corroborating the existence of Republican-Iranian meetings in Paris, the task force had little choice but to reject that information.

The later witnesses included journalist David Andelman, the biographer for French intelligence chief Alexandre deMarenches. Andelman recounted deMarenches's admission that he had helped Reagan's campaign chief, William Casey, set up the Paris meetings. The task force noted that two other French intelligence officials corroborated that account. But the alleged Paris meetings still were judged a fiction largely because of Bush's redacted Secret Service records.

In the final days of the investigation, even Russia's Supreme Soviet weighed in with a confidential report buttressing the Paris charges. The Russian report claimed that Soviet intelligence was aware of Republican meetings with Iranians in both Madrid and Paris in 1980. The Russian report stated that Bush had attended the Paris meeting in October 1980. The task force's response to the Russian report, which Hamilton had requested, was simply to hide it from public view. It was stuck in a box of investigative records that I dug through in late 1994.[101]

W hile the Paris meeting remains one of the most controversial parts of the October Surprise allegations, other documentary evidence proves that Bush did have a direct role in the October Surprise monitoring. I also found evidence of that in Richard Allen's confidential notes.

According to those handwritten records, Bush called Allen at 2:12 p.m., Oct. 27, 1980, with a worried message from former Texas Gov. John Connally. A onetime-Democrat-turned-Republican, Connally was hearing some disturbing news from his Middle Eastern contacts: the possibility that Carter might yet pull off a pre-election hostage deal.

Bush ordered Allen to check out Connally's tip. When Allen knew more, he was to relay the information to "Shacklee [sic] via

---

[101] The Russian report was prepared by Sergei Stepashin, who became Russia's prime minister in May 1999. For the full Russian report, see Parry's *The October Surprise X-Files*.

Jennifer." The Jennifer was Bush's longtime assistant Jennifer Fitzgerald. "Shacklee" was Theodore Shackley, the legendary CIA covert ops specialist known as the "blond ghost." Though Connally's warning proved to be a false alarm, the notation indicated that Shackley was representing Bush on the sensitive October Surprise issue.

Shackley also had close ties to active-duty CIA personnel inside the Carter White House. As Saigon station chief during the Vietnam War, Shackley was the boss of Donald Gregg. In 1980, Gregg was the CIA representative on Carter's National Security Council. According to Ben-Menashe, Gregg and another key CIA officer, Robert Gates, assisted in the Paris contacts with the Iranians. Gregg and Gates both have denied the allegation.

But like Bush, Gregg had trouble establishing an alibi for Oct. 19, 1980. Then, when Iran-contra investigators put Gregg on a polygraph and asked whether he took part in the October Surprise operation, Gregg's denial was judged deceptive.

As the former head of the CIA's covert operations against Fidel Castro, Shackley had strong contacts, too, inside the right-wing Cuban community. One of those associates was former CIA officer Felix Rodriguez, a.k.a. "Max Gomez," who also worked with Gregg and Bush at the CIA.

After Carter's defeat, Vice President Bush emerged as an important foreign policy adviser to President Reagan. Many of Bush's former CIA associates filtered into key roles as well. Gregg became the vice president's national security adviser. Gates advanced quickly as one of CIA director William Casey's golden boys, rising first to the top of the analytical division and then to be deputy director. This close-knit team around Bush had a hand in nearly every important foreign policy initiative of the Reagan administration. Their fingerprints also were found on virtually every national security scandal.

According to a 1995 deposition by Reagan national security aide Howard Teicher, Gates joined in a secret operation in the 1980s to funnel sophisticated military equipment to Iraq via Carlos Cardoen, an arms dealer in Chile with close ties to Gen. Pinochet.

"Under CIA director Casey and deputy director Gates, the CIA authorized, approved and assisted Cardoen in the manufacture and sale of cluster bombs and other munitions to Iraq," Teicher wrote in the affidavit submitted as part of an arms-smuggling case in federal court in Florida.

Teicher stated, too, that to help Iraq in its war with Iran, Bush conveyed secret tactical recommendations to Saddam Hussein through Egyptian President Hosni Mubarak. Gates and Bush have denied enlisting third-country support for arming Iraq in the 1980s, although Reagan-Bush officials did acknowledge passing along sensitive battlefield intelligence to help Saddam in his eight-year-long war against Iran. But the press has never questioned Bush in any detail about the Iraqi arms operation.

Other of Bush's old CIA associates surfaced in other national security controversies. Shackley went into private business in the 1980s but kept a hand in the Middle East power game. The former CIA official made some of the initial contacts that led to secret U.S. arms shipments to Iran in the mid-1980s -- and eventually to the arms-for-hostage scandal known as the Iran-contra affair.

On the contra front, another ex-CIA officer, Felix Rodriguez, stepped in when the Reagan administration needed help in funneling secret support to the Nicaraguan contra rebels. Placed in the region by Gregg, Rodriguez reported directly to Gregg and Bush about developments in El Salvador, where the contra resupply operation was based.

The Rodriguez connection proved troublesome when Bush insisted, implausibly, that he was "out of the loop" on Iran-contra. Rodriguez, Gregg and Bush all denied that Rodriguez had ever mentioned the contra supply operation although one memo for a three-way meeting cited "resupply of the contras" as a topic. Bush has never been questioned about his knowledge of contra-connected drug trafficking, despite the smuggling allegations that surrounded Felix Rodriguez's Cuban-American contingent.

B ush's links to South American underworld figures also extends through Rev. Sun Myung Moon's business-political-religious empire. In the 1960s and 1970s, Moon's Unification Church developed close ties to organized crime figures in Asia and South America. In 1980, Moon's organization collaborated with a right-wing military putsch in Bolivia that turned that country into the region's first narco-state.

Over the next two decades, Moon poured hundreds of millions of dollars into conservative political organizations. Though losing an estimated $100 million a year, Moon's *Washington Times* newspaper became a flagship of the conservative movement. Yet, according to Moon's close associates and court records, Moon has financed his operations, in part, with vast sums of cash smuggled into the United States as well as through a suspected money-laundering base in Uruguay.[102]

In recent years, as his religious mission in the United States has shrunk to about 3,000 members, Moon has grown bitterly anti-American. In speeches, he has denounced the United States as "the kingdom of Satan" or as "Satan's harvest." In one speech on Aug. 4, 1996, Moon decried American "individualism" and declared that "the world will reject Americans who continue to be so foolish. Once you have this great power of love, which is big enough to swallow entire America, there may be some individuals who complain inside your stomach. However, they will be digested."[103]

Despite this anti-Americanism, Bush has maintained close ties to Moon and *The Washington Times.* In 1991, when Wesley Pruden was named the new editor, Bush invited Pruden to a private White House lunch "just to tell you how valuable the *Times* has become in Washington, where we read it every day."[104] Once out of office, Bush went to work for Moon as a paid speaker in Asia, the United States and South America. Bush's office has refused to divulge how much Moon's organization paid Bush, but a source close to Moon put the total as high as $10 million.

Bush proved especially valuable when Moon launched a newspaper in South America. The theocrat confronted a skeptical reception because of his past support for the region's brutal military dictatorships and evidence linking Moon associates to the drug trade. On Nov. 22, 1996, Bush came to the rescue. He flew to

---

[102] See Nansook Hong's *In the Shadow of the Moons* and *iF Magazine*, Nov.-Dec. 1997, Sept.-Oct. 1998 & Nov.-Dec. 1998.
[103] See *iF Magazine*, Sept.-Oct. 1997.
[104] *The Washington Times,* May 17, 1992.

Buenos Aires and paved the way for Moon with Argentine president Carlos Menem.

Bush also was the keynote speaker at a gala reception for the new newspaper, *Tiempos del Mundo*. With Moon sitting just a few feet away, Bush lavished praise on the theocrat. "I want to salute Reverend Moon, who is the founder *of The Washington Times* and also of *Tiempos del Mundo*," Bush declared.

"A lot of my friends in South America don't know about *The Washington Times*, but it is an independent voice. The editors of *The Washington Times* tell me that never once has the man with the vision interfered with the running of the paper, a paper that in my view brings sanity to Washington."

Bush's praise thrilled Moon's supporters. "Once again, heaven turned a disappointment into a victory," proclaimed the *Unification News*, the church's internal newsletter. [Dec. 1996] But Bush's claim of journalistic independence at *The Washington Times* was false. Since the paper's inception in 1982, editors and reporters have resigned in protest over editorial interference by Moon's lieutenants. The first editor, James Whelan, resigned in 1984 confessing to "blood on my hands" for giving Moon legitimacy.

Former President Bush, however, seemed to have no such qualms. One source close to the Bush camp said the ex-president saw the value of building an alliance with the powerful Moon organization, as an asset for his son's presidential run.

Given the failure of the Washington press corps to hold the Reagan-Bush administrations accountable for much these past two decades, the ex-president might have good reason to assume that the pattern will continue through 2000 – and maybe, that the "lost history" will stay lost forever.

INDEX

15th of September
    Legion, 37, 42, 226
ABC News, 102, 266
Abourezk, James, 279,
    283
Abrams, Elliot, 45-46, 123,
    136
Accuracy in Media, 46,
    61, 136, 180
Achenbach, Joel, 187-188
Adams, James, 245
Aerocondor, 166
Afghanistan, 50, 72
African National
    Congress, 14
Agency for International
    Development, 47, 51
Agent Orange, 11
Agronsky and Company,
    77
Aguado, Marcos, 181, 213,
    234
Allen, Paul, 71-72
Allen, Richard, 286- 288
Allende, Salvador, 174
Altmann, Klaus, 39
Amador, Carlos, 215- 217,
    220
Americas Watch, 22, 24,
    98
Anderson, Jack, 255
Anderson, Terry, 110, 117
Aplicano, Hector, 162,
    170
Arana, Arnoldo Jose
    "Frank", 237
Arce-Gomez, Luis, 39-41
Archivos, 16, 21-23
Argentina, 5, 10, 14, 37-
    42, 74, 174, 240, 280, 292

Arms Export Control
    Act, 87, 146
Arms Supermarket, 141, 160-
    162, 170-171
Artime, Manuel, 233
Assad, Hafez, 151
Associated Press, The, 12,
    28, 32, 46, 73, 80, 84-86,
    89, 92, 94-96, 104-105,
    109-111, 114-117, 121-
    124, 127-130, 133, 137,
    266, 270
Atala, Sonia, 40
Atlacatl Battalion, 44
Banco de Credito, 202
Banzer, Hugo, 40
Barbie, Klaus, 39-41, 201
Barger, Brian, 13, 84-96,
    104, 107, 109-110, 114-
    115, 121-122
Barnes, Fred, 96-97, 100-
    102
Barnes, Michael, 54, 116,
    117
Barreda, Felipe and
    Maria, 57, 97
Bay of Pigs, 165, 173, 228,
    233, 235
Bell, General J. Franklin,
    7
Belli, Humberto, 63
Ben-Menashe, Ari, 286,
    289
Berger, Samuel "Sandy",
    276
Bermingham, Robert A.,
    137
Bermudez, Enrique, 37,
    43, 101, 170, 182, 194-
    197, 209-210, 215, 226,
    236

Blandon, Oscar Danilo,
42-43, 182, 185-188, 193-
195, 208, 210
Blum, Jack, 117-118
Bo Hi Pak, 200-201
Boccardi, Louis D., 117
Boggs, Hale, 254-255
Boland Amendment, 66,
82, 114, 131
Boland, Edward P., 66, 73
Bolivia, 38-43, 194, 204,
227, 240, 291
Bonner, Raymond, 4, 44-
46, 102, 269
Boren, David, 275, 277
Borge, Tomas, 189
Bosch, Orlando, 173-174
Boston Globe, The, 70
Boxer, Barbara, 197
Brigade 2506, 165
Brinkley, David, 149
Bristow, Alan, 262
Brody, Reed, 77-78, 96- 97
Bromwich, Michael, 207-
223
Brosnahan, James, 155-
156
Buchanan, Patrick, 78
Bueso-Rosa, Jose, 170
Bui Dhien, 259
Burnes, Karen, 102
Bush, George H. W., 10-
11, 101, 122-123, 140-
141, 146-151, 155-158,
161, 174-175, 180-181,
206, 221, 243-244, 252-
253, 263, 269-292
Bush, George W., 280
Buzenberg, Bill, 72
Cabezas, Carlos, 190, 210-
211, 228
Calderon, Roberto, 221
Calero, Adolfo, 73, 82,
170, 191, 209, 237-238
Calero, Mario, 238-239
Camarena, Enrique, 237
Cannistraro, Vincent,
183-184
Cardoen, Carlos, 289- 290
Carey, David, 274, 277
Carlucci, Frank, 130
Carr, Steven, 93-94

Cartaya, Guillermo
Hernandez, 165-167
Carter, James, 11, 28, 252,
262-263, 280, 284-285,
288-289
Carter, Jimmy, 18, 19
Carver, George, 284
Casa Sanchez,
Maximillano, 160
Casey, William J., 12, 36,
43, 60-62, 65-66, 70, 74,
80, 82, 91, 99, 115-116,
119, 129, 136, 139, 146,
162, 202-204, 241, 245,
252, 273, 276-277, 289,
290
Castillo, Celerino, 177,
216-219
Castro, Fidel, 20, 161, 164-
166, 173-174, 231- 234,
289
Castro, Frank, 42, 69, 94,
232-235
CBS News, 71, 121, 271
Central American Task
Force, 105, 184, 218, 229
Central Intelligence
Agency, (See CIA)
Ceppos, Jerry, 188-191
Cerezo, Vinicio, 177
Cesar, Octaviano, 213-
214
Chambers, Whitaker, 257
Chamorro, Adolfo
"Popo", 212-214, 234
Chamorro, Edgar, 53- 59,
63, 65, 73-74, 84
Chamorro, Roberto
"Tito", 213
Chanes, Francisco, 93- 94,
232
Channell, Carl "Spitz",
117
Chapin, Frederic, 23- 24
Chardy, Alfonso, 61, 85,
103
Cheney, Dick, 134
Chennault, Anna, 259-
261
Chiaie, Stafano della, 39
Chile, 10, 279, 281, 283, 289
Christian, David, 161
Church, Frank, 11

CIA, 5-14, 19-22, 28, 35, 38-43, 49-69, 72-74, 82-94, 97-99, 104-112, 115-124, 129-132, 135-149, 155-156, 160-198, 202- 253, 262, 270-284, 289-290
Civilian-Military Assistance, 89
Clark, William, 50
Clarke, Maura, 31
Clarridge, Duane "Dewey", 35-37, 54-57, 60, 64-66, 155-156, 241
A Spy for All Seasons, 35
Cline, Ray, 284
Clinton, William, 15, 26, 27, 155, 158, 224, 253, 263, 264, 275, 276, 277, 278
CNN, 123
Cocaine Coup, 38-41, 204
Cocaine Politics, 40, 43, 232-233
Cockburn, Alexander, 245
Cohen, David, 274, 277
Cohen, Richard, 157
Cohen, William, 82, 139, 230
COINTELPRO, 250
Cold War, 3-7, 11, 27- 29, 53, 145, 164, 173, 178, 180, 248-249, 253, 256-257, 268
Colombia, 67, 119, 124, 163, 165, 213, 215, 220, 235-237
Colson, Charles, 260
Committee in Solidarity with the People of El Salvador, 69-70
Congressional Black Caucus, 182
Connally, John, 288- 289
Consortium, The, 28, 158, 243
contras. See Nicaragua. See Nicaragua
Contreras, Joseph, 135, 136
Contreras, Manuel, 280, 283
Copeland, Miles, 262

Corr, Edwin, 217-218
CORU, 233
Corvo, Rene, 94, 231- 235
Costa Rica, 37, 42-43, 60, 69, 87, 90-95, 98, 103-104, 130, 163, 168-169, 175, 181, 196, 198, 208-216, 220-235
Crowley, Monica, 263
Cruz, Arturo, 82
Cuba, 164-167, 173, 177, 232- 233
Dailey, Peter, 115-116
death squads, 37, 39
deBorchgrave, Arnaud, 184-185
Defense Intelligence Agency, DIA, 17, 24
Dellamico, Mario, 161-162, 170
DeLoach, Cartha, 261
DelValle, Enrique, 159, 170-171
DelValle, Eric, 171
Derian, Pat, 18
deTriquet, Thomas, 219
Deutch, John, 182-183, 277
Dickey, Christopher, 58-59
Dickson, Peter W., 276, 278
DISIP, 173
Dole, Robert, 149, 155-156, 263
Donovan, Jean, 31
Dornan, Robert K., 271
Dowling, Thomas, 98- 99
Doyle, Kate, 24, 189
Drug Enforcement Administration, 39- 41, 66-67, 93-94, 161, 164, 169, 177, 184, 190, 203-204, 208- 209, 213-223, 231, 236-240
Duarte, Napoleon, 177
Dubro, Alec, 199
Duemling, Robert, 164
Dupart, Louis, 229, 230, 241
Duran, Gerardo, 213- 215
Durenberger, David, 99
Dutton, Robert, 176

Earl, Robert, 164
Eisenhower, Dwight David, 145, 271-272
El Flaco. See Terrell, Jack
El Mozote, 44-47
El Salvador, 4, 10, 14, 31, 33, 36, 44, 46, 51- 53, 60, 71, 80-82, 150, 163, 172, 175-176, 215-219, 234, 239, 268-271, 290
Ellsberg, Daniel, 251, 256, 258
Enders, Thomas, 45- 46
Endless Enemies, 165
Evans, Rowland, 123
Fagoth, Steadman, 239
Federal Bureau of Investigation, 69-70, 92, 103-107, 112-114, 119, 167, 170-177, 196, 210, 227, 232, 235, 237, 241, 253-255, 260-261, 284
Feldman, Jeffrey, 103- 108, 176
Fernandez, Joe, 91, 104, 130, 168-169, 175, 230
Ferrara, Salvatore John, 251
Fiers, Alan, 105-108, 156, 184, 218, 230- 231, 241
Fitzgerald, Jennifer, 289
Foley, Tom, 156
Fooling America, 28
Ford, Gerald, 255, 281
Ford, Ita, 31
Fort Holabird, 18
Fort Huachuca, 270
Freedom House, 63, 76
Freedom of Information Act, 11, 69, 249, 253
Friends Peace Committee, 70
Frigorificos de Puentarenas, 91, 94, 163-164, 221, 229, 231
Frixone, Donaldo, 238
Frogman Case, 68, 125, 196
FRONTLINE, 12
Gannon, John, 274, 277
Garcia Meza, Luis, 200-201

Gasser, Erwin, 39
Gasser, Jose Roberto, 39, 200
Gates, Robert, 136, 239, 273-277, 289-290
Gejdenson, Sam, 99
Gentry, John A., 275, 278
George, Clair, 155-156
Gilstrap, Wiley, 283
Glibbery, Peter, 93
Gomez, Ivan, 190, 227-228
Goodman, Melvyn, 273, 275, 278
Gorbachev, Mikhail, 152
Grasheim, Walter, 217-218
Greener, William I., 62
Greentree, Todd, 45
Gregg, Donald, 140- 141, 149-150, 161, 175, 289-290
Gregorie, Richard, 124
Gregory, Dick, 182-183
Greve, Frank, 269
Guatemala, 4, 10, 14- 26, 53, 177, 210, 216, 219
Guerrilla Army of the Poor, EGP, 20
Guevara, Ernest "Che", 173
Guglielminetti, Raul, 38, 42
Guillermoprieto, Alma, 44
Haig, Al, 32, 36
Haldeman, H.R., 256- 257, 261
Hall, Fawn, 110, 128
Halper, Stefan, 284- 285
Halperin, Morton, 252
Hamilton, Lee, 114, 221, 252
Hart, Gary, 82
Hasenfus, Eugene, 120-123, 127, 176-177
Hay-Adams Hotel, 79
Healy, Marta, 213
Hedges, Michael, 183- 184
Henderson, David, 286
Herman Hernandez, Roger, 239
Hermann, Kai, 201

Hersh, Seymour, 179, 259-260
Hill, Charles, 147
Hiss, Alger, 256-258
Hitz, Frederick, 187, 193, 204-205, 224-243
Hodel, Georg, 191-192
Hoffman, Clare E., 250
Holbrooke, Richard, 141
Honduras, 14, 37, 43, 57-60, 74-75, 87, 89, 93, 98, 141, 160-162, 169-172, 177, 182, 194, 204, 210-211, 216, 225, 236-240
Hoover, J. Edgar, 254-255, 260
House Intelligence Committee, 73, 114
Hughes, John, 22
Huk rebellion, 7-8
Hull, John, 42, 93-94, 104, 208, 213-214, 220-223, 232-234
Humphrey, Hubert, 259-260
Hurtado-Candia, Hugo, 40
Hyde, Alan, 239-240
iF Magazine, 28, 158, 191, 243, 246
Ilopango airbase, 81- 82, 120, 123, 163, 172, 175-176, 215-220, 234, 239
In These Times, 137
Indonesia, 6, 10, 13
Iran, 10, 12, 28, 50-51, 62, 76, 85, 98-99, 103-107, 117, 128-141, 145-148, 155-163, 170, 173, 176-177, 180, 184-185, 218-219, 229- 230, 237-239, 262, 275, 284, 289-290
Iran-contra, 12, 28, 50- 51, 62, 76, 85, 98-99, 103-107, 117, 129- 141, 145-147, 155- 162, 170, 173, 176- 177, 180, 184-185, 218-219, 230, 237- 239, 275, 289-290
Isikoff, Michael, 143
Israel, 54, 87, 146, 151
Jacobowitz, Daniel "Jake", 76

Jacobsen, David, 154
Jacobsen, Ernst, 67
Johnson, Lyndon, 259-261, 272
Justice Department, 69, 83, 103, 105, 117- 119, 125, 142, 145, 170, 196, 203, 207, 212, 217, 225, 227, 234-235, 254, 258
Kagan, Bob, 115
Kaplan, David E., 199
Kass, Stephen L., 22- 23
Kazel, Dorothy, 31
Kellner, Leon, 104-105, 108
Kelly, J. Michael, 43
Kennedy, John F., 27, 272
Kerry, John, 38, 96, 105-108, 112, 117-119, 123-125, 133, 140- 143, 169, 181, 221, 231-232, 235, 241, 244
Kim Jong-Pil, 199-200
Kirkpatrick, Jeane, 12, 32
Kissinger, Henry, 256-259, 262
Kodama, Yoshio, 199
Kolt, George, 274
Kondracke, Morton, 102
Korten, Patrick, 104
Krauthammer, Charles, 102
Kurtz, Howard, 187, 189, 191
Kutler, Stanley I., 255
Kwitny, Jonathan, 165
La Negra, 58
La Prensa, 64
La Republica, 160
Lagana, Greg, 103
Lake, Anthony, 277
Landau, George, 282- 283
Lansdale, Edward G., 7-9, 12, 76
Lebanon, 72, 117
Leiwant, David, 104
Lernoux, Penny, 167
Letelier, Orlando, 174, 279-280, 283-284
Levine, Michael, 39-41, 200
   Big White Lie, 40
   Deep Cover, 39

Lewinsky, Monica, 5, 27, 224
Lewis, Charles, 86, 94- 96, 109-110, 115
Libya, 88
Lippert, Ron, 222-223
Littledale, Kris, 117
Longon, John, 15-16
Los Angeles Times, The, 101, 143, 189, 225, 243, 246
Lucas Garcia, Fernando Romeo, 19
Lugar, Richard, 118, 125
Lynch, Jim, 274
Mabry, Philip, 70
Mackenzie, Angus, 248-253, 264
Maclean, John, 286
Madison, Joe, 183
Mafia, 11, 41, 164, 166, 178
Marchetti, Victor, 251
Marshall, Jonathan, 40, 232
Martin, Ronald, 102, 161-162, 168, 170-171
Matta Ballesteros, Juan, 237
Matthews, Christopher, 149
Matthews, Linda, 9
Mayerfeld, Ernest, 197
McClintock, Michael, 8
McCoy, Alfred W., 178-180
McFarlane, Robert, 75, 82-87, 129, 146-147, 151, 154
McGehee, Ralph, 252
McGovern, George, 260
McKay, John, 45
McLaughlin Group, 77
McLaughlin, John, 274, 277
McManus, Doyle, 189
McNeil, Francis, 91
Mears, Walter, 84
Mechanic School of the Navy, 40
Medellin cartel, the, 66-69, 94, 119, 164, 180, 204, 212-213, 228-229, 232, 235, 238
Medina, Ramon, 122, 175, 177

Meese, Edwin, 104, 129, 134, 146-147, 176, 238
Mejia Victores, Oscar, 23-24
Melendez, Jorge, 222
Menem, Carlos, 292
Meneses, Jairo, 210
Meneses, Norwin, 42, 43, 186, 193-195, 208-210, 215, 220, 226
Messick, Rick, 241
Messing, Andy, 127- 128, 271
Meyer, Cord Jr., 179
Meza, Luis Garcia, 41
MHCHAOS, 250-251
Miami Herald, 61, 85, 103, 109, 111, 173
Milian Rodriguez, Ramon, 164, 181, 229, 232
Miller, Jonathan, 71, 76, 78
Mingolla, Alfred Mario, 201
Minh, Ho Chi, 9, 178
Miranda, Enrique, 195
Mitchell, John, 256, 259-261
Moffitt, Ronni, 174, 279
Molina, John, 159-172
Molina, Pablo, 167-171
Monge, Luis Alberto, 92
Moon, Sun Myung, 41, 199-201, 281, 290-292
Morabia, Nan, 162-163
Morales, Jorge, 212- 214, 220, 234
Morales, Ricardo, 42, 219
Mubarak, Hosni, 290
murder manual. *See* Psychological Operations in Guerrilla Warfare
Murdock, Rupert, 62
My Lai, 179, 249
Nakasone, Yasuhiro, 151
Narodny Bank, 166
National Defense Council, 127
National Public Radio, 71-72
National Security Agency, 130

National Security
   Archive, 24
National Security
   Council, 12, 49-51, 61,
   70, 78-79, 82-87, 90, 93,
   103, 110-112, 115-116,
   128-134, 139, 146-147,
   184, 205, 225, 228-232,
   250, 289
Neutrality Act, 87, 104,
   203, 236
New Republic, The, 96,
   100-102, 158, 220
New York magazine, 88
New York Times, The, 44,
   46, 73, 86, 104, 133, 137,
   143, 179- 180, 183, 189,
   204, 225, 243-244, 255,
   269
Newsweek, 12, 78, 102,
   130-136, 266, 283
Nicaragua, 5, 31, 35-36, 51-
   56, 59-71, 77, 82- 88, 92,
   95-97, 100-101, 111, 120-
   121, 125, 127, 135-136,
   173, 184, 190-195, 208-
   209, 212- 214, 220, 226,
   234, 236, 238, 243, 265,
   273
   contras, 5, 13, 28, 35- 38,
      42-43, 52-78, 82-120,
      124-142, 145- 150,
      155-164, 168- 172,
      175-177, 180- 198,
      202-221, 224- 245,
      281, 290
Nicaraguan Democratic
   Force, 54, 57, 65, 73-75,
   93- 94, 162, 195, 198,
   209- 210, 215-216, 226,
   236-238
Nieves, Robert, 93, 169
Nixon, Richard, 179, 251-
   264, 267, 272
Noriega, Manuel, 90- 91,
   160, 167, 169, 171, 180-
   181
North, Oliver, 12, 66, 70,
   77-99, 103-117, 120-123,
   127-133, 136- 137, 140-
   143, 146-150, 154, 161-
   164, 168-172, 175-177,
   185, 187, 216, 218, 225,
   229-230, 234, 238, 271

Novak, Robert, 123
Nunez, Moises
   "Dagoberto", 221, 228-
   232
O'Neill, Thomas P. "Tip",
   119
Obando y Bravo, Miguel,
   88, 135-136
Ocean Hunter, 91, 229,
   231
Ochoa, Jorge, 119, 235,
   238
October Surprise, 28, 259,
   263, 284-289
October Surprise X-Files,
   The, 28
O'Dwyer-Russell, Simon,
   262
Office of Public
   Diplomacy for Latin
   America, 70, 100, 139
Office of Strategic
   Services, 178
Operation Condor, 282-
   284
Operation Tick-Talks, 42
Ortega, Daniel, 78
Ortega, Humberto, 190
Owen, Robert, 87, 104,
   111, 164, 187, 234
Owen, Robert W., 77
Pais, Frank, 164
Palacio, Wanda, 119, 123-
   126, 133, 163, 232, 238
Palestine Liberation
   Organization, 88, 285
Panama, 90-93, 159- 161,
   165-166, 169, 171, 180,
   269
Papas, Dimitrius, 92
Parker, Maynard, 134,
   141, 144
Pastora, Eden, 90, 94, 109,
   111, 169, 209, 212-213,
   219, 227, 234-235
Pell, Claiborne, 118, 125
Pena Cabrera, Renato,
   195-198, 209, 215
Pentagon Papers, 5, 11,
   251, 256, 258
perception management,
   12, 28, 43, 66, 70, 74, 131,

140, 144. *See also* public
   diplomacy
Pereira, Horacio, 210- 211
Peretz, Martin, 102
Perez, Jose, 237
Perez, Juan, 222-223
Peru, 210
Philippines, 7-8
Phoenix Program, 9- 10,
   179
Piedra, Alberto, 24
Pike, Otis, 11
Pinochet, Augusto, 279, 281,
   283, 289
PLO. *See* Palestine Liberation
   Organization
Plumbers, 251, 255-258
Poindexter, John, 85, 103,
   112, 115-117, 127-129,
   134, 146-148
Poland, 72
Polgar, Tom, 132
Posada Carriles, Luis,
   172-177
Powell, Colin, 130, 157
Project Democracy, 112
Project X, 9-10, 18
Propper, Eugene, 283
Psychological
   Operations in
   Guerrilla Warfare, 73,
   84-85
psychological warfare, 8-
   9, 12, 73, 76
public diplomacy, 12, 49-
   54, 60-61, 66, 70- 71, 77-
   78, 82, 86-88, 96, 99, 103,
   112, 115- 116, 120, 138-
   139, 180, 217, 246, 266
Puebla Institute, 63
Pumpkin Papers, 256
Quintero, Rafael "Chi
   Chi", 175-176
Quiroga, Marcelo, 40- 41
Ramirez Cervantes, Elias
   Osmundo, 18
Ramparts, 250-253
Raymond, Walter, 4, 44,
   49-51, 60-63, 70, 76, 99,
   115-116
Reagan, Ronald, 11- 12,
   15, 18-23, 27-28, 31-36,
   43-49, 52-54, 59-71, 74,

78-87, 101- 104, 107, 110-
   113, 116-119, 123, 126-
   134, 139-154, 158- 163,
   172, 180-181, 185-186,
   197, 202- 208, 211, 217,
   220- 221, 224-225, 228,
   234-235, 243-246, 252,
   263-277, 281, 284-286,
   289-290
Redman, Charles, 95
Regan, Donald, 82, 131,
   134, 146
Reich, Otto, 70-72, 76-77,
   87-88, 99, 100, 115, 139
Reider, Rem, 189
Reno, Janet, 167
Republic National Bank,
   162
Revell, Oliver "Buck",
   105-107, 113-114
Ribeiro, Osvaldo, 37
Ricevuto, Anthony, 222-
   223
Richard, Mark, 118, 125
Rider, James, 166-167
Rios Montt, Efrain, 20- 23
Rivas, Juan, 236-237
Robelo, Alfonso, 78, 82
Robinette, Glenn A., 112
Rockefeller, Nelson, 165
Rodriguez, Felix, 122-
   123, 140-141, 150, 161,
   173-176, 289-290. *See*
   Rodriguez, Felix
Rodriguez, Luis, 164, 221
Rolling Stone, 102
Rosenfeld, Stephen S., 13
Rosenthal, Abe, 46
Rudman, Warren, 139,
   230
Rupp, Heinrich, 286
Russoniello, Joseph, 197
Saddam Hussein, 281, 290
Saenz, Francisco Aviles,
   69, 196
San Jose Mercury News,
   181, 184, 191, 193, 242
San Pedro Sula (arms
   warehouse), 141, 160,
   170
Sanchez, Aristedes, 210
Sanchez, Fernando, 210-
   211

Sanchez, Troilo, 210
Sanchez-Reisse,
    Leonardo, 38, 41-42
Sandinistas, 35-37, 52- 58,
    61-71, 75-78, 82, 88, 90,
    96-100, 107, 117, 120-
    122, 136, 177, 189-190,
    194, 196, 209, 215, 220,
    226, 240- 241, 265
Sasakawa, Ryoichi, 199
Sawyer, Wallace "Buzz",
    122-123, 124
Schaufelberger, Albert,
    80-81
Schneider, Keith, 133,
    137-138
School of the Americas,
    10
Schorr, Daniel, 259
Scott, Peter Dale, 6, 40,
    232-233
Scowcroft, Brent, 134
SDECE, French
    intelligenc agency, 178
Seal, Barry, 66-67, 120
Secord, Richard, 175
Secret Service, 113, 286
Semerad, Kate, 47
Senate Intelligence
    Committee, 99, 118,
    187, 230, 275, 277
Sentelle, David, 148
SETCO, 237
Shackley, Theodore, 282,
    289-290
Shultz, George, 71, 146-
    147, 151
Silberman, Laurence, 148
Singlaub, John K., 83, 86,
    111, 162, 200
Small, Karna, 84-85
Smith, Wesley, 98
Smith, William French,
    43, 202-204
Snyder, Alvin A., 266- 268
Somoza, Anastasio, 52-54
Soto, Carlos, 164, 229
South Africa, 10, 14, 72
Southern Air Transport,
    119, 124, 163, 232, 238-
    239
Southern Front, the, 90,
    168, 212, 225-228, 234

Soviet Union, 14, 252, 254,
    257, 261, 265- 267, 272-
    275
Spadafora, Hugo, 90-93,
    168-169
Speakes, Larry, 270
Sporkin, Stanley, 197
St. Clair, Jeffrey, 245
Starr, Kenneth, 224
State Department, 19- 20
Steele, James, 150, 175
Stoltz, Richard, 237
Stone, Richard B., 23
Strickland, Lee S., 69, 196,
    211-212
Studley, Barbara, 162
Suarez, Roberto, 38- 39,
    227, 240
Sucre y Sucre, 159, 171
Suicida, 57-59, 97-98
Tambs, Lewis, 104, 235
TecNica, 70
Teicher, Howard, 289- 290
Tenet, George, 277
Terrell, Jack, 89-90, 103,
    112-114
Terrorist Incident
    Working Group, 112-
    113
The Babies, 92
The Historical
    Clarification
    Commission, 25
The Politics of Heroin in
    Southeast Asia, 178
Thibault, Andy, 183- 184
Thieu, Nguyen van, 259-
    260
This Week with David
    Brinkley, 77
Thomas, Evan, 130, 134,
    139-144
Tigrillo, 59, 101
Toensing, Victoria, 125
Tomuschat, Christian, 26
Torres, Ivan, 208
Tower, John, 129, 133- 134
Townley, Michael, 283-
    284
Trafficante, Santo Jr., 166
Trott, Stephen, 103

Truth and Reconciliation
  Commission (South
  Africa), 14
Turkey, 36
UniBank, 160, 165-167
Unification Church, 199
United Nicaraguan
  Opposition, 61
United States
  Information Agency,
  51, 61, 266
USA Today, 78
USIA
  United States Information
    Agency, 62, 266-268
Vaky, Viron, 16-17
Vaughn, Federico, 67- 68,
  190
Venezuela, 172-174
Vidal, Felipe, 221, 231- 232
Viet Cong, 9, 11, 173, 260
Vietnam, 8-11, 69, 127,
  145, 165, 178-180, 248-
  253, 256, 259, 264, 268,
  272, 277, 289
Vortex, 238
Walker, Greg, 271
Walker, William G., 268
Wall Street Journal, the,
  149
Wall Street Journal, The,
  46, 78
Walsh, Lawrence, 106,
  129, 140, 145-151, 154-
  158, 162-163, 173, 230,
  238
Walters, Vernon, 19, 282-
  283
Ward, Thomas, 201
Warren, Ellen, 139, 230,
  269
Washington Post, The,
  44, 58, 78, 84, 86, 102,

143, 158, 179-180, 183,
  185, 189, 191, 208, 225,
  243, 255, 259, 268
Washington Times, The,
  67, 149, 183-185, 202,
  291-292
Watergate, 5, 11, 102, 117,
  130, 132, 145, 158, 204,
  246, 253-264
Waters, Maxine, 182- 183,
  204-206
Webb, Gary, 181-194, 205-
  210, 244-245
Webster, William, 138
Weinberger, Casper, 146-149,
  155-157
Welch, Richard, 252
Weld, William, 118- 119,
  124-126
WFC, 160, 165-167
WFC Corp., 160, 165
Wheelock, Ricardo, 122
Whelan, James, 292
White, Clif, 116
White, Robert, 31
Wick, Charles Z., 61- 62,
  266
Wiley, Winston, 274, 277
Williams, Marjorie, 158
Wires, Harold, 222-223
Wirthlin, Richard, 53
Woolsey, James, 253, 277
World Anti-Communist
  League, 39, 83, 86, 200
World Court, 74, 112
Wright, Jim, 132
Yellow Rain, 50, 273
Zanides, Mark, 211
Zavala, Julio, 210-212
Zucker, Willard, 162- 163

About the Author

In the 1980s, investigative reporter **Robert Parry** broke many of the stories now known as the Iran-contra affair. Those stories included the first article about Oliver North's secret White House network. Parry also co-authored the first story about Nicaraguan contra-cocaine trafficking.

While working for *The Associated Press, Newsweek* and PBS Frontline, Parry has reported from such international hot spots as Grenada, El Salvador, Nicaragua, Iran, Israel and Haiti. His journalism awards include the George Polk Award for National Reporting in 1984. He also taught at New York University's Graduate School of Journalism.

Parry now edits the investigative publication, *iF Magazine.*

 **is the best new investigative magazine in America.**

investigates everything from national politics to the CIA, from the environment to the news media. And it does so with no punches pulled, 'without fear or favor.'

Find out what the excitement's about.
Subscribe below.

Order Form:

❏ Send 1 year (6 issues) of *iF Magazine*, **$25.**

❏ Send 2 years (12 issues) of *iF Magazine* for **$48.** (Includes free book, Robert Parry's *Lost History*, a $19.95 value.)

❏ Send me Issue(s):_____
 (Separate Issues of *iF Magazine*: **$6** each.)

❏ Send all available back issues of *iF*: **$50.** (Price in effect through the end of 1999)

❏ Parry's *October Surprise X-Files: The Secret Origins of Reagan-Bush Era,* **$15.95.**

❏ Parry's *Lost History: Contras, Cocaine, The Press & 'Project Truth,'* **$19.95.**

❏ Parry's *Trick or Treason: The October Surprise Mystery* for **$24.95.**

(Checks should be payable to The Media Consortium, Suite 102-231, 2200 Wilson Blvd., Arlington, VA 22201. Or call 1-800-738-1812 or 703-920-1802 with Visa/Mastercard.)

(Outside U.S., add $15 for extra postage.)

Name:_____

Address:_____

City/State/ZIP:_____

Visa/MC#:_____ Exp. Date:_____